The American Environment

Geographical Perspectives on the Human Past

General Editor: Robert D. Mitchell,
University of Maryland, College Park

THE AMERICAN ENVIRONMENT

Interpretations of Past Geographies

Edited by Lary M. Dilsaver and Craig E. Colten

ROWMAN & LITTLEFIELD PUBLISHERS, INC.

ROWMAN & LITTLEFIELD PUBLISHERS, INC.

Published in the United States of America
by Rowman & Littlefield Publishers, Inc.
4720 Boston Way, Lanham, Maryland 20706

British Cataloging in Publication Information Available

Library of Congress Cataloging-in-Publication Data

The American environment: interpretations of past geographies/
edited by Lary M. Dilsaver and Craig E. Colten.
p.   cm. — (Geographical perspectives on the human past)
Includes bibliographical references and index.
1. Man—Influence on nature—United States--History.
2. Environmental policy—United States—History. 3. United States—
Historical geography. I. Dilsaver, Lary M. II. Colten, Craig E.
III. Series
GF503.A44 1992
304.2'8'0973—dc20   92-12812   CIP

ISBN 0-8476-7753-2 (cloth : alk. paper)
ISBN 0-8476-7754-0 (pbk. : alk. paper)

Printed in the United States of America

The paper used in this publication meets the minimum requirements of
American National Standard for Information Sciences—Permanence of
Paper for Printed Library Materials, ANSI Z39.48–1984.

For Robin and Marge

Contents

List of Figures

List of Tables

Acknowledgments

The editors first encountered one another in 1977 with no premonition that they would one day collaborate on a project such as this. They attended classes together at Louisiana State University and took field trips across Dixie with a lively group of fellow students. Although historical geography had suffered at many institutions and what was then known as the "man–land" tradition had virtually vanished from many departmental curricula, LSU maintained strengths in these two endangered specialties. It was an exceptional time at an incomparable place and was extremely important in shaping the ideas of the editors. Our first debt of gratitude goes out to the LSU faculty, especially Sam Hilliard, and our peers there who provided a fertile seedbed for this project.

Over the past few years, as we began to lay the foundation for this work, many colleagues provided encouragement or participated in exploratory discussions at the annual AAG meetings. To them, we extend our sincere thanks.

Both administrative and technical staff of the Illinois State Museum provided exceptional support as well. Bonnie Styles and Bruce McMillan allowed this project to move forward and encouraged Colten's participation. Malinda Aiello and Tim Osburn undertook the tasks of text entry and word processing. At the University of South Alabama, Dean Lawrence Allen supported Dilsaver's participation with release time and special funding.

We also wish to thank the Academic Press and the *Georgia Journal of Science* for permitting us to reprint the articles by Ray and Trimble.

Finally, it has been a pleasure to work with the editorial staff of Rowman and Littlefield, particularly Jonathan Sisk and Lynn Gemmell, and with series editor Robert Mitchell, who provided useful comments, criticism, and guidance as we pushed the manuscript through to its final form.

Preface

Many of us take it as an article of faith that geography is that discipline which analyzes phenomena in a spatial context employing both human and physical factors as necessary.[1] The human–land approach to geographic analysis, in this view, is what allows us to deal effectively with environmental problems of the past and the present. But can there be any question that physical geography and human geography have been increasingly segregated over the past three or so decades?[2] No one denies that it is possible to deal with geographic problems which are *totally human* or *totally physical*, but many such problems are often exotic and sterile. Yet, a colleague and a leader in human geography recently stated to me that "physical geographers have nothing of interest to say to human geographers." While this appears extreme, much of the available evidence indicates that this attitude in some permutation is common, whether it is explicitly or implicitly manifested.

If one accepts the concept that historical geography is the spatial analysis of past landscapes, then it follows that the increasing physical–human dichotomy would show up there also, and it has. How is it, for example, that Donald Meinig, perhaps our leading historical geographer and who in 1968 wrote the exceptionally well-balanced and physically well-informed *The Great Columbia Plain*, could two decades later produce *Atlantic America*, which excludes most physical phenomena?[3] Indeed, Professor Meinig in a recent essay explicitly refers to historical geography as human geography,[4] and that sentiment has much support as evidenced by the literature of recent years. Moreover, Cole Harris has just presented constructs that seem to pull historical geography far from any physical consideration and environmental analysis.[5]

Perhaps it is a case of default, but much of the work of historical geography of environment over the past three decades has in fact been done by physical geographers (and cultural ecologists) who sometimes have had little or no training in historical geography, but who found that the data and methodology of historical geography were powerful tools for unraveling the processes of the recent past.[6] In a perspective on the field in 1980, four physical geographers concluded:

> We believe that no other group engaged in geomorphic research is as well qualified to grapple with the human factor [of environmental change] as are geographers. Our broad training in both physical and cultural systems and our appreciation of landscape change in the natural and human senses give us perspectives and insight that are rarely found in other disciplines. Geographers need to work closely with engineers and geologists in order to share with them such wide-ranging concepts as spatial analysis and emphasis on the man–land interface. These concepts are endemic to geography but they may be quite foreign to other workers.[7]

They further suggested that training in historical geography was indispensable for those researching the human–nature interface.

Ironically, it seems that the more recent "Great Retreat" of historical geographers from physical phenomena[8] has been complemented by a cautious advance of physical geographers into historical geography. Indeed, it seems that Meinig's plea for reinforcement of the ranks[9] has been partially filled, but the problem now seems to be the recognition of one's own troops. Perhaps one reason for the presence of so few historical geographers is the specialty's apparently exclusionist stance in the first instance.

But is using historical data and methodology to find answers and develop theory in physical geography any different from human geographers who use similar data and methods to develop social or economic models and theory? In fact, much of this work on the physical side remains invisible to "mainstream" historical geography. Seemingly, many historical geographers have constructed a pale against the incursions of physical geography, but some physical geographers have admittedly maintained a similar barricade on their side. In my view there is a parallel between the process-oriented physical geographer and the process-oriented human geographer, both working in past landscapes.[10] Perhaps these two groups represent the bounds of historical geography, but the core, lying in no-man's-land between the pales, is the landscape itself or better, the region (Fig. A). Some years ago, Wilbur Zelinsky wrote a provocative piece wherein he suggested that historical geographers were really regional geographers with a predilection for the past.[11] I believe this driving interest in the region, or the landscape itself, is actually the core of historical geography and is the flag about which we can rally. Both physical and human geographers reach toward that regional core to varying degrees, but few, if any, can single-handedly bridge the continuum.[12]

It is precisely this core, the region in its totality, that we have neglected too long, creating a vacuum in which the environmental historians

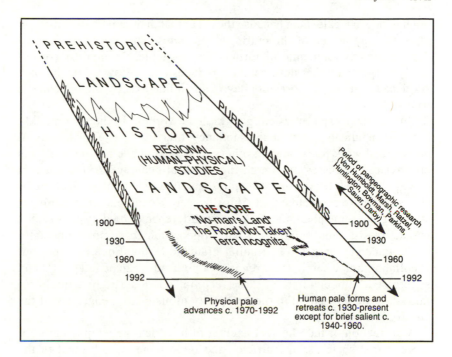

have been able to thrive. Their work varies greatly, ranging from superficial and impressionistic to quite sophisticated. A major problem is that many environmental historians miss much because they have apparently never studied environment in a systematic way (such as the content of a good introductory physical geography course). Rather, it appears that they have had some biology here and some geology there without an overview.[13] But it is ironic that geography—that social science with a long tradition of earth science[14]—should relinquish ground to a field like history with no physical underpinnings. The human–physical interface is a major strength of geography, and we should always speak from our strengths.[15]

Environmental history is often strikingly independent of geographical sources, both human and physical. Indeed, a recent review of environmental history relegates historical geography to a near-footnote status.[16] This impression is reversed by an inspection of Michael Conzen's *The Making of American Landscape*.[17] In that volume, the authors recognized and integrated the work of environmental historians. The reasons for this disparity are most interesting to speculate on, but I believe they have to do with the better-trained spatial perceptions of geographers with concomitant comprehension of what constitutes landscape and ability to assimilate the appropriate literature.

Human geographers may well recognize the role of physical factors but hesitate to tackle them because they fear that their expertise in matters physical may not be of the cutting-edge status. This does not seem to deter some environmental historians. For example, the myth is consistently perpetuated that deforestation reduces streamflow.[18] For the past six decades, however, foresters have known that exactly the opposite is true.[19]

On the other hand, physical geographers working in the past quickly come upon human factors such as tenancy, literacy, perceptions, cultural values, and work traits, among others, which can have profound effects on physical processes. Although the physical geographer may not feel adequate to treat these human factors in a state-of-the-art manner, he or she is still more competent to do this than, say, a geologist or an engineer studying the same phenomena. A strong inference to be drawn from this is that cross-training should be a part of geography programs, especially at the undergraduate and beginning graduate levels. Equally important is collaboration wherein the strengths of both sides can be integrated and synergized. Although both of these recommendations are perennial bromides, they are essential to the prosperity of historical geography of the environment.

A correction of the physical anemia in historical geography calls for more than a spate of long articles and large tomes which meet in the physical–human continuum, although many such works are necessary. In the meanwhile, however, more subtle but sophisticated recognition of the physical components of landscape can be highly effective. An example that falls to mind is, again, from Donald Meinig's *Atlantic America*. In mentioning Natchez, Mississippi, he notes the local "rich" soils (p. 282). I suspect that most anyone who has ever seen the wonderful architectural treasures of Natchez and environs would intuitively know that the area had "rich" soil, since local wealth there was frequently based on agriculture. How much more could have been conveyed if the word "loessal" had only been substituted for "rich." With no increase of manuscript length, knowledgeable readers from the Bukovina or Chad would immediately know bookfuls about the region. Not only would they know the fertility of the soil, but they would also recognize many other agronomic advantages and disadvantages, including the fact that rampant soil erosion is a constant threat. Of course, agronomy is as much cultural as physical so the further implications are evident. Readers would also know (or could easily find out) many engineering characteristics of the local soils. At first blush, this might appear to be a purely physical attribute, but consider just one effect on human occupance, trafficability. Road building and maintenance on loess is highly problematic so that transportation would have been considerably hampered until recent years. No geographer should be surprised that some local roads are deeply entrenched into the local loess.

The point here is that many physical terms and attributes are (or should be) part of the knowledge base of all geographers so that all characteristics accruing to them are immediately comprehended. Some might counter that such nomenclature is presumptuous and might exclude readers from other disciplines, but this argument does not seem to prevent some other disciplines, especially the social sciences, from using jargon that is often pedantic, pretentious, and far less informative. Given that the physical landscape is part of the sinew of historical geography, why do we persist in this self-mutilation? Is mainstream historical geography destined to become mere history with maps?

The historical geography of the environment presents unlimited opportunities. Few regions of the United States have been given intensive coverage and even those are always subject to potential revision, as the essay in this volume by Carville Earle shows. Certainly, revisionism should always be with us. The conventional wisdom about New England, perhaps the most studied region of the United States, was recently challenged by Michael Bell who contends that the soils, previously thought poor, are relatively fertile.[20] Yet another region for which revision may be appropriate is the Dust Bowl. Although Donald Worster's tendentious study[21] is informative and well written, there is yet much to say about that region by a physically oriented historical geographer and there is much information readily available. Under the aegis of the U.S. Department of Agriculture Soil Conservation Service, the late geographer C. Warren Thornthwaite and his associates laid strong foundations for a full understanding of that unfortunate regional disaster. The fruits of that research, now in the National Archives, remain apparently untouched.[22] Seeing all the physical and human features of the Dust Bowl brought together and analyzed in their spatial dimensions would be satisfying indeed. Most regions of the United States cry out for similar analysis, and the Thornthwaite collection reminds us that the availability of sources can sometimes be the catalyst for research direction. Ron Cooke and I have assembled a much too abbreviated guide to historical sources which we hope will help stimulate such regional research.[23]

Foreign areas require study both in their own right and to provide comparison and contrast. A wonderful opportunity, which opened up in the past two years, is the chance to study freely the former socialist areas of the USSR and eastern Europe.[24] Despite the problems, others have already succeeded to some degree in showing the environmental nightmare created by government ownership and exploitation of natural resources.[25] A common thread running through much of the recent environmental history is the idea that environmental degradation is the child of capitalism.[26] The parochialism of that theme would hardly seem to require comment, but it is not the first time that data were gathered to support preconceived notions.[27] Historical studies may now be designed to study the historical geography of resource management under sequential capitalist and socialist economic systems within the same region. Yet another approach is the historical contrast of the two economic systems which were operating simultaneously in eastern and western Europe. An excellent example of such a study would be an objective comparison of the American Dust Bowl and the 1950s Soviet "Virgin Lands" disaster in Kazakstan.

In summary, the overall trend of historical geography during the past three decades is not awfully encouraging, and in view of that trend, the present volume is especially welcome. From their stronghold of applied historical geography, Craig Colten and Lary Dilsaver have marshaled an array of papers which demonstrates the utility of the historical approach in the study and management of the environment. At once this collection shows that historical geography of the environment has never really died; more importantly, it signals a renewed interest in the field by workers whose lineage is from the human side of the continuum. Let us take steps to ensure that this collection is just the harbinger of a renewed movement.

Stanley W. Trimble
University of California–
Los Angeles

Acknowledgments

I thank Liisa Gardner for preparing the manuscript and Chase Langford for preparing the figure. Ongoing discussions with Ron Shreve were helpful.

Notes

1. M.G. Marcus, "Coming Full Circle: Physical Geography in the Twentieth Century," *Annals of the Association of American Geographers* 69 (1979): 521–32. D.A. McQuillan, "The Interface of Physical and Historical Geography," in *Period and Place*, A.R.H. Baker and M. Billinge, eds. (Cambridge: Cambridge University Press, 1982): 136–44. R.W. Kates, "The Human Environment: The Road Not Taken, the Road Still Beckoning," *Annals of the Association of American Geographers* 77 (1987): 525–34.

2. Some recent exceptions to this tendency are Andrew Goudie, *The Human Impact on the Natural Environment* (Cambridge: MIT Press, 1986) and B.L. Turner II, W.C. Clark, R.W. Kates, J.R. Richards, J.T. Matthews, and W.B. Meyer, eds., *The Earth as Transformed by Human Action: Global and Regional Changes in Biosphere over the Past 300 Years* (Cambridge: Cambridge University Press, 1990).

3. D.W. Meinig, *The Great Columbia Plain: A Historical Geography 1805–1910* (Seattle: University of Washington Press, 1968). D.W. Meinig, *Atlantic America, 1492–1800*, Vol. 1 of *The Shaping of America: A Geographical Perspective on 500 Years of History* (New Haven: Yale University Press, 1986).

4. D.W. Meinig, "Meinig's Reply," *Annals of the Association of American Geographers* 80 (1990): 622.

5. Cole Harris, "Power, Modernity and Historical Geography," *Annals of the Association of American Geographers* 81 (1991): 671–83.

6. For examples, see Goudie, *Human Impact* and S.W. Trimble and R.U. Cooke, "Historical Sources for Geomorphological Research in the United States," *Professional Geographer* 43 (1991): 212–28.

7. W.L. Graf, S.W. Trimble, T.J. Toy, and J.E. Costa, "Geographical Geomorphology in the Eighties," *Professional Geographer* 32 (1980): 270–84.

8. S.W. Trimble, "Environmental Impacts in the American Past," in Carville Earle and Lary Dilsaver, eds., "Foreword to Historical Geography: Accomplishments and Agenda of Its North American Practitioners," *Working Papers in Historical Geography No. 2*, AAG Historical Geography Specialty Group, 1988, 49–51. Republished in "Historical Geography," in *Geography in America*, G.L. Gaile and C.J. Willmont, eds. (Columbus, Mo.: Merrill, 1989), 156–91.

9. D.W. Meinig, "The Historical Geography Imperative," *Annals of the Association of American Geographers* 79 (1989): 79–87.

10. I am aware that many historical geographers would disagree strongly with this statement. See Cole Harris, "Power, Modernity and Historical Geography," and J.N. Entrikin, *The Betweenness of Place* (Baltimore: Johns Hopkins Press, 1990).

11. Wilbur Zelinsky, "In Pursuit of Historical Geography and Other Wild Geese," *Historical Geography Newsletter* 3 (1973): 1–5.

12. Both physical and human geographers reach toward that regional core to varying degrees but few can single-handedly bridge the continuum. Three mid-to-late-twentieth-century geographers who have successfully spanned the human–physical continuum are Carl Sauer, H.C. Darby, and Karl Butzer. In any case, enough of our number from both sides can reach across the center so that we can link hands and share our work.

13. On the other side of the continuum, physical geographers frequently note that earth scientists from other fields have never had such an overview, and such is often a revelation.

14. W.D. Pattison, "The Four Traditions of Geography," *Journal of Geography* 63 (1964): 211–16.

15. R.F. Abler, "What Shall We Say? To Whom Shall We Speak?" *Annals of the Association of American Geographers* 77 (1987): 511–24.

16.   P.G. Terrie, "Recent Work in Environmental History," *American Studies International* 27 (1989): 42–63.

17.   M.P. Conzen, ed., *The Making of the American Landscape* (Boston: Unwin Hyman, 1990).

18.   J.R. Stilgoe, *Common Landscape of America 1580–1845* (New Haven: Yale University Press, 1982), 317; William Cronon, *Changes in the Land: Indians, Colonists, and the Ecology of New England* (New York: Hill and Wang, 1983), 160.

19.   The most recent model indicates that complete deforestation of a stream basin will *increase* annual runoff by about 330 mm (13 in.) and, conversely, complete reforestation will *decrease* annual runoff by a similar amount. S.W. Trimble, F.W. Weirich, and B.L. Hoag, "Reforestation and the Reduction of Water Yield on the Southern Piedmont Since Circa 1940," *Water Resources Research* 23 (1987): 425–37.

20.   M.M. Bell, "Did New England Go Downhill?" *Geographical Review* 79 (1989): 450–66.

21.   D.E. Worster, *Dust Bowl: The Southern Plains in the 1930s* (Oxford: Oxford University Press, 1979).

22.   See the cartographic records of the U.S. Department of Agriculture, Soil Conservation Service, Climate and Physiographic [Research] Group, Record Group 114, entries 49, 57–75.

23.   Trimble and Cooke, "Historical Sources."

24.   I attempted a research project in Romania in the late 1960s but encountered not only government noncooperation but also government harassment of my contacts there.

25.   M.I. Goldman, "Environmental Disruption in the Soviet Union," in *Man's Impact on Environment*, T.R. Detwyler, ed. (New York: McGraw-Hill, 1971). V. Smil, *The Bad Earth: Environmental Degradation in China* (Armonk, N.Y.: M.E. Sharpe, 1984). D.R. Weiner, *Models of Nature: Ecology, Conservation, and Cultural Revolution in Soviet Russia* (Bloomington: Indiana University Press, 1988).

26.   For example, Worster, *Dust Bowl*; J.M. Petulla, *American Environmental History* (Columbus, Mo.: Merrill, 1988); Worster, "The Vulnerable Earth: Toward A Planetary History," in *The Ends of the Earth: Perspectives on Modern Environmental History*, Donald Worster, ed. (Cambridge: Cambridge University Press, 1989), 3–22.

27.   Two sources that quickly get to the heart of this matter are E.G. Dolan, *The Economic Strategy for Environmental Crisis* (New York: Holt, Rinehart and Winston, 1971) and T.L. Anderson and D.R. Leal, *Free Market Environmentalism*, Pacific Research Institute for Public Policy Working Paper 91-7 (Boulder, Colo.: Westview Press, 1991). Earle (in this volume) also makes some good points along this line. See, especially, note 2.

1

Historical Geography of the Environment: A Preliminary Literature Review[1]

Craig E. Colten and Lary M. Dilsaver

Stanley Trimble recently suggested that historical geographers have shown "signs of another 'Great Retreat'" from the study of human impacts on the environment.[2] Rather than a "great retreat," we submit that historical geographers have engaged in a protracted flanking maneuver or the "Great Sidestep." Historical perspectives on physical geography have been ever present, but this literature is extremely thin, and too seldom is it presented as historical geography; in truth it comes from elsewhere within or even outside the discipline. Furthermore, claiming historical geographers have retreated from studies of the physical environment implies a prior advance, or at the very least a fortified position from which to flee. But one can argue that there has never been a structured and deliberate approach to past environments. Certainly we can find excellent examples of investigations that treat the impact of human activity, but they are scattered in the literature of biogeography, geomorphology, climatology, cultural ecology, environmental history, and anthropology. The overwhelming emphasis in historical geography over the past twenty years has been on cultural, social, and economic theory. In such a context, the environment becomes a passive backdrop for the erection of a cultural landscape or an inert medium upon which economic and social systems operate.

George Perkins Marsh initially proposed that we investigate how man has "determined the material structure of his earthly home," but his appeal went unheeded by geographers for many years.[3] It is ironic, given the so-called "man–land" tradition in North American geography, that historical geographers have shown so little enthusiasm for topics dealing with the human environment.[4] The reworking of the environment is often presented as the imposition of a cadastral order or the planting of an

1

agrarian society. There has been ample discussion of the settlement of forests and prairies, but little analysis of the physical consequences. In terms of urban and industrial impacts, geographers have examined the social and economic organization of cities and regions, but they have seldom touched on the necessary and far-reaching physical alteration of the land that accompanied social and economic transformations.[5]

The observation that we have neglected physical geography is not new. In 1982, D. Aidan McQuillan wrote about the neglect of "some basic skills and traditional geographical concerns, such as the study of human responses to environmental challenges." He went on to issue a plea "to put more physical geography back into historical geography without giving up the concern for advancing social theory." Terry Jordan issued a similar call to action, "It is high time for historical geographers to end our half-century or more of neglecting physical environmental factors." And Donald Meinig recently lamented that environmental topics "have become dominated by other guilds of scholars."[6]

Through this collection of essays, we hope to address these appeals by presenting a selection of research findings that integrate human activities and environmental processes within the context of historical geography.

The Environment and Historical Geography

What are the lineages of environmental inquiry in historical geography? We see three organizing themes: (1) cultural landscapes, (2) environmental understanding and evaluation, and (3) resource use and management. Although each is easily recognizable, it is often difficult to categorize a single piece as fitting wholly within one tradition. Nevertheless, these three traditions represent the three articulated perspectives on human–environmental relationships during the past fifty years. Since 1940, each of the major figures in American historical geography has sketched a place for the study of past environments within the specialty. Yet, their intellectual offspring often have fixed their attention on other dimensions of the past or have smeared the outlines left by their mentors.

Carl Sauer offered the first explicit appeal for one of these "traditions" in his "Great Retreat" address. His reference, in 1940, was to the intellectual drift of geography away from geology and earth sciences. He saw the decline in physical studies, in part, as an attempt to distance geographic scholarship from the discredited environmental determinism, while carving out a unique academic focus. Yet, Sauer argued that competent human geographers need not withdraw from the study of physical geography, particularly in terms of his conception of historical geography. He outlined several subthemes which focused directly on humans as agents of physical change. Specifically, Sauer called for inquiry into the influence of settlement on climate, the role of society in shaping geomorphology, and its influences on the flora and fauna of a region.[7] Only in the latter realm of historical biogeography has there been much work done by human geographers.

The Sauer-inspired Berkeley school sought to explain the cultural landscape genetically—particularly in terms of plant and animal ecology. By tracing the introduction of exotic species or the imposition of agricultural practices on the land surface, Sauer and his students emphasized cultural alteration of the "natural" landscape.[8] Their work focused on the proliferation and utilization of introduced plants and animals, however, while overlooking the consequences to indigenous biotic, geomorphic, or hydrologic systems—although Sauer and his students certainly were not oblivious to this. Rather, with the goal of explaining the creation of the human landscape, they were free to dismiss the disruptive impacts of human activity.

In a special edition of the *Annals of the Association of American Geographers*, Homer Aschmann, H.F. Raup, and Howard Nelson exemplified the Berkeley approach by tracing the alteration of southern California from "wild" vegetation to an "artificial landscape," and it is exceptional for the Berkeley scholars in that it deals with urban, industrialized landscapes.[9] Throughout, it emphasized the cumulative effects of human action, stressing cultural processes rather than portraying humans as a force interacting with or disrupting natural processes.

While Sauer and students such as Jan Broek, Robert West, James Parsons, Carl Johannesen, and William Denevan produced a body of work that reflected his view of landscape genesis, their emphasis on the cultural landscape relegated preexisting physical features and processes to the status of malleable surfaces awaiting a cultural transformation.[10] Historical geography as practiced by Berkeley products has given close attention to past environments, but seldom in an environmental context. *Man's Role in Changing the Face of the Earth* provided a view into the awareness of environmental problems, but was not wholly representative of Berkeley historical geography.[11]

Cultural ecologists have carried forward the Berkeley tradition, which derived much influence from Marsh. From energy-budget investigations to the analysis of prehistoric agricultural systems, this mode of inquiry has retained a sharp focus on natural systems and human modification of the physical and biological terrain. Closely allied with anthropology, and especially archaeology, cultural ecologists have devoted much of their attention to traditional or prehistoric societies. In recent years Karl

Butzer has called for an expansion of this approach beyond non-western societies. He claims that "ecological sophistication and cultural expertise can be applied with equal profit in the First World as in the Third."[12] Anthropologists have found cultural ecology a useful framework for investigating human use of the earth, and it has been embraced in archaeological research.[13]

Ralph Brown initiated a second strand of interest in historical environments. He argued that "the past geography is only partly told when account has been taken of the cultural landscape. The picture must be extended to include the natural setting."[14] Although he never formally analyzed the impact of human activity on the natural environment, he certainly remained cognizant of topography, vegetation, soils, and climate, particularly as they were known or understood by contemporary occupants of a region. In *Mirror for Americans*, Brown emphasized contemporary geographic understanding.[15]

Although he was never a mentor to a subsequent generation of scholars or a direct influence in studies of environmental understanding, Brown's approach found indirect application in the work of numerous scholars whose publications bridged the other traditions. Brown's perspective embodied what J.K. Wright later referred to as geosophy.[16] The examination of how people came to know and evaluate their habitats falls into this category and became a viable approach to past environments with the acceptance of perceptual topics. Land quality and access to water played an important role in the selection of farmsteads in Pennsylvania,[17] and contemporary understanding of the relationship between forest and agricultural productivity has been a fertile topic for investigation in the prairie and western states.[18] Human assessment of the environment also appears in studies dealing with adaptation to new settings. Roy Merrens explored the emerging representation of North Carolina as more became known of its geographic realities.[19] Carville Earle has interpreted health problems encountered by settlers in Virginia as a consequence of imperfect understanding of the environment.[20] Jeffrey Roet reported that land selection on the Dakota frontier was not a function of soil quality and eventually led to dire consequences during drought.[21] There is much opportunity to draw this line of investigation into the twentieth century.[22]

Andrew Clark outlined a third approach to physical geography nearly forty years ago, and in many ways, it provides a perspective for the analysis of resource use and management. Clark pointed out that "the problems of resource use, including the use of the land for agriculture" were of special interest to geographers.[23] It may be impossible to characterize the work produced by the many historical geographers who studied under Clark's tutelage as reflective of a single approach, but for the most part it differed from the Berkeley tradition in its analysis of social and economic theory from a geographic viewpoint. Clark's students used geographical tools adeptly to question and reassess theories about natural resources offered by historians. Central to their analyses were natural resources and agricultural commodities, but frequently they were placed in the context of their economic value, not viewed as components of natural environmental systems. Robert Mitchell and Sam Hilliard dealt with agricultural production and wildlife procurement primarily as part of regional economic systems, with less emphasis on agroecosystems.[24] Even Arthur Ray, whose essay considering conservation programs promoted by the Hudson's Bay Company is important enough to be included in this volume, focused his work on the exploitation of natural resources as economic commodities.[25] McQuillan's study of settlement in Kansas, stands in contrast to much of Wisconsin-produced historical geography by focusing on ethnic adjustments made by pioneer groups in a new environmental setting.[26] There is nothing wrong with what we have summarized as Wisconsin approaches, but ample opportunity exists to reassess similar topics from different points of view. For example, it is possible to explore the heretofore unmentioned economic costs of environmental degradation and depletion of valuable resources. One could also consider human use of natural resources as a means of examining ecological theory.

Sherry Olson's *The Depletion Myth* offers a valuable review of the efforts to contend with an impending timber shortage and exemplifies the potential of a reexamination of resource consumption and management.[27] There have also been reviews of legislation dealing with public lands, such as federal programs designed to alter the vegetation of the arid west[28] or of human activity within regulatory systems, namely conservation of wildlife and rangelands.[29] Earle has reexamined the impact of Southern land ethic and soil conservation practices while Stanford Demars, Lary Dilsaver and William Tweed, and Ronald Foresta have given considerable attention to the federal administration of parks and wildlands.[30] There remain many important questions and issues in this area.

Related Contributions

Firmly rooted in the human–environment tradition, but professing no formal interest in historical questions, is the Gilbert White school of geographers. Influenced in part by Harlan Barrows, White and his students have created a substantive literature dealing with human efforts to control and adapt to natural systems.[31] Their work is functional or problem oriented and has served as a guide to public policy for over half a century. While not directed at seeking answers to historical problems, most of White's work and that of his students has a strong historical component. The retrospective viewpoint is essential to explain current conditions and to develop agendas for future resource management.

A recent volume, *The Earth as Transformed by Human Action*, exhibits many of the perspectives of the cultural ecologists and the natural resource management approaches.[32] This fine volume provides both a long-term and global perspective. The fundamental message is that over the past three hundred years the role of humans in altering the face of the earth has grown dramatically.

British geographers have offered an approach to past environments that parallels somewhat the Berkeley approach, although it is infused with a stronger historical orientation. The draining of the fens and the removal of forests loom large in English historical geography,[33] and both reflect the impress of human activity. Williams reported that Darby felt that "one could not divorce humankind from the natural scene."[34] This comment demonstrates an overwhelming emphasis on the landscape as a human creation, not as a system in which humans are significant players. The British literature, with a few notable exceptions, includes meager discussion of the consequences of the massive environmental disruptions produced by an urban and industrial society.[35]

As Trimble has argued, geomorphologists, biogeographers, and climatologists have evidenced great interest in human alteration of the natural environment. Scholars in these specialties have prepared a substantive body of material on historical ecology and climate. Lawson's examination of climatic change in the American West meshes tightly with the historical geography of settlement of the Great Plains.[36] Extensive work on stream-basin sedimentation by Knox and Trimble embody a lively, ongoing intellectual debate.[37] The reconstruction of past vegetative communities also adds considerable insight into past settlement patterns, but is infrequently undertaken by historical geographers.[38] Not only are historical geographers seldom engaged in such studies of historical ecology,[39] but such scholarship is all too often unfamiliar to historical geographers or remains unused by scholars interested in social and economic theory.

Environmental historians have instead been aggressive in the examination of environmental change and human action. Their work over the past few decades reflects an increasingly sophisticated understanding of environmental processes and the documentary sources used to reconstruct past environments. It is not uncommon to find climatologists, ecologists, and archaeologists cited in their bibliographies. They have offered outstanding scholarship, ranging from Cronon's regional treatment of colonial New England to Crosby's sweeping epic of the ecological impact of European expansion.[40] Indeed, the pursuit of environmental topics now supports several journals exclusively, including the *Environmental History Review* and *Forest and Conservation History*, while others such as the *Public Historian* draw heavily on this growing specialty. Environmental historians often cite Marsh and Sauer as guiding lights in their research, but they have not restricted themselves to traditional societies or forest removal.[41] Rather, they have launched into such unsavory topics as garbage and sewage.[42]

Efforts to manage the environment, particularly through various federal land and water agencies, have received rapidly burgeoning attention. Robert Dunbar, James Malin, Marc Reisner, and Douglas Strong have contributed histories of environmental manipulation which found large audiences.[43] National parks have become a particularly popular topic with important works by Robert Righter, Hal Rothman, and Alfred Runte.[44] National forests and federal forestry likewise have received serious attention by scholars such as David Clary, William Robbins, William Rowley, and Harold Steen.[45] Environmental historians have also tackled other agencies including the Army Corps of Engineers,[46] the Fish and Wildlife Service,[47] the Tennessee Valley Authority,[48] and the Bureau of Reclamation.[49] The U.S. Environmental Protection Agency (EPA) has also contracted for historical investigations of past waste-management practices.[50] Furthermore, some government agencies employ historians or regularly contract for "administrative histories," which devote varying amounts of attention to resource management policies and practices. The Forest Service has produced noteworthy histories of its Intermountain and Southwest regions,[51] while Barry Mackintosh and Linda Greene have provided useful park histories.[52] Historians for the Army engineers have published significant discussions of the Corps' environmental policies and impacts.[53] In addition, the EPA has begun to examine the long-term implications of its policies and hired an agency historian in 1991.[54] Perhaps too much environmental history deals with the politics of the environment, but this merely reflects a professional bias.[55] Regardless of this professional predilection, much of their work on environmental topics is assembled along the same academic front as our own work and there is a risk of historians' encircling our complacent troops.

Signs of Promise

There are, and have been, scattered signs of promise. Stanley Trimble's study of soil erosion in the Southern Piedmont has appeared in every major review of significant works in historical geography for more than fifteen years.[56] It has been lauded, yet never duplicated in another regional setting. Its importance lies in the fact that it analyzes direct interaction between human society and the earth's surface—namely, the erosive impacts of agricultural practices and the eventual arrest of erosion, through intentional and unintentional actions. Michael Williams and Graeme Wynn provide superb treatments of timber removal and timber economies.[57] Williams, in particular, who worked on a national scale, may help rekindle interest in the relationship between humans and natural resources, although both works are set within a context of cultural landscapes and economic development.

Discussions of the evolving geographic knowledge about critical environmental phenomena illustrate the value of historical analysis to current environmental problems such as urban heat islands, groundwater contamination, and agricultural practices.[58] A more common approach is to analyze historical processes and attitudes toward the environment. Sam Hilliard has explored the development of agricultural practices in coastal Carolina that reflect a sophisticated understanding of natural processes and also brought about tremendous change to the riparian wetlands.[59] Jeanne Kay has discussed ecological interpretations of native population change and also explored conservation traditions and practices.[60] Jordan has called for cultural ecological interpretation of settlement, although his efforts along this line have not fully integrated ecological with cultural interpretations.[61] Recent efforts have used historical travelers' accounts to reconstruct plant and animal life on remote islands.[62] On a grander scale, National Park Service and other public agency land-management practices have been the subject of extensive investigations.[63]

There have been sweeping treatments of human impact on and interaction with the environment.[64] Furthermore, studies of "land degradation" claim that the historical perspective is "indispensable" in explaining the political economy of human impacts on the environment.[65] The task of integrating this material into future work and exploring the theoretical questions it poses lies ahead.

A final promising trend is found in three historical geography surveys which all devote attention to physical geography. Most chapters in Robert Mitchell and Paul Groves's book include a discussion of climate and physical features. Furthermore, Michael Conzen's recent work included a chapter specifically on the environment—or the "grand stage" upon which human settlement occurred. Both recognized the large-scale transformations of land and landscape that took place under the direction of federal agencies such as the Corps of Engineers and the Soil Conservation Service.[66] The importance of physical topics is also amply illustrated in a forthcoming volume on the American West.[67] Thus, there is a literature that examines human–environment relations, but as we have been told time and again, there is a far greater role for historical geographers to play in this endeavor.

Areas of Opportunity

If we step back and look at the broad panorama of human–environment interaction, two fundamental questions emerge: (1) How have human pursuits transformed the environment? and (2) How have human social organizations controlled their environment? These questions reflect upon perhaps the two most important factors in environmental change over time. Both questions place the environment as the object of human activity and consider humans as important forces in its alteration. Historical geographies that ask these questions are not explaining the development of cultural landscapes or the establishment of an economic system; rather, they illuminate the creation of a humanized landscape, whether engineered by an industrial nation or crafted by a traditional society, and they examine the controlling mechanisms used to protect or plunder a territory.

The essays in this volume are structured to explore one or both of these questions. Our intent is to draw attention to the impact of human societies on the environment, to explore environmental change caused by human activity, and to consider the means of manipulating human actions that impinge on natural processes. Seldom are impact and management discrete or disassociated. One begets the other. The highly visible effects of soil erosion during the 1930s gave rise to a federal agency with the mission of managing soil resources. Flooding caused by urbanization and development of major floodplains eventually forced the Corps of Engineers to assume responsibility for flood-protection programs. These examples reflect the social response to human-induced environmental change. All too frequently the ultimate consequences of human activity are unanticipated or unpredictable. When changes in human use of the environment result in adverse impacts, however, there is frequently an adjustment in environmental management practices, or at least policies. In this scenario, impact gives rise to management.

Certain forms of environmental management can also lead to unintended or unimagined impacts. Public health authorities at the turn of the century welcomed the discharge of toxic effluent into waterways thinking it would reduce the danger of waterborne diseases. Since the 1940s, however, natural scientists urged the cessation of poisonous releases after recognizing the havoc they cause in biological communities. In parks

and forests early biological management policies instituted with immature science and wholly different goals led to the loss of meadows,
endangered species, and altered whole ecosystems.

Impacts and management touch all manner of environments and constitute the stuff of which geography is made. Land allocation policies,
for example, impart a cultural context to a countryside; they shape the
pattern and distribution of land holdings, thereby delineating the economic landscape. They reflect the imposition of a political order and
bespeak the underlying values and attitudes of a society toward its resources. These factors, interacting and ever evolving, shape the impacts
of human society. The slow-moving manner of resource management
policies and the incremental nature of human impacts demands historical
treatment of such subjects, and historical geography offers an ideal framework for their examination. Historians have maneuvered down this route-
way for some time now. Their emphasis has been on the political and
intellectual aspects of resource use and stewardship. Chris Hamlin, discussing the historian's approach to stream pollution, wrote that it is not
the pollution itself that concerns historians, but "the economic and
ideological landscape in which the pollution problem emerged."[68] The
shortcomings of the policy focus have been noted by historians,[69] and
this should encourage geographers to venture into the bountiful intellectual boulevard of past environments—bringing to bear their comprehension of environmental process. By addressing the environmental dimension of human impacts and management policies, historical geography
can blend its perspective with that of history and make a significant
contribution. Furthermore, it can open new horizons for examining human interaction with the earth's surface.

Historical Geography of the Environment: Essays

The following collection of essays portrays approaches and rich opportunities in environmental historical geography. The first two are older,
pioneering efforts. Stanley Trimble's study of sedimentation in the Alcovy River swamps illustrates the historic impact of human activity on
an environmental system. Arthur Ray, on the other hand, reviews nineteenth-century attempts to manage fur trapping and its resources in
Canada. Together, these two works demonstrate the contrasting approaches
and the opposing forces of impact and policy at work in the human environment. Eight new essays carry on this inchoate tradition.

The next three chapters explore the impacts and policies of primary
economic activity. Carville Earle offers a critique of past interpretations
of southern agricultural practices. He forcefully argues that the impacts
of soil erosion were cyclic, rather than persistent over time, and that

damaging episodes were not due to an oft-damned chronic insensitivity to agroecological conditions in the cotton belt. Richard Francaviglia offers a landscape classification system for areas of mineral extraction. His work employs the rich cultural landscape tradition in historical geography, but broadens the scope to encompass the massive disruptions caused by twentieth-century technologies. Finally, Martha Henderson's work provides a rare contrasting perspective as it explores how major shifts in federal Indian policy found expression in logging and timber production on reservation lands and their spatial and environmental effect.

The second section illuminates the consequences of deliberate environmental policy. First, David Hardin examines the impact of an agricultural society on native wildlife in colonial Virginia and traces the policies that emerged to contend with both the disappearance of valuable game and the proliferation of pests. Olen Paul Matthews focuses on the legal means used to control limited water resources in the semiarid west and the results of disparate policies within the watershed of an interstate stream. By contrast, Craig Colten argues that pollution-control policy in Illinois was unable to keep pace with the environmental effects of industrial wastes. This signifies, he contends, that policy alone is an inadequate barometer of environmental management.

The final section discusses efforts by society to maintain environments that it deems important, not for primary economic needs, but for recreation and preservation purposes. Klaus Meyer-Arendt examines the social responses to changing coastal conditions. He asserts that policy follows human-induced change and that successive alterations in management strategy lead to unforeseen environmental consequences. These, in turn, inspire sometimes contradictory policies that cope with only one facet of environmental conditions. The National Park Service, with its mandate to provide access to and protect wild areas, is the focus of Dilsaver's essay. He traces the development of measures in four National Park units to manipulate visitation and thereby protect sensitive environments.

In 1956, Carl Sauer wrote, "Wherever men live, they have operated to alter the aspect of the Earth, both animate and inanimate, be it to their boon or bane."[70] These essays represent a continuation and a restatement of this geographic perspective on past environments, merging policy analysis with environmental management, and the consequences they reap.

Acknowledgments

We would like to gratefully acknowledge Stanley W. Trimble, D. Aidan McQuillan, and Carville Earle for providing critical remarks to a earlier version of this essay.

Notes

1. This literature review is not intended as an exhaustive summary of works in the fields of historical geography or environmental history. Rather, it represents a selection of significant works that reflect the focus of this work—in terms of both the long-term development of the field and recent efforts primarily in the United States.

2. Carville Earle and Lary M. Dilsaver, eds., "Historical Geography," in *Geography in America*, G.L. Gale & C.J. Willmont, eds. (Columbus, Mo.: Merrill, 1989), 156–91.

3. George P. Marsh, *The Earth as Modified by Human Action* (New York: Scribner, Armstrong, 1876). For a discussion of Marsh's early impact and discussions of topics related to his concerns, see William L. Thomas, ed., *Man's Role in Changing the Face of the Earth*, 2 vols. (Chicago: University of Chicago Press, 1956), esp. Vol. 1, xxviii–xxxvii.

4. There has been an amorphous and disjointed literature that touched on the subject throughout the twentieth century. Examples include L.C. Gottschalk, "Effects of Soil Erosion on Navigation in the Upper Chesapeake Bay," *Geographical Review* 35 (1945): 219–38; A.E. Parkins, "Indians of the Great Lakes and their Environment," *Geographical Review* 6 (1918): 504–12; Gordon Sweet, "Oyster Conservation in Connecticut, Past and Present," *Geographical Review* 31 (1941): 591–608; Glenn Trewartha, "Second Epoch of Destructive Occupance in the Driftless Hill Land," *Annals of the Association of American Geographers* (hereafter *Annals AAG*) 30 (1940): 109–42; Hildegard Binder Johnson, "The Location of German Immigrants in the Middle West," *Annals AAG* 41 (1951): 1–41.

5. A significant exception by the historian William Cronon is *Nature's Metropolis: Chicago and the Great West* (New York: W.W. Norton, 1991).

6. D.A. McQuillan, "The Interface of Physical and Historical Geography: The Analysis of Farming Decisions in Response to Drought Hazards on the Margins of the Great Plains," in *Period and Place*, A.R.H. Baker and Mark Billinge, eds. (Cambridge: Cambridge University Press, 1982), 136; Terry Jordan, "Preadaptation and European Colonization in Rural North America," *Annals AAG* 79 (1989): 494; D.W. Meinig, "The Historical Geography Imperative," *Annals AAG* 79 (1989): 82.

7. Carl O. Sauer, "Foreword to Historical Geography," *Annals AAG* 31 (1941): 1–24.

8. Carl O. Sauer, *Seeds, Spades, Hearths, and Herds* (Cambridge: MIT Press, 1952); *Northern Mists* (Berkeley, Calif.: Turtle Island, 1968); *Northern Spanish Main* (Berkeley: University of California Press, 1969); *Seventeenth Century North America* (Berkeley, Calif.: Turtle Island, 1980).

9. Homer Aschmann, "Evolution of a Wild Landscape and Its Persistence in Southern California," *Annals AAG* 49 (1959): 34–56; H.F. Raup, "Transformation of Southern California to a Cultivated Land," *Annals AAG* 49 (1959): 58–78; Howard J. Nelson, "The Spread of an Artificial Landscape in Southern California," *Annals AAG* 49 (1959): 24–32.

10. Jan O.M. Broek, *The Santa Clara Valley, California: A Study in Land-*

scape Changes (Utrecht: Oostoek, 1932); Robert C. West, "Folk Mining in Columbia," *Economic Geography* 28 (1952): 323–30; James J. Parsons, "Human Influences on the Pine and Laurel Forests of the Canary Islands," *Geographical Review* 71 (1981): 253–71; Carl Johannessen et al., "The Vegetation of the Willamette Valley," *Annals AAG* 61 (1971): 286–302; William Denevan, "Livestock Numbers in Nineteenth Century New Mexico and the Problem of Gullying in the Southwest," *Annals AAG* 57 (1967): 691–703.

11. Thomas, *Man's Role*.

12. K.W. Butzer, "Cultural Ecology," in *Geography in America*, 205.

13. Donald L. Hardesty, *Ecological Anthropology* (Reno: University of Nevada Press, 1977); Karl W. Butzer, *Archaeology as Human Ecology: Method and Theory for a Contextual Approach* (Cambridge: Cambridge University Press, 1982); George P. Nicholas, ed., *Holocene Human Ecology in Northeastern North America* (New York: Plenum Press, 1988).

14. Ralph H. Brown, *Historical Geography of the United States* (New York: Harcourt, Brace & World, 1948), iii.

15. Ralph H. Brown, *Mirror for Americans* (New York: American Geographical Society, 1943).

16. John. K. Wright, "Terrae Incognitae: The Place of Imagination in Geography," *Annals AAG* 37 (1947): 1–17. For an example see, Martyn Bowden, "The Perception of the Western Interior of the United States, 1800–1870: A Problem in Historical Geosophy," *Proceedings of the Association of American Geographers* 1 (1969): 16–21. Also, David Lowenthal and Martyn Bowden, eds., *Geographies of the Mind: Essays in Historical Geosophy* (New York: Oxford University Press, 1976).

17. Although Lemon's work did not focus on this aspect of settlement exclusively, it was an important contribution. See J.T. Lemon, *Best Poor Man's Country: A Geographical Study of Early Southeastern Pennsylvania* (Baltimore: Johns Hopkins University Press, 1972). Of a similar nature is H.B. Johnson, "The Location of German Immigrants in the Middle West."

18. Douglas R. McManis, *The Initial Evaluation and Utilization of the Illinois Prairies, 1815–1840* (Chicago: University of Chicago Geography Department Research Paper 64, 1964); T.G. Jordan, "Between the Forest and Prairie," *Agricultural History* 38 (1964): 205–16; R. Sauder, "Patenting an Arid Frontier: Use and Abuse of the Public Lands in Owens Valley, California," *Annals AAG* 79 (1989): 544–69.

19. H. Roy Merrens, "The Physical Environment of Early America: Images and Image Makers in Colonial South Carolina," *Geographical Review* 59 (1969): 530–56.

20. Carville Earle, "Environment, Disease, and Mortality in Early Virginia," *Journal of Historical Geography* 5 (1979): 365–90.

21. Jeffrey B. Roet, "Land Quality and Land Alienation on the Dry Farming Frontier," *Professional Geographer* 37 (1985): 173–82.

22. M.J. Bowden, "Geographical Changes in Cities Following Disaster," in *Period and Place*, 114–26.

23.   Andrew Clark, "Historical Geography," in *American Geography: Inventory and Prospect*, P. James and C. Jones, eds. (Syracuse: Syracuse University Press, 1954), 71–105.

24.   Robert D. Mitchell, *Commercialism and Frontier: Perspectives on the Early Shenandoah Valley* (Charlottesville: University Press of Virginia, 1977) and Sam B. Hilliard, *Hog Meat and Hoecake: Food Supply in the Old South, 1840-1860* (Carbondale: Southern Illinois University Press, 1972).

25.   A.J. Ray, *Indians in the Fur Trade* (Toronto: University of Toronto Press, 1974).

26.   A.D. McQuillan, *Prevailing over Time: Ethnic Adjustment on the Kansas Prairie, 1875–1925* (Lincoln: University of Nebraska Press, 1990).

27.   Sherry H. Olson, *The Depletion Myth: A History of Use of Railroad Timber* (Cambridge: Harvard University Press, 1971).

28.   Walter M. Kollmorgen, "The Woodman's Assaults on the Domain of the Cattleman," *Annals AAG* 59 (1969): 215–39 and C. Barron McIntosh, "Use and Abuse of the Timber Culture Act," *Annals AAG* 65 (1975): 347–62.

29.   Bret Wallach, "Logging in Maine's Empty Quarter," *Annals AAG* 70 (1980): 542–43 and "Sheep Ranching in the Dry Corner of Wyoming," *Geographical Review* 71 (1981): 51–63; also see, Lydia M. Pulsipher, "Resource Management Strategies on an Eighteenth Century Caribbean Sugar Plantation," *Florida Anthropologist* 35 (1982): 243–50.

30.   Carville Earle, "Myth of the Southern Soil Miner," in *Ends of the Earth: Perspectives on Modern Environmental History*, Donald Worster, ed. (Cambridge: Cambridge University Press, 1989), 175–210; Lary M. Dilsaver and William Tweed, *Challenge of the Big Trees: A Resource History of Sequoia and Kings Canyon National Parks* (Three Rivers, Calif.: Sequoia Natural History Association, 1990); Stanford E. Demars, *The Tourist in Yosemite, 1855–1985* (Salt Lake City: University of Utah Press, 1991); Ronald Foresta, *America's National Parks and their Keepers* (Washington, D.C.: Resources for the Future, 1984). Also, Michael Williams, *Americans and their Forests: A Historical Geography* (Cambridge: Cambridge University Press, 1989).

31.   For a discussion of the Barrows influence in American historical geography, see William A. Koelsch, "The Historical Geography of Harlan H. Barrows," *Annals AAG* 59 (1969): 632–51. The influence of Barrows on White and his students is discussed in Robert W. Kates and Ian Burton, eds., *Geography, Resources, and Environment*, Vol. II (Chicago: University of Chicago Press, 1986).

32.   B.L. Turner et al., eds., *The Earth as Transformed by Human Action* (Cambridge: Cambridge University Press, 1990).

33.   H.C. Darby, "The Changing English Landscape," *Geographical Journal* 117 (1951): 377–94 and *The Changing Fenland* (Cambridge: Cambridge University Press, 1983); Michael Williams, *Americans and their Forests*.

34.   Michael Williams, "Historical Geography and the Concept of Landscape," *Journal of Historical Geography* 15 (1989): 92–104.

35.   K.L. Wallwork, *Derelict Land: Origins and Prospects of a Land-Use*

Problem (London: David and Charles, 1974) and John Sheail, "Underground Water Abstraction: Indirect Effects of Urbanization on the Countryside," *Journal of Historical Geography* 8 (1982): 395–408.

36. Merlin P. Lawson, *The Climate of the Great Desert: Reconstruction of the Climate of the Western Interior United States, 1800–1850* (Lincoln: University of Nebraska Press, 1974). See also D.W. Moodie and A.J.W. Catchpole, "Valid Climatological Data from Historical Sources by Content Analysis," *Science* 193 (1976): 51–53.

37. J.C. Knox, "Human Impacts on Wisconsin Stream Channels," *Annals AAG* 67 (1977): 323–42; "Historical Valley Floor Sedimentation in the Upper Mississippi Valley," *Annals AAG* 77 (1987): 224–44 and Stanley W. Trimble, "On 'Valley Floor Sedimentation in the Upper Mississippi Valley' by Knox," *Annals AAG* 79 (1989): 593–601. See also Stanley W. Trimble, *Man-Induced Soil Erosion on the Southern Piedmont, 1700-1970* (Ackeny, Iowa: Soil Conservation Society of America, 1974) and "Changes in Sediment Storage Transport in Coon Creek Basin Driftless Area Wisconsin, 1853–1975," *Science* 214 (1981): 181–83.

38. Kenneth Thompson, "Riparian Forests of the Sacramento Valley," *Annals AAG* 51 (1961): 294–315; T.R. Vale, "Vegetation Change and Park Purposes in the High Elevations of Yosemite National Park, California," *Annals AAG* 77 (1987): 1–18; John Vankat, "Fire and Man in Sequoia National Park," *Annals AAG* 67 (1977): 17–27; Conrad J. Bahre and David E. Bradbury, "Vegetation along the Arizona Sonora Boundary," *Annals AAG* 68 (1978): 145–65; Daniel W. Gade, "Weeds in Vermont as Tokens of Socioeconomic Change," *Geographical Review* 81 (1991): 153–69. Also, Carville Earle, *The Evolution of a Tidewater Settlement System: All Hallow's Parish, Maryland, 1650-1783* (Chicago: University of Chicago, Department of Geography, 1975).

39. L. Wester, "Invasions and Extinctions on Masatierra: A Review of Early Historical Evidence," *Journal of Historical Geography* 17 (1991): 18–34.

40. William Cronon, *Changes in the Land: Indians, Colonists, and the Ecology of New England* (New York: Hill and Wang, 1983). Studies of a similar nature include Richard White, *Land Use, Environment, and Social Change: The Shaping of Island County, Washington* (Seattle: University of Washington Press, 1980) and Timothy Silver, *A New Face on the Countryside: Indians, Colonists, and Slaves in South Atlantic Forest, 1500–1800* (Cambridge: Cambridge University Press, 1990). A.W. Crosby, *Ecological Imperialism: The Biological Expansion of Europe, 900–1900* (Cambridge: Cambridge University Press, 1986).

41. The literature is reviewed in Donald Worster, ed., *Ends of the Earth: Perspectives on Modern Environmental History* (Cambridge: Cambridge University Press, 1989). For a critique of the current status of the specialty, see Donald Worster, "Transformations of the Earth: Toward an Agroecological Perspective in History," *Journal of American History* 76 (1990): 1087–1106.

42. Martin V. Melosi, *Garbage in the Cities: Refuse, Reform, and the Environment, 1880–1980* (College Station: Texas A & M University Press, 1987); Joel A. Tarr, "The Search for the Ultimate Sink: Urban Air, Land, and Water

Pollution in Historical Perspective," *Records of the Columbia Historical Society of Washington, D.C.* 51 (1984): 1–29.

43. Robert G. Dunbar, *Forging New Rights in Western Waters* (Lincoln: University of Nebraska Press, 1983); James Malin, *Grassland of North America: Prolegomena to Its History* (Glouchester, Mass.: Peter Smith, 1967); Marc Reisner, *Cadillac Desert: The American West and Its Disappearing Water* (New York: Penguin Books, 1986); Douglas Strong, *Tahoe: An Environmental History* (Lincoln: University of Nebraska Press, 1984).

44. Robert W. Righter, *Crucible for Conservation: The Creation of Grand Teton National Park* (Boulder: Colorado Associated University Press, 1982); Hal Rothman, *Preserving Different Pasts: The American National Monuments* (Urbana: University of Illinois Press, 1989); A. Runte, *National Parks: The American Experience*, 2nd ed. (Lincoln: University of Nebraska Press, 1987) and *Yosemite: The Embattled Wilderness* (Lincoln: University of Nebraska Press, 1990).

45. David A. Clary, *Timber and the Forest Service* (Lawrence: University of Kansas Press, 1986); William G. Robbins, *American Forestry: A History of National, State, and Private Cooperation* (Lincoln: University of Nebraska Press, 1985); William D. Rowley, *U.S. Forest Service Grazing and Rangelands: A History* (College Station: Texas A & M University Press, 1985); Harold K. Steen, *The U.S. Forest Service: A History* (Seattle: University of Washington Press, 1976).

46. Arthur E. Morgan, *Dams and Other Disasters: A Century of the Army Corps of Engineers in Civil Works* (Boston: Porter Sargent, 1971) and Garrett Power, "The Fox in the Chicken Coop: The Regulatory Program of the U.S. Army Corps of Engineers," *Virginia Law Review* 63 (1977): 503–59.

47. Arthur McEvoy, *The Fisherman's Problem: Ecology and Law in the California Fisheries 1850–1890* (Cambridge: Cambridge University Press, 1986); Philip Scarpino, *Great River: An Environmental History of the Upper Mississippi, 1890–1950* (Columbia: University of Missouri Press, 1985); Peter Matthiessen, *Wildlife in America*, 2nd ed. (New York: Penguin, 1987); Frank N. Egerton, "Missed Opportunities: U.S. Fishery Biologists and Productivity of Fish in Green Bay, Saginaw Bay and Western Lake Erie," *Environmental Review* 13 (1989): 33–63.

48. Daniel Schaffer, "Managing Water in the Tennessee Valley in the Post-War Period," *Environmental Review* 13 (1989): 1–16.

49. Micheal C. Robinson, *Water for the West: The Bureau of Reclamation, 1902–1977* (Chicago: Public Works Historical Society, 1979).

50. William J. Jewell and Belford L. Seabrook, *A History of Land Application as a Treatment Alternative: A Technical Report* (Washington, D.C.: U.S. Environmental Protection Agency, Office of Water Program Operations, 1979) and Vary Coats et al., *Nineteenth Century Technology—Twentieth Century Problems: A Retrospective Mini-Assessment* (Washington, D.C.: National Technical Information Service, PB 82-242058, October 1982).

51.   Thomas Alexander, *The Rise of Multiple-Use Management in the Inter-mountain West: A History of Region 4 of the Forest Service* (Washington, D.C.: U.S. Department of Agriculture, U.S. Forest Service, 1987) and Robert D. Baker, Robert S. Maxwell, Victor H. Treat, and Henry C. Dethloff, *Timeless Heritage: A History of the Forest Service in the Southwest* (Washington, D.C.: U.S. Department of Agriculture, U.S. Forest Service, 1988).

52.   Barry Mackintosh, "Assateague Island National Seashore: An Administrative History," (Washington, D.C.: U.S. Department of the Interior, National Park Service, History Division, reproduced typescript, 1982) and Linda W. Greene, *Historic Resource Study: Yosemite*, 3 vols. (Washington, D.C.: U.S. Department of the Interior, National Park Service, 1987).

53.   Albert E. Cowdrey, "Pioneering Environmental Law: The Army Corps of Engineers and the Refuse Act," *Pacific Historical Review* 44 (1975): 331–49 and Martin Reuss, "Atchafalaya," *Environment* 30:4 (May 1988): 7–11, 36–44.

54.   U.S. Environmental Protection Agency, Office of Policy, Planning and Evaluation, *Unfinished Business: A Comparative Assessment of Environmental Problems, Vol. I, Overview* (Washington, D.C.: February 1987).

55.   See Worster, "Transformations of the Earth."

56.   Stanley Trimble, *Man-Induced Soil Erosion*.

57.   Michael Williams, *Americans and their Forests* and Graeme Wynn, *Timber Colony: A Historical Geography of Early Nineteenth Century New Brunswick* (Toronto: University of Toronto Press, 1980).

58.   W.B. Meyer, "Urban Heat Island and Urban Health: Early American Perspectives," *Professional Geographer* 43 (1991): 38–48; C.E. Colten, "A Historical Perspective on Industrial Wastes and Groundwater Contamination," *Geographical Review* 81 (1991): 215–28; D.A. McQuillan, *Prevailing over Time*.

59.   Sam B. Hilliard, "Antebellum Tidewater Rice Culture in South Carolina and Georgia," in *European Settlement and Development in North America*, Paul Gibson, ed. (Toronto: University of Toronto Press, 1978), 91–115.

60.   Jeanne Kay, "The Fur Trade and Native American Population Growth," *Ethnohistory* 31 (1984): 265–87; and Jeanne Kay and C. Brown, "Mormon Beliefs about Land and Natural Resources," *Journal of Historical Geography* 11 (1985): 253–67.

61.   Terry Jordan, "Preadaptation and European Colonization."

62.   L. Wester, "Invasions and Extinctions."

63.   L.M. Dilsaver and William Tweed, *Challenge of the Big Trees*; and Stanford Demars, *The Tourist in Yosemite* and T.R. Vale, "Vegetation Change and Park Purposes." Another important contribution to this literature is William L. Graf, *Wilderness Preservation and the Sagebrush Rebellion* (Lanham, Md.: Rowman & Littlefield, 1990).

64.   I.G. Simmons, *Changing the Face of the Earth: Culture, Environment, History* (Oxford: Basil Blackwell, 1989) and Andrew S. Goudie, *The Human Impact on the Natural Environment*, 3rd ed. (Cambridge: MIT Press, 1990).

65.   Piers Blaikie and Harold Brookfield, *Land Degradation and Society* (New York: Methuen, 1987).

66.   Robert D. Mitchell and Paul A. Groves, eds., *North America: The Historical Geography of a Changing Continent* (Lanham, Md.: Rowman & Littlefield, 1987) and Michael P. Conzen, ed., *The Making of the American Landscape* (Boston: Unwin Hyman, 1990).

67.   William Wyckoff and Lary Dilsaver, *Historical Geography of the Mountain West* (Lincoln: University of Nebraska, forthcoming).

68.   Christopher Hamlin, *What Becomes of Pollution? Adversary Science and the Controversy on the Self-Purification of Rivers in Britain, 1850–1900*, William H. McNeil and Peter Stansky, eds. (New York: Garland Publishing, 1987), 10.

69.   Donald Worster, "Transformations of the Earth."

70.   Carl Sauer, "The Agency of Man on Earth," in Thomas, *Man's Role*, 49.

**Part One
Early Explorations in Impact and Policy**

2

The Alcovy River Swamps: The Result of Culturally Accelerated Sedimentation

Stanley W. Trimble

The Alcovy River is a Georgia Piedmont stream which originates in mid-Gwinnett County and flows through Walton and Newton Counties. Along the main stream are several thousand acres of swamp and marsh. These swamps have been recently described as "a primeval mystery land that was created before the Indians came to Georgia."[1] An intensive investigation by this writer in the Oconee River watershed directly to the east of the Alcovy River has shown that most swamps and marshes in that area are man-made.[2] Based on this information and a study of the Alcovy watershed, most of the Alcovy swampland appears to have been created since the time of European settlement, which began in 1814. Briefly, the process whereby swamps are culturally induced is as follows.

The Georgia Piedmont, an erosional tinderbox of steep slopes, easily eroded soils, and intense rainfall, was settled by Europeans who brought with them the twin torches of clean-cultivated crops and poor conservation methods. Erosion was accelerated to many times the geologic norm, and streams that had once been clear and flowed over bedrock soon were choked by sediment. Because Piedmont soils are rather coarse (30 to 75 percent sand and coarser materials), most sediment was carried as bedload, causing the bed and banks of the stream to be built up, often above the level of the valley floors, flooding the bottomland. Even if not flood-

Editors' Note: This paper has been widely cited over the years as an example of how historical documents can be used to reconstruct human impacts on the environment. Furthermore, we feel it represents a pioneering effort, and for these reasons, we chose to include it here. It originally appeared in the *Bulletin of the Georgia Academy of Sciences* 28 (1970): 131–41 and is reprinted with permission.

ed, the once fertile and valuable bottomlands were usually covered by coarse, infertile sediment. This accelerated erosion and sedimentation continued unabated until recently, when decreases in row crops, an increase in forests, and implemented conservation practices combined to stop most soil erosion.

For this study only the continuous belt of swamps along the main stream, as shown in Figure 2-1, will be under consideration.[3] The data examined to reconstruct the former landscapes are both historical and geographic.

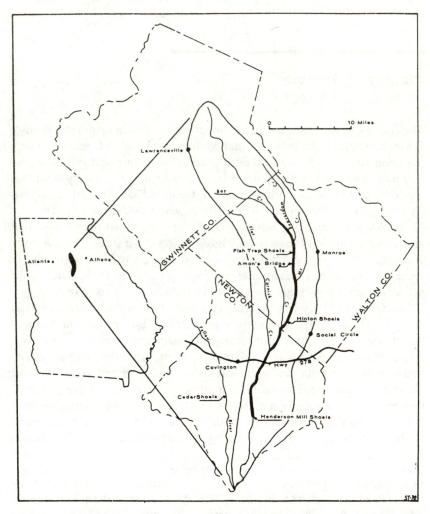

Figure 2-1. The Alcovy River Swamps study area. The heavy line denotes the main stream portion under investigation.

Investigation of Historical Data

In order to gain a picture of the pre-European settlement landscape, the original plats of survey on file in the Office of the Surveyor General of Georgia were inspected.[4] These plats are accurate, large-scale maps of the presettlement landscape with certain features noted such as streams, lakes, swamps, and ponds. To ensure accuracy, surveyors were under a bond of $10,000. Thus, any stream valley swamps, wetlands, or other land unsuitable for agriculture should have been recorded. In addition to the plats of survey themselves, the surveyor's field notes were also inspected by the writer to corroborate the plats.

Within the study area, only two stretches of swamp were noted by the surveyors, both in Walton County and both approximately two miles long.[5] Other than these two areas, the bottomland in the study area was apparently suitable for agriculture. Figure 2-2 is a copy of the plat of the mouth of Cornish Creek, an area which is at present a well-developed swamp.

Another significant feature of streams at the time of survey was the well-defined stream channel. Presently, the stream channel is often braided and is almost nonexistent in several places, especially downstream from the mouth of Cornish Creek. The evolvement of such a braided channel would indicate massive stream and valley sedimentation since the plats of survey were completed.

The suitability of the Alcovy bottomlands for agriculture is dramatized by the premium prices they brought at the time of settlement. A systematic sampling of land lot prices in Walton and Newton counties indicated that Alcovy bottomland prices per acre were usually from three to six times those of the upland.[6] Anita B. Sams, author of *Wayfarers in Walton*, records that the "purchase prices for the standard 250 acre lots ranged from $40 to $2,000 with bottom lands on the Alcovy bringing the best prices."[7] Moreover, Sams also states that "the banks of the Alcovy were favored sites for homes."[8] Thus, not only were the Alcovy bottomlands especially favored for agriculture, but they were often the sites of the farmsteads.

The clearing of the Piedmont soils, however, soon had its effects. Sir Charles Lyell, the observant British geologist, passed to the south of the study area in 1845. He stated that the Ocmulgee River into which the Alcovy flows had been clear, even during floods, until the upstream area had been settled and cleared by Europeans.[9] Lyell also noted the rapidity with which Piedmont soil eroded and gullied after being cleared.[10]

It appears evident that the formation of swamps along the Alcovy had progressed little by about 1850. George White, the author of two antebellum Georgia gazetteers, was able to record in 1849 that, in Walton

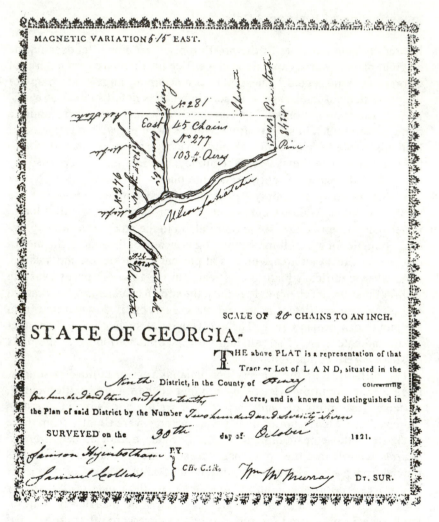

Figure 2-2. Original Land Survey Plat of the Confluence of Cornish Creek with the Alcovy (Ulcofauhatchee River), dated October 30, 1821. (Source: Original Plat Book, AAAA, page 284. Office of the Surveyor General, Georgia State Records and Archives, Atlanta, Georgia.)

County, "first quality lands are on Alcovy river, Jack's and Hard Labour Creeks." For Newton County, White noted that "the most productive lands lie on the rivers."[11] In 1855, a committee was appointed to appraise the Cedar Shoals on Yellow River four miles west of the present Alcovy swamp. In describing the surrounding landscape, the commission reported that "the face of the country is very free from swamps or marshes of any description."[12]

The first travel accounts of anyone crossing the study area were those of Sherman's troops in November 1864. During their traverse across Georgia, most unit commanders noted landscape features, especially swamp streams which would have afforded a difficult crossing.[13] Of approximately 140 accounts of units passing through the study area, only two mentioned swamp conditions on the Ulcofauhatchee (Alcovy) River.

The greater part of Sherman's Fourteenth Corps crossed the Alcovy just east of Covington, probably at the present Highway 278 crossing. This site was a ford for a pioneer road which possibly succeeded an old Indian trail. It is noted on the 1821 plats of survey as "McGourk's Road Crossing."[14] The west bank at this site, presently a swamp one-half mile wide, was the campsite for several thousand troops on November 17–18, 1864.[15] Sherman himself spent the night at this crossing.[16] No swamps or wet ground were noted by troops crossing at this site on November 18, 1864. However, swampy conditions were recorded by two units crossing on November 19. One of these accounts of November 19 described the Alcovy: "The stream is not very deep, rapid, without making a swamp on either side of the stream for a considerable distance."[17] It is perhaps important to note that it had rained during the night of November 18–19, 1864, possibly affecting the stream level on the 19th.[18] Although the present bridge and its approach over the bottomland swamp at this site is approximately one-half mile long, Sherman's engineers reported that they were able to cross on a pontoon bridge eighty feet in length.[19] Nonetheless, it is quite probable that swamps had begun to develop in the area by about 1865. Erosion had been proceeding for almost fifty years, and only a few feet of channel aggradation could possibly have caused large areas of bottomland to be inundated. Further, this part of the stream has a very low gradient and would have been especially suscep- tible to sedimentation.

Troops of Sherman's Twentieth Corps crossed the Alcovy upstream near Social Circle (probably at Hinton's Shoal) and noted no swamps. All of these troops had crossed the Alcovy by November 18.

In 1882 a survey was made of waterpower in the United States, and the Alcovy River was included. The surveyor noted no swamps on the Alcovy, but he reported that the river was "sluggish."[20] He did, however, mention Hinton's Shoal in Walton County, noting that the shoal had a fall of five feet. The head of this shoal is presently (May 1970) under eigh- teen inches of water at normal stream flow. Thus, the river has aggraded a minimum of six and one-half feet at this point since 1882.

A U.S. Geological Survey topographical map, *Monroe, Georgia* (1:125,000), surveyed in 1891, indicates swamp or marsh along much of the lower two-thirds of the study area. This map would indicate that swamps were becoming extensive by 1891. The stream channel, however, is shown as well defined and unbraided.

In 1901 a soil survey was made of the Covington area including part of the study area. It notes that the "larger streams are bordered by belts of meadow land [recent alluvium], often marshy, and subject to overflow at flood time."[21] The surveyor noted that much of the bottomland was being cultivated at that time and that more would be except for frequent flooding. The very recentness of overbank deposition is clearly pointed out by the surveyor; he notes that "leaves, twigs, and decaying branches of trees are found to a depth of three or four feet."[22] This much recent overbank deposition would have indicated an even greater depth of channel deposition. The map that accompanies this survey does not indicate the extent of swampy or marshy areas. It does, however, indicate a house located at the mouth of Flat Creek, an area which is now covered by extensive, well-developed swamps.

An agriculture drainage survey completed by the Georgia Geological Survey in 1917 reported that "pockets" of bottomland comprising two thousand acres along the Alcovy River in Walton County was swamped or was overflowed too often to be of agricultural use.[23] A detailed report for Newton County was unfortunately not given. Several miles of streams in the Alcovy watershed were ditched during the period 1917 to 1935 in order to regain bottomlands lost to swamping. A passage in the Drainage Records of Walton County vividly portrays the bottomlands in the Alcovy watershed in 1919 before being ditched:

> The bottom lands on these streams have become so wet that it is now almost impossible to till or cultivate any of them, a great proportion of these lands have been abandoned and are growing up in willows, some has never been in cultivation and is growing large timber, while a part is in pasture and some small parts are still planted in corn.[24]

The ditching lowered the base levels of tributary streams, causing them to empty their sediment into the ditched channels. Also the upland erosion continued unabated. The result was that the ditched channels, some as deep as twenty feet, soon refilled and the bottomlands again became swamps.

An important but forgotten landscape feature brought to light by the drainage records was Fish Trap Shoals, which, before being covered by sediment, were located just upstream from the present Highway 138 bridge in Walton County. These shoals were described in 1915 as having "sufficient fall to take the water away at a level much lower than the surface of the bottom land."[25] Fish Trap Shoals are presently (May 1970) covered by over sixteen feet of sediment.

An erosion survey of the study area in 1935 reported that severe erosion had started soon after settlement. Land abandonment, an especially significant source of sediment because the gullying removed the coarse saprolitic material, had begun before the Civil War. At the time of the survey in 1935, it was noted the "pine trees 75 years old were observed on several old fields that had lost over 75 percent of the surface soil."[26] The abandonment of land became even more pronounced later on:

> Large areas of abandoned land occur on the upper watershed of the Alcovy River, especially on the steeper slopes bordering the larger streams. Many of these areas were cleared during the period at the end of the World War, when high cotton prices prevailed.[27]

The material removed from both abandoned and actively cultivated land soon had its effect on the streams. The survey stated:

> Many of the formerly productive flood-plain soils have been ruined by deposits of sand and silt; stream channels have become clogged with sands and clays. The channels of the upper Alcovy River and its tributaries are more completely filled with sand than the channels of the other large streams in the area. Practically all the bottom land along the Alcovy River has been covered by sand, or the channel has become so clogged with sand that the bottom lands are now swamps. According to farmers in this vicinity, good corn crops were grown only 20 years ago on bottom lands that are now swamps, worthless for cropland. On Little Flat Creek, a tributary of the Alcovy River, a millpond has been completely silted up and is now planted to corn. Silting of bottom lands has been less destructive along Yellow and South Rivers, probably because these have a gradient steeper than that of the Alcovy.[28]

Elderly people still living in the study area can remember many bottomland areas being cultivated or used for pasture which have been transformed into swamp over the past sixty years. Mr. J.W. Thompson of Between, Georgia, for example, remembered the bottomland downstream from Amon's Bridge in mid-Walton County as being "almost like a park" in 1910. The bottoms were used as a wooded pasture so that the tall virgin oaks, pines, sweetgums, and hickories grew with little undergrowth. The land was not wet but was overflowed too often to grow crops. This land had become swamp by 1935. Another specific site recalled by Mr. Thompson was a road that crossed the Alcovy just downstream from the mouth of Bay Creek. This road is now covered by a one-hundred-acre lake. Mr. Thompson also stated that as a youth he had heard old-timers relate having cultivated bottomland in the nineteenth century which had become swampland by the early part of the twentieth century.[29]

Examination of Geomorphological Factors

Several types of historical evidence have been examined to show that the Alcovy River has been aggrading, causing adjoining lowlands to be inundated and thereby creating new swampland. An examination of physical factors indicates that the Alcovy River would have necessarily *had* to aggrade during the past 150 years. The erosion survey completed in the middle 1930s reported that the study area had lost an average of over six inches of soil to erosion since European settlement.[30] The sedimentologist estimated that 43 percent of the total soil lost was deposited in streams and on bottomlands to an average depth of three feet.[31] In reality, however, most of the sediment would be deposited in or near the streams, an area comprising only a fraction of the total bottomland. Thus, the river could easily have aggraded ten to fifteen feet or more in many places, such as is the case at Fish Trap Shoals. If these figures appear unreasonable, it might be instructive to compare the Alcovy with two similar rivers for which culturally accelerated sedimentation has been more thoroughly documented.[32]

The Mulberry River and the North Oconee River (upstream from Athens) are in the upper Oconee River watershed just east of the study area and are similar to the Alcovy watershed in terms of soils and rainfall intensity. The Alcovy study area, however, has had a larger percentage of the total area in row crops, tenancy (which leads to poor soil conservation) has been more prevalent, and most importantly, the Alcovy River has a lower stream gradient.[33] Whereas the average mainstream gradient of the Mulberry River is 6.8 feet per mile and that of the North Oconee River, 4.6 feet per mile, the Alcovy River has an average gradient of only 3.5 feet per mile. It is, therefore, theoretically probable that the Alcovy River would have undergone more sedimentation than either the Mulberry or the North Oconee River. Moreover, this sedimentation would probably have begun to occur at an earlier date.

The Mulberry River, by actual measurement, has aggraded from three to seventeen feet along its entire length, thereby inundating several thousand acres of bottomland. Of the many bedrock shoals that were visible fifty to seventy-five years ago, not one may be seen today. The North Oconee River has aggraded its bed to depths of up to eighteen feet. Of the many shoals once extant, only one, Hurricane Shoals, now remains visible. Only two long-term index measurements were found for the Alcovy River. At Fish Trap Shoals, as previously noted, the river has aggraded over sixteen feet, while at Hinton Shoals the river has aggraded at least six and one-half feet. Geomorphologically speaking, a shoal is a point of least aggradation. Therefore, twenty feet of aggradation in many stretches of lower gradient would not be an overestimate in the opinion of this investigator. Probably the only way to determine accurately the depth of aggradation along the entire Alcovy is to employ Carbon 14– or pollen-dating methods, which are difficult and expensive processes.

Meanwhile, the Alcovy River continues to aggrade. The head of Hinton Shoals, now under eighteen inches of water, was visible as late as 1959. People living in the area state that the swamps are becoming larger. Inasmuch as there is little sediment coming from upland erosion, the sediment may be coming from tributaries that are beginning to degrade themselves. In the upper Oconee River watershed, it was ascertained that as a result of diminished erosion and resulting diminished sediment load, lower-order tributaries are degrading. The sediment is being transported to larger streams where the lower stream velocity allows redeposition.[34] If the same process is taking place in the Alcovy River watershed, the mainstream Alcovy will continue to aggrade for some time to come, and the area of swampland will continue to increase.

Summary

At the time of settlement of the Alcovy River watershed by Europeans, it appears, with two noted exceptions, that the bottomland along the river was relatively dry, fertile, and prized by the settlers. Moreover, the stream appeared to have had a well-defined channel and banks. Some settlers, in fact, chose the banks of the Alcovy as a site for their farmsteads. Sediment from the erosion of newly cleared and poorly farmed uplands soon began to fill the streams. The channel of the main stream had built up enough so that swamping of some bottomlands was apparent by the time of the Civil War.[35] Because of continued sedimentation and stream aggradation, the area of swamps and marsh has increased through the years and may continue to increase for some time to come. The flora and fauna of these swamps have developed to the point that the swamps are now mistakenly considered to be "natural" and to be thousands of years old.

Acknowledgments

The author wishes to thank Mrs. Pat Bryant and Mr. Marion Hemperley of the Office of the Surveyor General. The investigation would have been impossible without their assistance. Thanks also goes to Mr. Jim Huff, geologist with the Soil Conservation Service, Athens, Georgia, for the extended loan of several documents used for this study. The author is indebted to Professors Kirk Stone and James Woodruff, Messrs. A.P. Barnett and Jim Huff, and Dr. Donal Hook for their critical reading of the manuscript. Appreciation is due the National Science Foundation for financial support during this study. Finally, I should like to thank my wife, Alice, who so willingly typed the many drafts of the manuscript.

Notes

1. G.T. Bagby, "Our Ruined Rivers," *Georgia Game and Fish* 7 (1969): 2–16.

2. S.W. Trimble, "Culturally Accelerated Sedimentation on the Middle Georgia Piedmont" (M.A. thesis, University of Georgia, 1969).

3. From the mouth of Gap Creek in northern Walton County downstream to Henderson Mill Shoals southeast of Convington.

4. Georgia State Records and Archives Building, Atlanta, Georgia.

5. One area of swamp was upstream from the mouth of Beaverdam Creek, while the other was upstream from the mouth of Mountain Creek.

6. See, for example, Purchases of Fractions in Gwinnett, Habersham, Hall, Rabun, and Walton Counties sold in 1821 under the Act of December 22, 1820, Original Plats in the Records of the Office of Surveyor General, Georgia State Records and Archives Building, Atlanta.

7. Anita B. Sams, *Wayfarers in Walton* (Doraville, Ga.: Foote and Davis, 1967), 109, see also 112 and 285. Based on her historical research, Mrs. Sams stated that she also believed the Alcovy River swamps to have come into existence since European settlement. Interview with author, August 13, 1970.

8. Sams, *Wayfarers in Walton,* 6.

9. Sir Charles Lyell, *A Second Visit to the United States,* Vol. 1 (New York: Harper and Brothers, 1849), 256.

10. Ibid., Vol. II, 28–31.

11. G. White, *Statistics of the State of Georgia* (Savannah: W. Thorne Williams, 1849), 581 and 450.

12. Report of the Committee Sent to Georgia to Examine the Cedar Shoals Water Power, (Boston: Farwell and Co., 1855). De Renne Collection, Special Collections Room, Main Library, University of Georgia, Athens.

13. *The War of the Rebellion, A Compilation of the Official Records of the Union and the Confederate Armies,* 128 Volumes (Washington, D.C.: 1880–1901). Series I, Vol. XLIV, 37–361. Also consulted were the several diaries and books concerning Sherman's march through Georgia.

14. Book LLL, 256, plat 219, Original Plats in the Records of the Office of Surveyor General, Georgia State Records and Archives Building, Atlanta.

15. *War of the Rebellion,* Vol. XLIV, 50, 163, 194, and 270.

16. W.T. Sherman, *From Atlanta to the Sea* (Bungay, Suffolk: Richard Clay and Co., 1961), 164.

17. E.L. McCormick, E.G. McGehee, and Mary Strahl, eds., *Sherman in Georgia* (Boston: D.C. Heath and Co., 1961), 35.

18. *War of the Rebellion*, Vol. XLIV, 213; and M.A.D. Howe, *Marching with Sherman: Passages from Letters and Campaign Diaries of Henry Hitchcock* (New Haven: Yale University Press, 1927).

19. *War of the Rebellion*, Vol. XLIV, 60.

20. U.S. Bureau of the Census, Tenth U.S. Census, *Reports on Water Power of the United States* (Washington, D.C.: 1880), 156.

21. H.W. Marean, *Soil Survey of Covington Area, Georgia* (Washington, D.C.: U.S. Department of Agriculture, Bureau of Soils, 1901), 331.

22. Ibid., 336.

23. H.H. Barrows and J.V. Phillips, "Agricultural Drainage in Georgia," *Geological Survey of Georgia Bulletin* No. 32 (Atlanta: 1917), 103.

24. Volume, Drainage Records, 60, Office of the County Clerk, Walton County Court House, Monroe, Georgia. In addition to reclaiming farmland, the records indicated that ditching would "improve the public health by draining breeding places for malaria mosquitoes and improve the roads that cross the district, allowing the RFD carriers to make their appointed rounds" (p. 9).

25. Volume, Drainage Records, 8. Mr. J.W. Thompson of Between, Georgia, could also vaguely remember these shoals. Interview with author, May 2, 1970. A sixteen-foot sand probe failed to reach the bedrock at the site of the shoals.

26. P.H. Montgomery, *Erosion and Related Land Use Conditions on the Lloyd Shoals Reservoir Watershed, Georgia* (Washington, D.C.: U.S. Department of Agriculture, 1940), 7.

27. Ibid., 17.

28. Ibid., 16.

29. Mr. J.W. Thompson, interview with author, May 2, 1970. Mr. Thompson, who has hunted and fished along the Alcovy River for over sixty years, furnished the investigator with several other examples of stream aggradation. Mr. Oscar Barton, also of Walton County, could remember fields and roads which are now covered by swamps. For the sake of brevity, these additional examples have not been included in this study.

30. Montgomery, Erosion and Related Land Use, 21. In an area of 905,024 acres, 467,200 acre-feet of soil were estimated to have been lost to erosion.

31. Studies of accelerated sedimentation in the Southeast have shown that, by 1940, most erosional debris had accumulated within approximately ten miles of the point of upland origin. Stafford C. Happ, Gordon Rittenhouse, and G.C. Dobson, *Some Principles of Accelerated Stream and Valley Sedimentation*, U.S. Department of Agriculture, Technical Bulletin No. 695, 1940, 116. Also, Montgomery, Erosion and Related Land Use, 23.

32. Stanley W. Trimble, "Field Reports to Accompany Trimble" and "Culturally Accelerated Sedimentation," 6–26 and 43–54. Manuscript folder located in the Special Collections Room, Main Library, University of Georgia, Athens. This is a collated set of field reports concerning twenty-two investigation sites in the upper Oconee River watershed.

33. Trimble, "Culturally Accelerated Sedimentation," 52–62.

34.   Ibid., 79–91.

35.   That some of the swamps are as much as one hundred years old seems to be corroborated by botanical evidence. The largest water tupelo trees in the study area (trees that need inundation to succeed other plants) appear to be approximately one hundred years old. Dr. Donal Hook, Plant Psychologist, S.E. Forestry Experiment Station, Forest Science Laboratory, Athens, Georgia, Interview with author, August 11, 1970.

3

Some Conservation Schemes of the Hudson's Bay Company, 1821–1850: An Examination of the Problems of Resource Management in the Fur Trade

Arthur J. Ray

Current interests in the plight of many Indian groups, and the concern with ecologically directed conservation efforts, have stimulated a reexamination of the North American fur trade. As part of this reexamination, the record of the attempts by the Hudson's Bay Company to adopt and effect a conservation policy for beaver and other furbearers in the early nineteenth century deserves careful consideration.

In this paper attention will be focused upon the beaver conservation schemes that the Hudson's Bay Company tried to introduce in Western Canada between 1821 and 1850 under the direction of Governor George Simpson. For this study the lands that lay within the company's Northern Department (Fig. 3-1) have been chosen. The problems that Governor Simpson and the company faced in their efforts to husband beaver populations in this region were similar to those they faced in other areas and/or in the management of other resources.

Trade Rivalries and the Destruction of Fur and Game Resources, 1763–1821

The period between 1763 and 1821 was the time when fur-trading rival-

Editors' Note: This chapter represents an early effort to examine natural-resource conservation in the context of the colonial economy of North America. It originally appeared in its entirety in the *Journal of Historical Geography* 1 (1975): 49–68 and is reprinted here with permission.

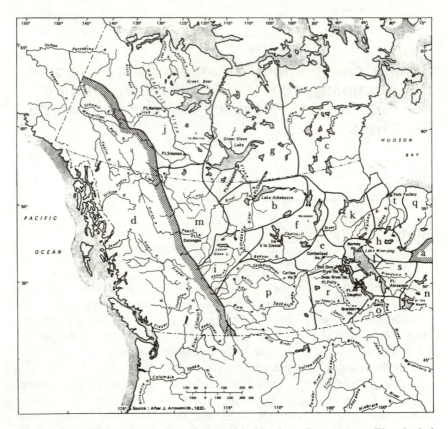

Figure 3-1. The Hudson's Bay Company's Northern Department. The shaded line shows the limits of the Northern Department. Letter codes: a, Albany; b, Athabasca; c, Churchill; d, Columbia; e, Cumberland; f, English River; g, Great Slave Lake; h, Island; i, Lesser Slave Lake; j, Mackenzie River; k, Nelson River; l, Norway; m, Peace River; n, Rainy Lake; o, Red River; p, Saskatchewan; q, Severn; r, Swan River; s, Winnipeg; t, York.

ries were sharpest in Western Canada as the Hudson's Bay Company struggled with competitors, most notably the Montreal-based traders operating in groups known as the North West and XY Companies, for the Indians' furs. This competition forced these companies to expand their operations territorially, and it encouraged them to increase the numbers of posts that they maintained in the various districts. Therefore, not only were the local furbearing animals intensively trapped, but heavy hunting pressure was brought to bear on large game animals also as the Indians attempted to satisfy the mushrooming logistical requirements which this expansion of trading networks generated. Consequently, when the Hudson's Bay and North West Companies merged in 1821, bringing this period of cut-throat competition to an end, whole territories had been laid to waste, and the resource base of the fur trade and the food supplies of the Indians had been seriously undermined in many sections. This was particularly the case in the wooded country adjacent to, and south of, the Churchill River in the Northern Department (Fig. 3-1). The situation was most acute in the area to the east of Lake Winnipeg and the Red River. For example, the annual report for the Hudson's Bay Company's Rainy Lake District submitted in 1822 stated:

> The large game animals are the Rein Deer and Moose, but in such small numbers that the natives cannot kill enough to supply themselves with leather for their moccasins and snow shoes.[1]

Not only was leather scarce, food was said to be in such short supply that many of the Indians had abandoned the region rather than face starvation. Those who remained were reported to have been preoccupied with food-gathering activities and therefore had little time to devote to trapping the few remaining furbearing animals.[2]

The Indians faced similar hardships in the Winnipeg, Norway, Island Lake, York, Nelson River, Cumberland, and English River Districts, and Governor Simpson said that these problems were stimulating an emigration of population. Most of the Indians relocated near the Red River Colony, the Indian Mission at Norway House at the northern end of Lake Winnipeg, or in the grassland sections of the Red River, Swan River, and Saskatchewan Districts where food was plentiful.[3] The pace of this outward migration was such that Governor Simpson expressed the fear that unless it was slowed in some manner, the woodland Indian population would no longer be large enough to provide the company with the hunters and trappers it required.[4] In the Lesser Slave, Peace, Athabasca, Great Slave, and Mackenzie River Districts the depletion of game does not appear to have been a serious problem before the 1830s, judging from the letters which the traders in charge of those districts wrote to Governor Simpson.[5]

Conservation Strategies Before 1841

It is clear that when Governor Simpson assumed control of the Canadian operations of the Hudson's Bay Company in 1821, years of overhunting and trapping had left the trade of many areas on a precarious footing. Yet, he was convinced that effective countermeasures could be taken. Reflecting this optimism, in his 1822 report to the Governor and Committee in London he wrote:

> The country is without doubt, in many parts exhausted in valuable furs, yet not to such a low ebb as has been generally supposed and by extending the trade in some parts and nursing others, our prospects are by no means unfavourable.[6]

Since beaver had long been the staple in trade, Simpson focused his efforts on "nursing" them back.

One of the cornerstones of his conservation program involved the curtailment of trapping operations in overhunted districts, while at the same time the company traders were encouraged to extend the trade into new areas. In the Northern Department this meant that the fur trade was to be vigorously prosecuted in the Mackenzie River District, particularly in the mountainous western and northwestern portions of the district, while in most of the territories lying to the south of the Churchill River a variety of approaches were used in an attempt to ease the trapping pressure on the remaining beaver. Recognizing the difficulties of obtaining Indian consent to local moratoriums on beaver hunting for reasons which will be discussed subsequently, Simpson began to shift trading posts around within the districts in accordance with the fluctuations of fur returns. For example, in 1824 he closed Fort Dauphin and the Swan and Red Deer River posts in the Swan River District and Brandon House in the Upper Red River District (Fig. 3-1). To replace these four posts he opened Fort Pelly, which was centrally located to serve both districts, including the Qu'Appelle River valley (Fig. 3-1). Besides cutting the company's operating costs in these overexploited areas, Simpson believed these actions would, "remove the Indians from exhausted tracts of country which will recruit, to parts which have of late been little hunted."[7] The Governor based this assumption on the belief that the Indians would gravitate toward Fort Pelly, giving the other parts of the district a chance to recover. Similar moves were made elsewhere.[8] Generally, these moves did have a positive effect, and in the Swan and Upper Red River areas for instance, furbearers, especially beaver, were reported to be rebounding by 1826. In part this rapid recovery was due to the fact that the closing of Brandon House and Fort Qu'Appelle had the unexpected effect of leading many Assiniboine and Plains Cree to discontinue trapping activities altogether. Instead, it encouraged these two groups to "follow the Herds of Buffolo wherever they go depending on their Bows and Arrows."[9] Simpson added:

> So many Indians being therefore withdrawn leaves a great portion of that country [Swan River District] to recruit, but the improvement is very slow

as of late years it was scarsly [sic] possible to trace a vestige of Beaver on the Assiniboine River in any of its feeders; they now however begin to appear and if left undisturbed for a few years there is no question that important advantages will result.[10]

Besides shifting post locations in response to changing local resource conditions, the traders also attempted to swing the focus of Indian trapping activities from beaver to other furbearing species. In doing this, the Hudson's Bay Company traders tried to take advantage of the fact that the populations of all of these animals fluctuated a great deal irrespective of the intensities of hunting pressures. Frequently, the oscillations of population in one species did not parallel those of another, but rather complemented them. Furthermore, there was a considerable variation in the amplitude and duration of these population cycles in the different animal species. Governor Simpson was quick to note this phenomenon, and he sought to exploit it by having the Hudson's Bay Company traders encourage the Indians to concentrate their trapping activities on one furbearing species as it approached a population peak, leaving others, usually beaver, to recoup their losses in the interim.

This practice was particularly well suited to the boundary waters area of Ontario and Minnesota, southern Manitoba, and central Saskatchewan. The hydrography of much of this area is characterized by rivers and lakes that have extensive shallow water margins which provide ideal habitats for muskrat and beaver. By the 1820s nearly all of the beaver and other prime fur animals had been trapped out of this country, and the fur trade was heavily dependent on muskrat.[11] Of all of the furbearers, this animal exhibited the greatest fluctuations in numbers. Significantly, the oscillations of muskrat populations were closely tied to short-term variations in rainfall and runoff. Living in the shallow waters of lakes and rivers and having no control over local water levels, they were more sensitive to water level changes than were the beaver. High water can limit the growth of aquatic plants which the animal feeds upon, principally rootstocks, cattails, bulrushes, and arrowhead plants, while low water may cause ponds to freeze to the bottom during winter. When the latter occurs, many muskrat starve to death since, unlike the beaver, they do not store food. Low water was an additional problem since it seems to have favored the outbreak of disease. For instance, in 1824 Simpson reported that water levels were low in the Cumberland Department (Fig. 3-1) and, as a consequence, "produced a disease among the Rats that destroyed them by the thousands as heaps were found dead on opening their houses this spring."[12] As a result of this epidemic the muskrat returns of the Cumberland Department declined from 150,000 skins in 1823 to 70,000 skins in 1824.[13] On many other occasions low water levels were said to have produced epidemics that killed many muskrat. In all probability, the disease that broke out under these circumstances was tularemia.[14]

While muskrat populations thus frequently suffered heavy losses, they rebounded quickly with more favorable moisture conditions. The female muskrat may have up to five litters a breeding season and may produce as many as eleven offspring in each litter. In contrast, the female beaver mates in February, bears her young in May, and usually nurses only four cubs per litter. The higher fertility rates of the muskrat allowed them to recoup their population losses much more rapidly than the beaver.[15]

Since the variations of muskrat populations were closely tied to moisture conditions, the traders often used fluctuations in local water levels to make predictions about their future muskrat returns and to plan short-term management strategies on a district basis. For instance, as noted previously, it was very dry in eastern Saskatchewan and western Manitoba in 1824, and low water levels along the lower Saskatchewan River led to a precipitous drop in the muskrat trade of the districts adjoining it, particularly the Cumberland Department. In 1825 more humid conditions returned, ending a two-year drought, and spring flooding along the lower Saskatchewan was extensive that year. This flooding led Simpson to predict that the muskrat would soon reappear in considerable numbers in the Cumberland Department. However, because of the severity of the preceding drought and the intensive trapping pressure that had been exerted on the dwindling muskrat population, he believed that it would not be until 1826 that the recovery would be strongly felt in the returns from the district. Indeed, it was not until 1827 that a marked improvement was reported. By the latter date, higher muskrat returns were being registered throughout eastern Saskatchewan and southern Manitoba.[16]

During this wet phase the Indians were encouraged to turn their attention to muskrat once more in the hope that other fur animals, particularly beaver, would have a chance to recover. For example, when discussing the returns of the Swan River area in 1827 (Fig. 3-1), Simpson reported:

> This District has improved more during the past year than any other . . . which is to be accounted for by the excellent hunts made in Rats while the returns of other furs have fallen off materially particularly in the article of Beaver; this reduction . . . is owing to the measures taken by Chief Factor Clarke to protect it, who discovering that the natives could find ample employment in rat hunting since the year 1823/24.[17]

Fortunately for the Hudson's Bay Company, the market for muskrat skins was strong in Eastern Canada and the United States during the 1820s, and in this instance their conservation scheme paid immediate economic dividends.[18]

The principal difficulty of attempting to exploit the oscillations of muskrat populations to give the beaver periodic respites from heavy trapping related to the fact that the amplitudes of the muskrat cycles were never of sufficient duration to allow the beaver to make a substantial recovery. Simpson was aware of this problem. In 1827 he wrote that although the Indians of the Cumberland District had begun to focus their trapping operations on muskrat, he doubted that it would prove to be very beneficial to future beaver returns from that area since the beaver population was so depleted that it would take many years to recuperate.[19] Simpson's doubts proved well founded. Eighteen twenty-eight was a dry year once again. This led him to write:

> I much fear there will be a considerable falling off next year on this branch of our Trade [Muskrat] as the present season has been hitherto unusually dry, and the Marshes and pools which they frequent are from that cause become stagnant which will engender disease and in all probability destroy them.[20]

Although Simpson's prediction of poor muskrat returns from eastern Saskatchewan and southern Manitoba in 1829 proved to be wrong, persistent low water levels did result in a substantial decline of this trade throughout the region in 1830.[21]

Besides shifting post locations and attempting to exploit alternative fur resources under favorable conditions, the Hudson's Bay Company employed a number of other strategies to manage the dwindling beaver trade. One of these efforts was directed toward encouraging and cajoling the Indians to stop trapping beaver during the summer season when pelts were of little value. Accordingly, in his 1822 report to London, Governor Simpson wrote, "the Indians have been informed that the skins out of season will not be taken off their hands."[22] During the competitive period before 1821 they had been accustomed to bringing in summer beaver to obtain alcohol and other items whenever they required them. Thus, the Indians were not willing to readily accept this abrupt departure from well-established trading practices. Because of this Indian reluctance, many of the company's district heads (called factors) apparently made little effort to enforce the new rule in the 1820s and early 1830s. As late as 1836, the London directors complained to Simpson that too many out-of-season skins were still being sent home from the Bay.[23]

In subsequent years, some of the factors did make a more earnest attempt to obtain Indian compliance with the regulation. Some of them—such as George Gladman, who was stationed at Norway House in the mid-1840s—

resorted to rather dramatic, and questionable, tactics to demonstrate their resolve on this matter to the Indians. In his letter to Governor Simpson dated June 21, 1844, Gladman wrote, "an Indian brought me a Beaver skin the other day/the animal being recently killed/this being against the rule I slapped his face with it."[24] There can be little doubt that such demeaning treatment would have left a strong impression upon the minds of the local Indians. However, for reasons that will be discussed subsequently, it is unlikely that the Indians discontinued their summer beaver hunts even if they did stop bringing summer pelts to the posts.

In the hopes of curbing the indiscriminate nature of Indian trapping (with respect to ages of beaver) and reducing the effectiveness of their operations, Simpson believed that the use of steel traps and castoreum bait, a trapping technique that came into general usage in the 1790s, should be discontinued.[25] Concerning this subject, in 1822 he wrote:

> The use of Beaver Traps should have been prohibited long ago, they are the scourge of the Country and none will, in the future, be given out except for new Districts exposed to opposition and frontier establishments.[26]

Thus, the further trade of steel traps in the Northern Department was banned except in areas near the United States border and the Red River Colony where the Indians could obtain them from alternative suppliers.

Most of the conservation schemes outlined thus far had little chance of success unless the local company traders were committed to the company's long-term goal of placing the fur trade on a sustained-yield basis. Yet there was always the temptation on the part of individual traders to increase their fur intakes on a short-term basis and therefore "look good" in the company's eyes in terms of profits. Also, the Indians living in one district could trade their furs in another near by if the local trader was too zealous in his efforts to implement conservation measures. In order to deal with these problems, Simpson and the governing council for the Northern Department (which was composed of the chief factors of the various districts) decided upon a more coercive plan of action. In 1826 they introduced a quota system for the beaver trade of the Northern Department (Table 3-1). Under this scheme, the average annual beaver returns were calculated for each of the fourteen districts of the department for a three-year period between 1823 and 1825. In 1826 each district was allowed to take in a percentage of its annual trade during the base period. In the case of two districts, those of the Lower Red River and Rainy Lake (Fig. 3-1), beaver quotas were not established because of the close proximity of American traders. In other districts, the fur intake was reduced by from between one-fifth to one-half of what it had been (Table 3-1). Governor Simpson indicated that all of these quotas

Table 3-1
Fur Quotas for 1826

Beaver assorted	Athabascan	Saskatchewan Lesser S. Lake Ft. Assininboine	English River	Cumberland	Swan River and Upper Red River	Lower Red River	Winnipeg
Outfit 1823	7,726	7,800	1,757	272	663	30	44
Outfit 1824	5,479	6,493	1,201	303	644	37	123
Outfit 1825	6,186	6,896	1,078	397	433	80	76
Returns in beaver for 3 years	19,391	21,189	4,036	972	1,740	147	243
Equal to an average per annum of	6,463	7,063	1,345	324	580	49	81
Less	1/5	1/5	1/2	1/2	1/4	—	1/5
	1,292	1,412	673	162	145	—	27
Not to exceed for outfit or 1826	5,171	5,651	672	162	435	—	54

(continued on next page)

Table 3-1
Fur Quotas for 1826
(continued)

Beaver assorted	Lac la Pluie	Norway House	Island Lake	Severn	Nelson River	Churchill	York Factory
Outfit 1823	826	138	352	660	794	447	504
Outfit 1824	735	7	187	368	1,003	317	370
Outfit 1825	501	26	152	211	702	342	285
Returns in beaver for 3 years	2,062	171	691	1,239	2,499	1,106	1,159
Equal to an average per annum of	687	57	230	413	833	368	386
Less	—	1/2	1/2	1/2	1/2	1/2	1/2
	—	29	115	207	417	184	193
Not to exceed for outfit or 1826	—	28	115	206	416	184	193

Source: HBC D 4/89.

would be rigidly enforced with the exception of that of the Saskatchewan District.

The quota for the Saskatchewan District was not enforced because the beaver returns of that department came largely from the Piegan Indians, who obtained their pelts by trapping, trading, and raiding south of the international boundary. Few beaver were taken by the Indians living north of the border because the animal had been nearly trapped out in many sections of the Saskatchewan region, especially in the country to the north of the North Saskatchewan River. Also, the Hudson's Bay Company traders were instructed to discourage the Indians living in the latter areas from taking any more beaver. Thus, by not enforcing the quota, Simpson was hoping to underwrite part of the cost of "nursing" the beaver back in the Saskatchewan District by drawing upon the resources of the American territories to the south.[27]

In brief, during the 1820s the Hudson's Bay Company undertook a series of initiatives that were intended to place the beaver trade on a sustained-yield basis. Yet, in spite of the fact that a variety of approaches were attempted, beaver populations continued to decline. . . .

Changes in the Conservation Program After 1841

Because of the general failure to achieve any significant success in its beaver conservation program before 1841, the Governing Council for the Northern Department issued a series of new rules and regulations that were intended to halt the continuing decline of beaver. The quota system introduced in 1826 had failed for the reasons that already have been outlined. Consequently, in 1841, the council decided to impose a more stringent allotment plan. By the ninetieth resolution in council it was ruled that

> the Impoverishment of the Country in the article of Beaver is increasing to such an alarming extent that it becomes necessary to take effectual measures for providing an immediate remedy to that and it is [resolved] That the gentlemen in charge of Districts and Posts be strictly enjoined to discourage the hunting of Beaver by every means in their power and that not more than half the number collected Outfit 1839 be traded during the Current and two succeeding Outfits at the undermentioned Districts and Posts.[28]

In order to put "teeth" into this regulation and discourage company men from ignoring it as many had the earlier quota system, the council issued an additional resolution (number 91) which stated:

As a further remedy for the evil, if it be found that gentlemen disregard this institution, as they have done many others issued from time to time for the same object it is [resolved] That the Governor and Committee be respectfully advised to give notice of retirement from the Service to such Gentlemen as may not give effect to the Spirit and the letter of the resolution now passed for the preservation of Beaver.[29]

In an effort to obtain Indian compliance with this new restriction on beaver trapping, the council decided to offer them a positive inducement to hunt other fur animals (the "small furs"). Accordingly, it was decided that

in order to encourage the Indians to greater exertions in hunting other Furs and that they may not suffer any privation in consequence of the proposed restriction it is [Resolved] That all Indians at Posts where the restriction exists and who do not kill Beaver be paid in Goods the value of 10 skins or Made Beaver for every 9 skins in small Furs they trade in the Course of the Year.[30]

Thus, the Indians were offered a premium on the small furs that they trapped.

Since these new regulations virtually banned the trapping of beaver in the Northern Department in the lands adjacent to and north of the Saskatchewan–Nelson River system, there was a mixed reaction to them on the part of the company employees.[31] Donald Ross, who was stationed at Norway House, had advocated the implementation of an effective conservation plan in his letters to Simpson prior to the passage of the resolutions. Not surprisingly, therefore, he approved of the new regulations and argued for their continuance in subsequent years.[32] John Lee Lewis who was in charge of Fort Simpson in the Mackenzie River District did not share Ross's view and was an outspoken critic of the new measures. Pressing his case with Simpson, in November of 1842 he wrote:

Drawing your attention for the moment to the restriction on killing Beaver within this District, which I hope by the Minutes of next summers Council to see rescinded, and that we be permitted to return to our usual means of making Packs, the McKenzie is still rich in the article of Beaver and our forbidding the Indians killing [beaver] only makes them generally discontented and tends very little to their preservation, and with many of them cannot be prevented in this hard country, a half starved and famished Indian . . . be it Beaver, or any other kind of food that come in their way, they must and will kill and if we do not take the skins from them after; they can I do assure you balk little at our refusal, for soon they convert the same into warm and comfortable clothing for themselves and Families, and when on a Winter day facing a cold N.W. blast at the Thermo 50 or

60 below zero, they find that they are the gainers and not us, by the present law and regret not our flimsy Blankets or Capots.[33]

Although some of the objections Lewis raised were legitimate, the governing council went ahead with its initial plan of trying the new scheme for a three-year period. By most accounts, this program was a success. During the summer of 1842, James Hargrave reported from York Factory that the Indians living in his district were responding favorably to the premium being paid on small furs and he was optimistic that the plan would work.[34] On August 16, 1843, Don Ross wrote from Norway House that the trapping restrictions were having all of the desired effects and that beaver cuttings and other evidence of the animal's presence were becoming common along the canoe route between Norway House and York Factory. For these reasons he was in favor of extending the ban another two years beyond the expiry date in the summer of 1844.[35] A similar recovery was under way in the territories lying to the northwest. On January 1, 1844, Colin Campbell said that the Indians had informed him that since the beaver-hunting restrictions had been put into effect, the animal had made a comeback and was more numerous in the Athabasca District than it had been in many years.[36]

During the spring of 1844 the subject of the restrictions occupied the attention of most of the district traders since the trial three-year period was coming to an end. Because of the widespread success of the plan and the mounting Indian pressure to relax the rules, most of the district heads favored reintroducing a modest quota system. Regarding this topic, R. Mackenzie Simon wrote to Governor Simpson from Ile à la Crosse on March 2, 1844, informing him:

> Our Chipewyans are now very anxious about killing Beaver. When the Beaver Nursing system was established in -40- I told them it was to continue in force for three years, without killing one Beaver if they could avoid it; but after that period, would be allowed to kill a certain number annually. I would like now that you would be pleased to inform me what Number that should be. . . . We have dealings with 300 Indians in this District, and I think if they could give an average 2 Beaver Skins each, annually, large and Small it would be as much as the District could well afford.[37]

Similar pressures were being felt elsewhere, and the same kinds of questions were being asked. Even Donald Ross at Norway House, who had championed a continuation of the ban beyond the original termination date the previous year, had modified his views and, in March of 1844, expressed the belief that a relaxation of regulations would have to be made the next time the council met.[38]

The London directors shared this view and in a letter dated March 4, 1844, they suggested to Simpson that

> in order to test in a satisfactory manner the improvement reported, it may perhaps be proper to relax for a season, in two or three districts, the prohibition with regard to beaver hunting, and you will determine in council in what districts such a relaxation shall take place, which of course is to be acted upon only in the winter, the issue of traps for all the depots being strictly prohibited.[39]

Therefore, the Governing Committee in London was willing to permit beaver trapping once again as long as the restrictions against summer hunting and the use of steel traps remained in force.

Having obtained this approval from London, the council for the Northern Department met in June of 1844 and passed a resolution which stated that in order to test the degree of improvement since the restrictions had been in effect

> the Gentlemen in charge of the several districts of the Northern Department, be permitted to trade all seasoned Beaver, ascertained to have been hunted during the winter and by the use of the Ice Chisel only.[40]

Although the council's resolution permitted beaver trapping in all districts, rather than in a selected two or three as the London directors suggested, the latter did not oppose it. They were willing to wait a year and assess the results.[41]

The Decline of the Beaver Trade

Ironically, at the very time the Company's conservation program was beginning to bear fruit, the market for beaver pelts in Europe started to decline as the silk hat replaced the felt hat. Having long been accustomed to viewing beaver pelts as a trade staple, the London directors of the company were slow to adjust to change. Rather, they initially regarded the shift away from beaver felt hats as temporary. Thus, on April 1, 1843, they wrote to Simpson, informing him:

> From an extraordinary break of fashion, the article [beaver pelts] . . . has of late fallen much into disuse in hat making, silk hats being principally worn at present, the consequence is that its value has greatly decreased in the market. . . . This depression is but temporary as no doubt exists that

Beaver hats will soon again come into general use, when of course amendment may be expected in the price.[42]

The London directors continued to hope that the beaver hat would regain its lost popularity. In fact, they were optimistic that their conservation efforts would bear fruit in such large returns of beaver pelts that it would lower the market price of beaver felt hats to a level that would make them cheaper than silk hats. This never happened, however, and the beaver hat failed to regain its lost popularity. The company directors then attempted to market beaver in other forms, principally as a fur similar to otter, mink, and other pelts, but these efforts were disappointing. Therefore, shortly after the Hudson's Bay Company began to achieve success in its effort to conserve beaver and conduct this trade on a sustained-yield basis, beaver pelts ceased to be a staple trade item.

Conclusion

After 1821 the Hudson's Bay Company initiated what must have been one of the earliest attempts in North America to put a primary-resource industry on a sustained-yield basis. In endeavoring to achieve this goal the company faced a number of serious problems. In some areas, particularly near the international border, it was confronted with opposition from American and Métis traders who did not have a long-range investment concern in the region and, consequently, were unsympathetic to the company's aims. Under these competitive conditions, which characterized the trade in most areas to the south of the border, management was not possible, and therefore the Hudson's Bay Company did not make a concerted effort to husband beaver in border regions. Rather, its efforts were concentrated in those lands where its monopoly was relatively secure.

Yet even in areas where it held a firm hand on the trade, the company was confronted with considerable obstacles since the fur trade was an industry in which two very disparate cultures took part. The Indians and the Europeans had fundamentally different views regarding future planning and the nature of, as well as the need for, game management. Many Indians believed that game would always be sufficient, provided that the appropriate rituals were followed. In contrast, the European traders maintained that game supplies could be assured only if man consciously husbanded them. Besides holding different views toward the need and nature of game management, the Indian and European concepts of land tenure differed. On an intratribal basis, land was a free resource and bands were free to hunt on each other's lands whenever the need arose, or whenever a given band was not exploiting a resource that was valued by a neighboring group. Hence, the notion of trespass held by Europeans was not held by the Indians in the Northern Department in precontact and early historic times. Thus, there were no traditional rules or customs among the Indians which a band could appeal to in order to justify limiting the access of their neighbors to resources found on their own lands. Furthermore, the egalitarian band organization of the Woodland Indians meant that there were no coercive Indian institutions that could have forced individual or group compliance to such rules had they existed. Under these circumstances, management was nearly impossible even in areas where the Hudson's Bay Company held a monopoly. It was in an effort to deal with these problems that the company attempted to alter Indian concepts of land tenure. Also, by using its economic power under monopoly conditions, the company imposed the authority system and regulations which were needed to control hunting activities. Thus, by pursuing these policies for reasons of self-interest and paternalism, the company played a major role in changing the Indian's way of life in some fundamental ways.

Acknowledgments

A shorter version of this paper was presented at the 1973 Algonquian Studies Conference in Green Bay, Wisconsin, April 6 and 7, 1973. The author would like to thank the Hudson's Bay Company for granting him permission to consult and quote from the company's records. I would like to thank the York University Cartography Office, especially Robert Ryan, for drafting the map.

Notes

1. This District was called the Lac la Pluie District at that time. Public Archives of Canada, Hudson's Bay Collection (hereinafter PAC HBC) B 105/e/2.

2. Lac la Pluie District Reports, 1822–25, PAC HBC B 105/e/2-5.

3. Governor George Simpson, Letters Outward, Report for the Northern Department, 1835, PAC HBC D 4/102, 42.

4. Governor George Simpson, Letters Outward, Report for the Northern Department, 1835, PAC HBC D 4/102, 43.

5. Simpson, Correspondence Inward, 1828–30, PAC HBC D 5/3. It should be pointed out, however, that food supplies had always been precarious in the Mackenzie River District, where the Indians depended heavily upon hare.

6. Simpson, Letters Outward, July 31, 1822, PAC HBC D 4/102, 42.

7. Simpson, Letters Outward, Report to London, Fort Garry, June 5, 1824, PAC HBC D 4/87.

8. Ibid., and Simpson, Report to London, York Factory, August 10, 1824, PAC HBC D 4/87.

9. Simpson, Letters Outward, Report to London, York Factory, August 20, 1826, PAC HBC D 4/89.

10. Ibid. During this period the Plains Indians became relatively independent of the Company. A.J. Ray, *Indians in the Fur Trade* (Toronto: University of Toronto Press, 1974).

11. Simpson, Letters Outward, Report to London, York Factory, August 20, 1826, PAC HBC D 4/89.

12. Simpson, Letters Outward, Report to London, York Factory, August 10, 1824, PAC HBC D 4/87.

13. Ibid.

14. Tularemia is an epizootic disease which causes hemorrhaging of the heart, lungs, and liver of the animal and usually death. Low water levels increase the concentration of tularemia bacteria and therefore increase the probability that muskrat or beaver will contract the disease. For a discussion of this disease (*Pasteurella tularensis*), see W.L. Jellison et al., "Epizootic Tularemia in the Beaver, *Castor canadensis,* and the Contamination of Stream Water with *Pasteurella tularensis,*" *American Journal of Hygiene* 36 (1942): 168–82. For a discussion of its effects on muskrat populations see P.L. Errington, *Muskrat Populations* (Iowa City: Iowa State University Press, 1963) and P.L. Errington, *Muskrats and Marsh Management* (Harrisburg, Pa.: Stackpole, 1961), 49–53.

15. Errington, *Muskrats and Marsh Management*, 35–37.

16. Simpson, Letters Outward, Report to London, York Factory, September 1, 1825, PAC HBC D 4/88. Besides the low ebb of the muskrat population of the Cumberland District, Simpson indicated that many of the Indians had scattered and he believed that this would adversely affect the department's returns for a year or two. In one of his reports for 1827, Simpson wrote that muskrat were increasing in the Cumberland, Swan River, and Winnipeg Districts. Simpson, Letters Outward, Report to London, York Factory, July 25, 1827, PAC HBC D 4/90.

17. Ibid.

18. Simpson, Letters Outward, Report to London, York Factory, September 8, 1823, PAC HBC D 4/86.

19. Simpson, Letters Outward, York Factory, July 25, 1827, PAC HBC D 4/90.

20. Simpson, Letters Outward, Report to London, York Factory, July 10, 1828, PAC HBC D 4/92.

21. Simpson, Letters Outward, Report to London, York Factory, August 26, 1830, PAC HBC D 4/97.

22. Simpson, Letters Outward, Report to London, York Factory, August 10, 1824, PAC HBC D 4/85.

23.   Simpson, Letters Inward, Hudson's Bay House, London, March 9, 1836, PAC HBC D 5/4.

24.   Simpson, Letters Inward, Norway House, June 21, 1844, PAC HBC D 5/11.

25.   R.F. Wells, "Castoreum and Steel Traps in Eastern North America," *American Anthropologist* 74 (1973): 479–83.

26.   Simpson, Letters Outward, Report to London, York Factory, July 31, 1822, PAC HBC D 4/85.

27.   Simpson, Letters Outward, Report to London, York Factory, August 20, 1826, PAC HBC D 4/85.

28.   York Factory, Minutes of the Council for the Northern Department, June 14, 1841, PAC HBC B 239/k/2.

29.   Ibid.

30.   Ibid.

31.   The ban did not apply to the Peel's River area of the Mackenzie River District. Simpson, Letters Inward, Peels River, December 20, 1841, PAC HBC D 5/6.

32.   Simpson, Letters Inward, Norway House, April 10, 1841, August 8, 1942, and August 16, 1843, PAC HBC D 5/6-8.

33.   Simpson, Letters Inward, Fort Simpson, November 25, 1842, PAC HBC D 5/7.

34.   Simpson, Letters Inward, York Factory, May 21, 1842, PAC HBC D 5/7.

35.   Simpson, Letters Inward, Norway House, August 16, 1843, PAC HBC D 5/8.

36.   Simpson, Letters Inward, Fort Chipewyan, January 1, 1844, PAC HBC D 5/10.

37.   Simpson, Letters Inward, Isle à la Crosse, March 2, 1844, PAC HBC D 5/10.

38.   Simpson, Letters Inward, Norway House, March 12, 1844, PAC HBC D 5/10.

39.   Simpson, Letters Inward, Hudson's Bay House, March 4, 1844, PAC HBC D 5/10.

40.   York Factory, Minutes of the Council for the Northern Department, June 10, 1844, PAC HBC B 239/k/2.

41.   Simpson, Letters Inward, Hudson's Bay House, March 4, 1844, PAC HBC D 5/10.

42.   Simpson, Letters Inward, Hudson's Bay House, April 1, 1843, PAC HBC D 5/8.

Part Two
Primary Economies and Resource Exploitation

4

Into the Abyss . . . Again: Technical Change and Destructive Occupance in the American Cotton Belt, 1870–1930

Carville Earle

Unrestrained capitalism has become something of a *deus ex machina* for the prevailing interpretations of American environmental history. While that argument doubtless contains a kernel of truth, the explanation that it offers is so vague in specification, so sweeping in scope, and so linear in trajectory as to constitute no explanation at all.[1] Much American environmental history is reduced to a morality play of good versus evil, of capitalist rapacity versus natural innocence. This makes for good drama, but bad history. It papers over occasional virtue with unending vice, the flash of wisdom with the derision of folly, and the periodically benign with the relentlessly malignant. In this version of history, the dramatic elements are remarkably rude: the *moral*, capitalist avarice and environmental abuse; the *plot*, three centuries of destructive capitalist occupance bracketed on either end by golden ages of ecological wisdom. In the interim between a romanticized Native American naturalism and an enlightened and embattled environmentalism, American capitalists allegedly ran roughshod over the landscape, despoiling as they went field and forest, water and air.

This one-dimensional environmentalist version of the past, I submit, is wrong for at least two reasons: first it misreads the dynamic and adaptive nature of American capitalism; and second it misapplies certain canons of causal and historical interpretation. In the first instance, the environmentalist text more or less writes off American capitalists as unadaptive, environmentally insensitive, and incapable of learning from their mistakes. Doubtless many of them lacked these capacities, but not always and not everywhere. In the second instance, the environmentalist interpretation disregards the enormous variability of American environmental behavior in time and space. Reintroducing the variables of space, time, and adaptability into the American past discloses at once an environmental history that is more problematic and an interpretation that is more satisfying.[2]

This chapter represents a continuing attempt to infuse temporal and spatial variability into the linear and aspatial mainstream of American environmental history. The exposition is less an apologia for capitalism—though that system has its moments—than an attempt to see the past clearly, to temper incantations of a unidimensional and all-powerful capitalism with counterevidence of environmental wisdom and sensitivity, even in cases when Americans (and capitalists) unwittingly abused their lands. And the evidence is ample indeed, especially (and paradoxically) in periods of real or imagined environmental abuse. In fastening attention on one of these cases—the southern cotton belt—I suggest that things are not always as they seem: that southern scholars almost always overlook the region's ecological wisdom, nearly as often misinterpret it as environmental abuse, and, when confronted by genuine environmental abuse, misattribute causality to capitalist avarice instead of to its more likely source in scientific agrarian reform.

I can think of no more apt illustration of history's little deceptions than the case of cotton planters in the nineteenth-century South. Few actors in American history have reaped as much scorn and contempt. They have been indicted for conducting a century-and-a-half campaign of environmental pillage that began with first settlement and lasted until the 1930s; tried as "robbers," "killers," or "miners" of the southern soil; and convicted, alas, as mere ciphers in a capitalist saga of unrelieved destructive occupance. The caricature of southerners as dumb and robotic is surely less than kind; it also happens to be wrong, and proving the case offers at least the satisfaction of turning the mirror on their accusers.[3]

Southern agrarian practices were, of course, more complex than environmental historiography usually allows. Indeed in the history of the southern environment one finds as much good as evil, wisdom as folly, and construction as destruction. And when destructive occupance did occur, environmental abuses were rarely, if ever, premeditated. Even in the most egregious cases of erosion, soil exhaustion, and deforestation, the environmental intentions of southern planters were well meaning, if uninformed. In presenting this brief on behalf of a more dynamic interpretation of capitalism and the environment, I intentionally bias the evidence against the argument by focusing on what may be the worst case of southern environmental abuse—the cotton belt in the period of accelerated soil erosion lasting between the 1870s and 1930. To be sure the cotton belt's unenviable record in these years has few peers in the annals of American environmental history, yet nagging questions remain: how did it happen? and why?

For scholars in the mainstream of southern environmental history, the answers are simple and obvious. This grievous epoch of accelerated erosion constitutes the apotheosis of capitalism, southern style. From that point of view, the exhausted and eroded soils, sediment-filled stream channels and bottomlands, abandoned land, and outmigration represent little more than a logical extension of an ancient regional legacy predicated on capitalism, plantation slavery, row-crop cultivation, and staple monoculture.[4] These claims of an unbroken continuity in southern environmental history stand or fall, however, on two unproven and controversial assertions: (1) that destructive occupance in the South was a linearly exponential process and (2) that southern planters blatantly (and premeditatively) abused the soil in their relentless pursuit of profit. These assertions are belied, however, by the historical and geomorphic record. As odd as it may seem to scholars enveloped in the myth of the soil miner, southern history affords several examples of when capitalist planters demonstrated especial sensitivity to the fertility of their soils. In these times, capitalist profits, ecological wisdom, and constructive occupance went hand in hand. Suspending disbelief affords a glimpse of these discontinuities in southern agrarian behavior and enables us to view afresh the catastrophic events that took place after 1870.

One of these constructive discontinuities occurred, in fact, on the eve of this epoch of destructive occupance. Merely acknowledging the presence of a measure of ecological wisdom in antecedent agrarian practices poses a series of knotty questions on their displacement: Why, for example, did postbellum cotton planters abandon an antebellum system of crop rotation which maintained profits and soil fertility in favor of a system of cotton monoculture, commercial fertilizers, and the accelerated erosion entrained by these innovations? What did planters expect of this new agrarian system? On what basis did they judge the new system as superior to its benign predecessor? Who introduced these innovations and who adopted them? When? Where? And why? And what were the environmental consequences, anticipated and real, of this new agrarian system? Or, to put it more precisely, how did these new agrarian practices translate into accelerated soil erosion and sedimentation? And lastly, how strong is my countercase for agroecological discontinuity? Are the several cycles observed in the agronomic history of the cotton belt—cycles of destructive occupance before 1840 and between the 1870s and 1930 and benign occupance in between—corroborated in the geomorphic record of valley sediments?

These queries reintroduce a sense of the problematic into southern environmental history. They compel us to ask why anyone, least of all southern agrarians, would have set about destroying the very lands that sustained them in a single-minded pursuit of profit. The truth of the matter, as we shall see, is that the havoc they wrought between the 1870s and 1930 was unintended. Southerners, in adopting this new system of commercial fertilizers and monoculture, saw themselves more as foot soldiers in an enlightened and scientifically legitimated agrarian reform than as ciphers in an unfolding capitalist dynamic. How could anyone, least of all an ordinary planter or cropper, have resisted the righteousness of agrarian reform, championed as it was by planter elites, state agricultural societies and bureaus, and fertilizer companies, all of whom genuinely believed that soil fertility would be maintained, cotton yields would increase dramatically, and rising profits would usher in a new and revitalized South?

These were the dreams that southerners dared to dream. To understand why they did not come true, why the dreams of well-intentioned reformers were turned into an ecological and social nightmare, invites a rethinking of this epoch of destructive occupance. I begin with a frontal assault on the linear version of southern history. In demonstrating the discontinuities and periodic alternations in southern environmental behavior, I simultaneously reposition the accelerated erosion between the 1870s and 1930 in macrohistorical context. Thus positioned, this period seems less a climacteric for three centuries of unrelieved destructive occupance and capitalist avarice than a periodic interlude of ill-conceived agrarian reform.

Macrohistorical Alternations in Southern Environmental Occupance, 1600–1870: A Context for the Cycle of Accelerated Erosion, 1870–1930

Southern agriculture is at once the most maligned and the most misunderstood of American agroecological systems. Perhaps because of its enduring commitment to the production of staples—tobacco, rice, indigo, and cotton—for a capitalist world system, this system has always seemed more responsive to the imperatives of the market than to those of ecological systems. Fair enough, but critics of capitalism go a step beyond, eliminating all differences of degree and imposing instead an adversarial disjunction between nature and capitalist economy. Intricate and subtle agrarian strategies are reduced to zero-sum trade-offs between nature and economy. Among other obvious omissions, this reductionist model makes no room for the contingent relations between profits in capitalist agrarian systems, on the one hand, and soil fertility, on the other. Since success in the one depends invariably upon ecological wisdom in the other, we should not be surprised that a refined sense of the interdependence of nature and economy is deeply rooted in the subsoil of southern history. Indeed, it would be remarkable if these sensibilities were lacking.

Perhaps the earliest indications of southern ecological wisdom emerged among tobacco planters in the colonial Chesapeake region. Faced with declining profits and falling yields during the last third of the seventeenth century, these planters introduced an ingenious agroecological system. This system of land rotation achieved three aims: it ensured the viability of the tobacco economy, maintained soil fertility, and retarded soil erosion. Devised as a replacement for a tottering system of continuous cultivation plagued by declining yields and low quality and price (due to manuring, which fouled the taste of the tobacco leaf), the new system restored the fertility of worn-out tobacco soils through a long fallow.

The system of land rotation maintained soil fertility by cycling worn-out land into a long fallow and recycling twenty years hence these old fields back into tobacco. The system, which was especially effective in the Chesapeake region given the high land–labor ratio, worked as follows. The typical worker cleared two or three acres of land, planted it in tobacco for two or three years followed by corn and small grains for another two or three years. The worn-out land was then turned into a long fallow ("old fields") of twenty years or so while nature and ecological succession restored plant nutrients to the exhausted soil. At that point, the tree-covered "old fields" were cleared again and the cycle began anew. On a land-abundant frontier, the twenty to twenty-five acres per worker required for the conduct of this mobile agrarian system was modest indeed.[5]

Land rotation's ecological virtues notwithstanding, this novel agrarian system made a bad impression on Chesapeake visitors. Unaware of the system's role in maintaining tobacco yields and mitigating soil exhaustion and erosion, these sojourners saw instead an ephemeral and disordered landscape. They lamented the scene of unkempt fields littered with stumps and branches and punctuated by irregularly spaced tobacco hills, of ragged old fields in various stages of ecological succession, of dilapidated and unpainted tobacco houses, and of primitive and slovenly methods of cultivation based on hoes, axes, and servile labor.[6]

In their eagerness to voice disapproval of the Chesapeake agrarian system, however, these observers too readily overlooked the several ecological functions that it fulfilled. In the first place, the system required a modest amount of cleared and cultivated land, usually no more than seven to nine acres per worker with two or three in tobacco and five or six in corn and small grains. Second, the system's field architecture, with its chaotic surface of tobacco hills, stumps, and branches, impeded runoff and sediment transport. Third, hoe cultivation and hilling, by confining tillage around the tobacco hillocks rather than over the entire field as in plow culture, served as a further retardant to soil erosion. Fourth, land rotation restored soil fertility naturally (botanically) through long fallows and ecological successions of grasses, shrubs, and second-growth forest. As a consequence of these functions, the environment along the tobacco coast enjoyed nearly a century of constructive occupance. The soils of the Chesapeake region experienced neither appreciable erosion or exhaustion.[7]

Visitors to the area never quite understood the ecological functions of the land-rotation system, and accordingly, their criticism had little effect. The system's demise traces rather to the critique of indigenous agrarian reformers who in the flush of revolution and American independence felt embarrassed by landscape appearances. Rejecting shifting cultivation as a "primitive" form of agriculture, these postrevolutionary reformers championed a new agrarian system based on Enlightenment science and English and French "high farming" systems. The new system replaced hoes with plows, hilling with clean tillage, land rotation with crop rotation, natural succession and long fallows with organic fertilizers—and soon after, constructive occupance with destructive occupance.

While the necessity of these reforms remains an open question—land pressure seems unlikely given the availability of fifty acres or more per worker—the fact of the matter is that planters rapidly installed the new system. Environmental problems arose, however, when many planters implemented some but not all of the reforms. When small planters and tenants eagerly introduced plows and clean tillage and eschewed their complements of organic manures and soil-building crops such as turnips and clovers, they issued an open invitation to soil erosion and exhaustion.[8]

The environmental consequences of elite reform were soon apparent in a region stretching from the Chesapeake to the Carolina piedmont. In the wake of the diffusion of the plow and the partial adoption of other reforms, soil fertility and crop yields declined, soil erosion accelerated, and rivers and harbors silted up. By the mid-1830s, this society of threadbare planters, poor whites, free Negroes, and hired and plantation slaves had begun to unravel. Desperate times called in turn for radical solutions, and each of the region's several classes advanced their own— solutions that ranged from Nat Turner's bloody slave insurrection to Hinton

Rowan Helper's viciously racist apologia for poor whites to George Fitzhugh's ideology of paternalist enslavement for everyone, save the planter elite. Such were the extremist ideologies of native sons in a landscape scarred and impoverished by well-meaning but ill-advised agrarian reforms. In retrospect, it is frightening to imagine the speed with which these reforms had worn out the landscape and displaced the republican ideology of the Founding Fathers with the embittered ideologies of class interest and conflict.[9]

Nor were the decades between 1780 and 1830 kind to environments elsewhere in the South. A similar pattern of destructive occupance (though for quite different reasons) unfurled on the cotton frontier of the lower South. On the heels of the cotton gin, the dramatic rise in cotton prices, and their joint stimulus to upland short-staple cotton and slavery, the cotton frontier spread swiftly across the Deep South, from the South Carolina backcountry across central Georgia, into the black belts of Alabama and Mississippi, and onto the alluvial flats of the lower Mississippi Valley.

If ever agrarian capitalism in the South was truly unrestrained and the pursuit of profit rode roughshod over environmental sensitivity, it was in these halcyon days. Planters cultivated cotton continuously until soils wore out, at which point they abandoned these lands for good and shifted cotton onto new land. And when all of their plantation had been exhausted, they pulled up stakes, migrated to new lands on the edge of the cotton frontier, and repeated their destructive sequence. This strategy of "vicious cultivation" held several consequences: many ordinary planters grew rich (or as W.J. Cash puts it, they acquired both blue blood and pedigree); the institution of slavery, whose viability was in doubt in the 1780s, was reinvigorated; and soils were used, abused, and abandoned at a phenomenal rate (the rate of frontier expansion in the lower South surpasses all other regions in this period).[10]

All of this came to an abrupt end in the long depression of the 1830s and 1840s. The collapse in the cotton market proved sobering to planters long accustomed to high cotton prices, hell-bent expansion, and environmental abuse. Planters everywhere spoke of agrarian reform. They cast about desperately for ways of transforming this rootless and exploitive agrarian system while simultaneously preserving their commitments to cotton and slavery. From among the many innovations presented for consideration, the least well known but perhaps the most fundamental was a system of crop rotation. This system proved fundamental in the sense that it enabled planters to retain their commitment to cotton and slavery, to remain fixed on their plantations, to cultivate the same soils again and again, and to maintain soil fertility as well as yields and profits. Probably originating in northern and central Mississippi shortly after Leibnez's 1838 discovery of the nitrogen-fixing capacity of leguminous plants, this clever system rotated land worn out by cotton with land restored by leguminous cowpeas intercropped with corn. Cowpeas constituted the critical element in the system.[11]

This system offered several advantages for cotton planters: it restored soil nitrogen, cotton's most critical plant nutrient, through the planting of cowpeas every third year; it improved the soil structure and hence infiltration and drainage when cowpea vines and/or plants were plowed under (put another way, "green manuring" reduced runoff and erosion); it retarded erosion by providing ground cover on corn land during months of high precipitation and runoff (July and August); it provided provender (cowpeas) for hogs and subsistence (corn) for humans, horses, and mules; and, lastly, it maintained soil fertility and yielded crops and profits that equaled or surpassed cotton monoculture.

The cotton–corn–cowpeas rotation was deceptively simple in its operation. On soils of moderate fertility, the rotation called for planting cotton and corn in a ratio of two acres to one up to the tillage capacity of eighteen acres per worker (the amount of acres an ordinary worker could cultivate during the two-month period of tillage, given prevailing rates of cultivation and the practice of tilling each field thrice). In the first year, twelve acres went into cotton and six into corn intercropped with cowpeas—usually after the third tillage of corn in early July, but sometimes in April or May after corn had made "a start." In the second year, six acres were rotated out of cotton and into corn–cowpeas and six remained in cotton. In the third year, the six acres that had remained in cotton for two years went into corn–cowpeas and the other twelve went into cotton; and so on in ensuing years.

The new system enjoyed widespread popularity, judging from the consistency of cotton–corn acreage ratios and from the increased output of the system's byproducts—corn, cowpeas, and hogs. Although the rotation ratio varied slightly from place to place—depending on soil fertility, soil recuperation rates, and cultivation methods—the practice of planting two acres of cotton to one of corn was fairly widespread throughout the cotton belt during the 1840s and 1850s, except in the fertile alluvial soils in the Mississippi Valley south of Memphis. Widespread adoption of this new agrarian system likewise helps to account for the notable regional gains in collateral commodity outputs, namely corn, cowpeas, and hogs. All of which is testimony to the swift advance of this ecologically wise and economically profitable agrarian system on the eve of the American Civil War.[12]

This desperately compressed narrative of southern agrarian history offers several caveats for southern environmental change in general and the ensuing half-century (1870s–1930) of destructive occupance in particular. The first of these is that southern environmental history was not linear; second, that constructive and destructive modes of environmental occupance alternated periodically in response to a combination of socio-economic crises, agrarian innovation and its diffusion; and third, that the planters' environmental intentions were usually well meaning, if sometimes (notably in cases when agrarian innovation was legitimated through the invocation of science) ill conceived and uninformed. It is a mistake, in other words, to assume that capitalist and ecological systems are inherently incompatible. A better case can be made, I believe, for a dialectical cycling of constructive and destructive occupance—a cycling that merges the bookish reforms of agrarian elites with our most destructive phases of American environmental occupance. Fortunately for the South, their reforms did not endure. As their corrosive environmental impacts became apparent in the ensuing half-century of their hegemony, these highly publicized reforms were swiftly shoved aside in favor of the ecologically sensitive agrarian innovations of practical—and better-informed—men.

Into the Abyss: Fertilizers, Monoculture, and Destructive Occupance, 1870–1930: The Guano Craze and Its Seductions

But the tables were reversed in the confusion and uncertainty that followed the Civil War. The environmental wisdom of crop rotation rapidly gave way to agrarian reform. Planters, abetted by science, the state, and the fertilizer industry, instituted a new and ill-fated agrarian system in the eastern cotton belt. Within a decade and a half after the war they had abandoned the botanic system of crop rotation and replaced it with an agrarian system based on cheap commercial fertilizers and cotton specialization (and, in some cases, monoculture). Concentrated initially in central Georgia and the uplands of that state and South Carolina, this system spread rapidly through the cotton belt after 1880. Southern fertilizer expenditures increased from $11 million in 1880 to over $60 million by 1910 (Table 4-1). In the four core states in the cotton belt—South Carolina, Georgia, Alabama, and Mississippi—the annual expenditures for fertilizers rose some fivefold, increasing from over $8 million to $42 million in the same period. The core-state share of southern fertilizer expenditures thus stood at 76 percent in 1880 and 70 percent in 1910 (Table 4-2). Concurrently, planters increased their specialization in cotton. In the core states, cotton acreage nearly doubled (83 percent in-

Table 4-1

**Fertilizer Expenditures and Acreage and Producton of Cotton
and Corn in the Southern States, 1880–1910* (in '000s)**

Year	Fertilizer Expenditures	Cotton, acres	Cotton, bales	Corn, acres	Corn, bushels
1880	11,131	14,123	5,656	20,558	307,432
1890	17,566	22,789	8,505	21,394	380,152
1900	22,411	25,955	10,355	28,432	477,172
1910	60,459	29,729	9,983	27,610	448,346

*The states are Alabama, Arkansas, Georgia, Kentucky, Louisiana, Mississippi, North Carolina, South Carolina, Tennessee, and Texas.

Table 4-2

**Fertilizer Expenditures in the Core States of the Cotton Belt,
1880 and 1910**

State	Fertilizer Used (in $'000s)		Percentage of Increase in Fertilizer Used 1880–1910
	1880	1910	
South Carolina	2,660	15,132	468.8
Georgia	4,347	16,784	286.1
Alabama	1,201	7,631	535.4
Mississippi	278	2,702	871.3
All Core States	8,486	42,249	397.9

crease) while corn acreage rose by just 39 percent. The ratio of cotton acreage to corn acreage, a useful surrogate for the extent of diversification–specialization, thus increased from 1.15 in 1880 to 1.52 in 1910.[13]

It was assumed of course that cotton yields would increase dramatically—contemporary estimates put the increase at between 25 and 60 percent—but they failed to follow the script. In fact, cotton yields in the four core states were the same in 1880 and 1910 (Table 4-5; 0.38 bales of cotton per acre in both years). That is to say that the hundreds of millions of dollars invested in fertilizers (probably in excess of half a billion dollars) in this thirty-year period realized zero net gains in cotton yields. The failure of yields to keep pace with fertilizer investments and cotton specialization has several causes including inter alia destructive occupance, the nature of elite reform, the mysteries of soil and fertilizer chemistry, and such prosaic agrarian matters as available plant nutrients, soil texture, upland cultivation, and plant spacing in the row and the drill. But we are getting ahead of our story, which properly begins with the "guano craze" that swept the eastern cotton belt shortly after the fall of the Confederacy.

In the aftermath of war, planters in the eastern cotton belt embarked on one of the most dramatic transformations in southern agrarian history. These changes were set in motion by the end of hostilities, the unleashing of pent-up demand for cotton, and a promising rise in the price of cotton. While many southerners resumed planting cotton in the old way, that is, using the familiar system of a cotton–corn–cowpeas rotation, the planters in the eastern cotton belt struck out on a new course. Capitalizing on a combination of rising cotton prices and falling fertilizer prices, they began revamping the region's agrarian economy and ecology.

Cheap fertilizers provided the linchpin in their strategic calculations. The story begins with the postwar exploitation of inexpensive domestic sources of phosphate rock along the South Carolina coast. The first phosphate mines opened in 1868, and soon after entrepreneurs established a series of phosphate-based fertilizer plants near Charleston. The new fertilizers sold cheap, some $20 to $30 per ton, or half the price of imported Peruvian guano. For war-wracked planters, cheap fertilizer promised an unanticipated economic windfall. The cost of these manures was low and the returns were high, or so they concluded from the reports of state agricultural experts and the agents of fertilizer companies who persuasively claimed that fertilizers increased cotton yields by 25 to 60 percent—claims that may have been true at least initially for the peculiar environmental regime of the eastern cotton belt.[14]

The new system of fertilizers and cotton monoculture proved ineluctable under these circumstances. A "guano craze" soon after swept across

Georgia—which spent over $4 million for fertilizers in 1880 alone—and South Carolina. Planters and croppers swiftly abandoned the old system of crop rotation, crop diversification, and the botanic maintenance of soil fertility in favor of continuous cultivation, cotton specialization, and soil maintenance based on industrial chemistry. Crop combinations changed accordingly. In South Carolina, corn (and probably cowpea) acreage actually declined between 1880 and 1910; and in Georgia during the same span gains in cotton acreage (86 percent) far outstripped those in corn (34 percent).[15]

The eastern cotton belt constituted the vanguard of a new agrarian system, and for good reason. The region's principal advantage was proximity—proximity to fertilizer's main constituent, phosphate rock, to the plants near Charleston that manufactured the rock into fertilizer, and to low-cost rail transportation. Equally important was an environmental regime peculiarly well suited for phosphate-based fertilizers. The astonishing improvements in cotton yields demonstrated in the initial experiments with fertilizer are hardly surprising given the deficiencies in soil phosphorus and the abundance of spring precipitation for activating plant–nutrient exchanges precisely when cotton's demand for nutrients was most critical.[16]

In their euphoria over these results, planters, croppers, agricultural-experiment-station experts and fertilizer companies can be excused perhaps for overlooking the long-run deficiencies of their new elixir. None of them perceived the compositional imbalances in fertilizers which were overloaded with phosphorus and deficient in nitrogen, cotton's most vital nutrient. Although phosphate-based fertilizers improved cotton yields in the short run, sustained dependence on them led to chronic nitrogen depletion and modest net gains in yields in the long run. From the latter perspective, these fertilizers performed most effectively in the phosphorus-deficient soils of Georgia and South Carolina where yields increased by 33 percent and 10 percent, respectively, between 1880 and 1910. Westward, however, where soil phosphorus became more abundant, cotton yields were static (Alabama) or declining (by one-fourth in Mississippi). But in all cases the costs were steep indeed. Georgia's losses were least costly (if only by comparison to its neighbors); its 33 percent improvement in cotton yields coming at the expense of a 400 percent increase in fertilizer expenditures. The costs were even higher in the other core states, where fivefold to tenfold increases in fertilizer expenditures produced modest gains, at best, and substantial reductions, at worst.[17]

But cotton planters in the 1870s and 1880s had little reason to doubt the wisdom of their craze for guano. All of the scientific evidence, not to mention the rhetoric, conspired toward one unequivocal conclusion:

that the gains in cotton yields evident in the early experiments with commercial fertilizer would continue indefinitely. Planters and croppers acted accordingly, and in short order the guano craze swept across South Carolina and Georgia in the 1870s and 1880s and then into Alabama, Mississippi, Louisiana, and Texas.

This mantra for a new agrarian system advanced steadily westward between 1880 and 1910. As depicted in the first of the several decadal maps (Figs. 4-1 through 4-4), fertilizer usage in 1880 had marched triumphantly over the uplands of South Carolina and Georgia and had opened more modest inroads into eastern and central Alabama as well as in and around port cities along the Gulf coast. A decade hence, fertilizer had crept into the western uplands and extended its grasp to virtually all of Alabama save the most fertile lands in the black belt and the alluvial soils of the Tombigbee valley. Fertilizer's advance seems to have slowed down somewhat during the 1890s, though caution is advised since the change of pace may be an artifact of a general price deflation in that decade. What does seem certain from comparisons of the 1880, 1890, and 1900 maps is a spatial shift in the relative intensities of fertilizer usage, with the cotton belt of central Georgia using relatively less fertilizer per acre of cotton (perhaps owing to the decline in yields which followed their initial spike) and Mississippi and Alabama using relatively more.

Agrarian diffusion resumed in full force after 1900, however. By 1910 fertilizers were commonplace throughout Alabama, Mississippi (the Delta excepted), and a central swath of Louisiana. Moreover, usage had intensified in these areas as well as in Georgia, South Carolina, southeastern Louisiana, southern Mississippi, and portions of Texas. It was not unusual for fertilizer expenditures per cotton acre to exceed three dollars in many counties in South Carolina and Georgia and one dollar in neighboring Alabama.

The "guano craze" that began in Georgia and South Carolina in the 1870s had advanced across the length and breadth of the cotton south by 1910—save of course for the planters in the fertile alluvial soils of the lower Mississippi Valley south of Memphis who had little need for commercial manures. Planters, yeomen, croppers, and tenants eagerly adopted this agrarian innovation, and the extent of their enthusiasm is nowhere more apparent than in the prodigious amounts they were willing to expend—amounts that in the four core states of the cotton belt alone totaled in 1910 over $42 million and represented a fivefold increase in less than one generation.

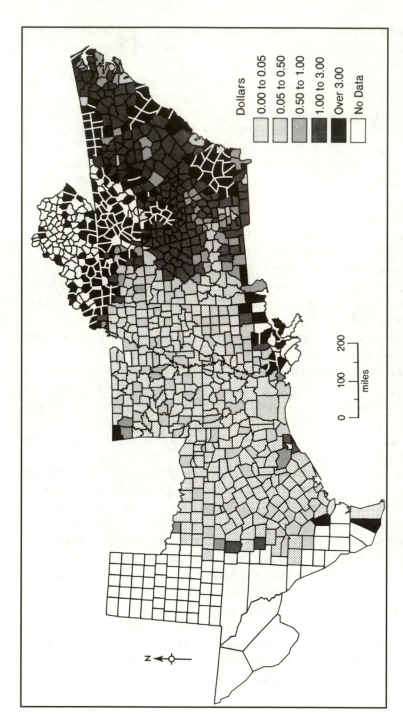

Figure 4-1. Fertilizer expenditures per cotton acre, 1880.

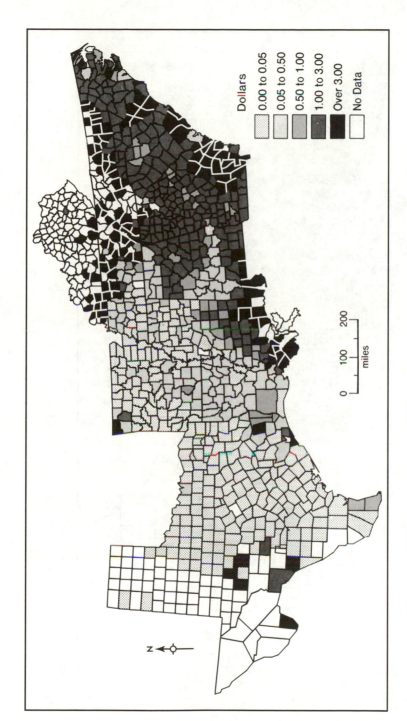

Figure 4-2. Fertilizer expenditures per cotton acre, 1890.

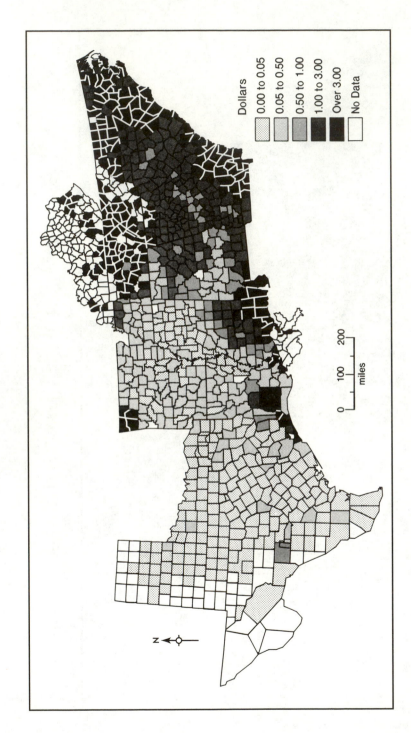

Figure 4-3. Fertilizer expenditures per cotton acre, 1900.

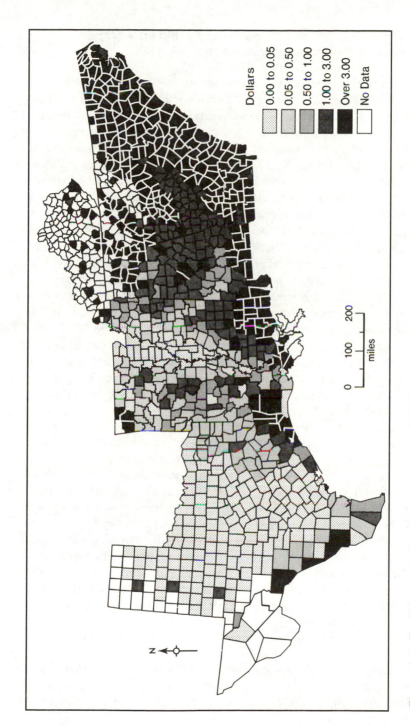

Figure 4-4. Fertilizer expenditures per cotton acre, 1910.

The Unintended Effects: Commercial Fertilizer, Agrarian Practice, and Destructive Occupance

The new agrarian system that spread across the cotton South between 1870 and 1910 entrained a series of unintended economic and environmental consequences. Perhaps the most obvious of these lamentable side effects centered on the economic inefficiencies inherent in the new system. At one level, the economic inefficiency of spending hundreds of millions of dollars on fertilizers in exchange for zero net gains in cotton yield hardly requires comment. But what is a bad situation when viewed in the aggregate looks even worse when these inefficiencies are reckoned in the planters' mode as net returns on a pound of cotton. In the four core states between 1880 and 1910, cotton output increased by 2,534,000 bales (roughly 500 pounds each) which, when valued at a farm price of $0.092 per pound, earned incremental gross revenues of $116.5 million. Achieving this additional income, however, required annual fertilizer expenditures of about $42.5 million in about 1910. Fertilizer expenditures thus amounted to 36 percent of incremental gross returns. These numbers meant that expenditures on fertilizers had pushed costs above the break-even price of cotton which traditionally stood at six or seven cents per pound. Adding three to four cents for fertilizers pushed the costs of production above the cotton price. Doubtless many southerners found that growing cotton, not to mention purchasing their corn on credit, was a losing proposition by 1910.[18]

Why then did they persist in doing so? One line of argument, which I have presented in detail elsewhere, runs as follows: in a volitional quest for higher profits, planters seeking to capitalize on the post–Civil War price boom and cheap fertilizers abandoned their diversified system of crop rotation in favor of cotton specialization. An initial spike in yields, attributable to phosphorus-laden fertilizers, encouraged even greater investments in fertilizers. But after a decade or so of heavy applications, nitrogen deficiencies in the fertilizers showed up in the form of falling yields. By that date, however, planters and croppers were locked into debt. In order to survive from year to year, they were forced to make advances on purchases of subsistence (corn) and fertilizer from local merchants and bankers in exchange for liens on next year's crop. The liens meant that in ensuing years planters would produce cotton with ever-increasing applications of commercial manure and ever-decreasing returns.[19]

No one in the 1870s and 1880s could have imagined that things would turn out as they did. In the euphoria of the guano craze and agrarian transformation, the future of planters in the eastern cotton belt looked

bright indeed. Their experience heartened others and served as a rehears-
al for what was to come in Alabama, Mississippi, and points west. There,
the promise of higher yields proved similarly ineluctable, and when initial
returns confirmed planter expectations, they too followed suit and adopted the new agrarian system.

The unintended ecological consequences of agrarian reform, if less
obvious, were equally damaging nonetheless. And of these consequences, none compared with the problem of accelerated soil erosion which
attended agrarian reform. The crux of the problem was that the new
agrarian system initiated a vast expansion of cotton acreage on lands
susceptible to accelerated soil erosion. Expansion was predicated on three
strategies ancillary to the new agrarian system: (1) cotton specialization
consequent to the adoption of fertilizers and the abandonment of the
cotton–corn–cowpeas rotation; (2) faster rates of cultivation; and (3) the
use of marginal lands consequent to fertilizer applications.

Theory affords some rough estimates of the relative contributions of
these three strategies to cotton acreage expansion between 1880 and 1910.
In the case of cotton specialization, let us assume that the new system
of cotton monoculture and fertilizers completely displaces the diversified system of crop rotation. The typical worker, accordingly, increases
acreage in cotton from twelve to eighteen (that is, six acres of corn–
cowpeas are shifted into cotton). His net gain of 50 percent in cotton
acreage probably represents the upper-bound effect of the switch to cotton
specialization. In practice, many planters and croppers continued to raise
corn and cowpeas, but it is a virtual certainty that they reduced the fraction of their output and acreage devoted to these and other diversified
crops.[20]

Faster cultivation methods also spurred the expansion of cotton acreage, but in this case the estimates are a bit trickier. While many planters
after the Civil War continued to cultivate row crops using the hoe and
human labor, the trend was toward faster methods of tillage. Even before
the war, planters had experimented with a variety of mule-drawn cultivators—scrapers of varying widths, shovel plows, and the like. After the
war, they adopted these faster methods in ever-increasing numbers. The
prevailing rate of cultivation increased from about three-quarters of an
acre per worker per day with the hoe to about one and a quarter acres per
day with the new cultivators and mules. Insofar as these rates are typical,
we can estimate their impact on row-crop acreage as follows: at the slower
rate of hoe cultivation, the typical worker cultivated 15.4 acres of row
crops in the two-month tillage season from mid-April to mid-June; at the
faster rate, using mules, scrapers, and plows, that same worker tilled

twenty-five acres in a season. In the examples at hand, faster cultivation methods effect a 60 percent increase in total acreage in row crops.[21]

The net result of these new agrarian methods, to summarize, is a doubling of cotton acreage, attributable in roughly equal portions to the strategies of fertilizer-induced cotton specialization and faster methods of tillage. In theory, faster methods of cultivation increase total row-crop acreage from between fifteen and eighteen acres to twenty-five; fertilizers and ensuing cotton specialization increase cotton acreage from between ten and twelve to twenty-five—only half of which is purely attributable to specialization.

The third source of cotton acreage expansion accrues from the entry of new and marginal lands into production. These increases are difficult to estimate with any certainty, and for the moment they may be regarded as the residual gains that remain once allowance is made for gains attributable to fertilizer and cultivation methods.

These theoretical estimates of cotton expansion are more or less corroborated by changes reported in the agricultural censuses between 1880 and 1910. In the four core states of the cotton belt, cotton acreage increased by 84 percent during this thirty-year period—slightly less than our hunch of a doubling of cotton acres (Table 4-3). The increase reported in the census, in turn, may be divided into gains attributable to (1) increased cotton specialization and fertilizer usage and (2) a combination of faster rates of cultivation and expansion into new lands. The impact of the first of these, cotton specialization, is estimable from the change in the fraction of cotton and corn acreage (Table 4-4). This fractional measure of specialization increases from 1.15 acres of cotton per acre of

Table 4-3

**Changes in Cotton and Corn Acreage in the Cotton Belt
Core States, 1880–1910 (acreage in '000s)**

State	Cotton Acreage			Corn Acreage		
	1880	1910	% Change	1880	1910	% Change
South Carolina	2,106	2,557	21.4	1,571	1,556	-0.9
Georgia	2,616	4,874	86.3	2,515	3,364	33.7
Alabama	2,330	3,730	60.1	2,056	2,540	23.5
Mississippi	865	3,403	293.5	743	2,092	181.6
All Core States	7,917	14,564	84.0	6,885	9,552	38.7

Table 4-4
Net Gains in Cotton and Corn Acreage and the Impact of
Specialization on Cotton Acreage in the Core States
of the Cotton Belt, 1880–1910

State	Net Gains ('000s of acres)			Cotton acres/ Corn acres		Percentage of Gain in Cotton Acreage Attributable to Specialization*
	Cotton	Corn	Row Crops	1880	1910	
South Carolina	451	-15	436	1.34	1.64	104.7
Georgia	2,258	849	3,107	1.04	1.44	61.4
Alabama	1,400	484	1,884	1.13	1.47	60.9
Mississippi	2,538	1,349	3,887	1.16	1.62	38.5
All Core States	6,647	2,667	9,314	1.15	1.52	55.4

*The increment of cotton acreage attributable to specialization is calculated in three steps: first, estimate total cotton acreage attributable to specialization in 1910 by multiplying the ratio of cotton and corn acreage in 1910 by total corn acreage in 1910; second, estimate the absolute increment attributable to specialization by subtracting acreage in cotton in 1880 from the estimate in step 1; and third, estimate the proportionate increase attributable to specialization by dividing the estimate in step 2 by the total increment of cotton acres and multiplying the quotient by 100.

corn in 1880 to 1.52 in 1910. Of the cotton acreage added between 1880 and 1910, this fractional increment (increased specialization) alone accounts for some 3.68 million acres or 55.4 percent of the net gain. The balance, some 45 percent, is attributable to faster cultivation and the introduction of new lands. Specialization's role in cotton acreage expansion thus seems somewhat larger in practice than in theory.

The impact of fertilizers and cotton specialization varied, however, from one state to another between 1880 and 1910. In these years, South Carolina led the way toward specialization as corn acreage decreased absolutely and cotton acreage increased by 128 percent. Elsewhere, specialization's gains for cotton acreage were less spectacular, ranging from 60 percent in Georgia and Alabama to just 39 percent in Mississippi. In achieving these gains, of course, planter expenditures on fertilizer ballooned in 1910 to over $15 million per year in South Carolina and Georgia, some $7.6 million in Alabama, and $2.7 million in Mississippi. The resemblances in the spatial trends of fertilizer expenditures in 1910 and the earlier diffusion of fertilizer usage (1880–1910) are uncanny. Their coincidence implies two important, if provisional, conclusions: (1) that expenditures on fertilizer increased significantly with the length of use and application; and (2) that the gains in cotton acreage in Mississippi and Alabama owe as much, if not more, to the entry of marginal lands into cultivation than to fertilizers and specialization.[22]

These conclusions in turn hint at a differentiation of the cotton belt into two more or less distinct regions of fertilizer usage: an eastern one that used fertilizers for the purpose of achieving a monocultural system and a western one that deployed fertilizers in order to expand cotton culture into marginal uplands. If my suspicions are correct, then the environmental consequences of this new agrarian system may have been greatest in the western states of Alabama and Mississippi where the expansion of row-crop cultivation onto upland soils encountered soils that were highly susceptible to surface wash and the ensuing erosion of coarse subsoil material. In these marginal uplands, it would appear, fertilizer use had set the stage for an epoch of accelerated erosion unmatched in southern history.

The stagnation in southern cotton yields affords a glimpse of the gravity of the region's environmental problems. The hundreds of millions of dollars spent on fertilizer notwithstanding, cotton yields in the four core states had not changed appreciably between 1880 and 1910 (Table 4-5). Many factors help to explain this lack of improvement, and most of them can be traced to the misuse or abuse of the soil—problems such as chronic deficiencies in soil nitrogen resulting from the abandonment of cowpeas and the deployment of phosphate-based fertilizers; deteriorations in

Table 4-5
Cotton Yields in the Core States of the Cotton Belt, 1880 and 1910

State	Yield of Cotton Bales per Acre of Cotton	
	1880	1910
South Carolina	0.45	0.50
Georgia	0.31	0.41
Alabama	0.30	0.30
Mississippi	0.59	0.33
All Core States	0.38	0.38

soil structure and infiltration capacity as a consequence of reductions in humus hitherto sustained by the plowing under of harvested and hog-rooted cowpea plants; and accelerated soil erosion resulting from the cultivation of wider rows, increased cotton acreage, and hillier land.

In the especially damaged uplands of Mississippi, Alabama, and Georgia, erosion rates accelerated dramatically as planters pushed cotton cultivation onto poorer land with steeper slopes and, worse, planted their crop "thin" (wide rows) on the assumption that fertilizers would compensate for the inherent infertility of their soil. In Mississippi, for example, over 60 percent of the increase in cotton acreage seems to have resulted from the opening up of new lands. When compared to the fertile soils of the black belt or the Delta, the uplands were marginal: soils were less fertile, slopes were steeper, and thin veneers of topsoil in the A horizon were underlain by erodible subsoils of coarse, sandy material. In antebellum times, planters had bypassed these marginal uplands in favor of productive bottomlands, but after the war and the introduction of cheap fertilizers, that strategy was reassessed.[23]

Henceforth, they subscribed to the revolutionary notion of the possibility of achieving soil parity through differential fertilizer application. A modest expenditure of fertilizer, they now believed, would render marginally productive lands as fertile and as productive as rich bottomlands. The implementation of this revolutionary idea had two immediate consequences for the uplands: (1) the expansion of cotton production into easily eroded uplands and (2) the extension from the flatlands to the hill country of the conventional wisdom on planting "thick" or "thin," that is, the choice of the proper spacing for cotton plants in the row and the "drill" (the columns as it were) on infertile and fertile soils, respectively. Both of these consequences would make immense contributions to accelerated erosion in the upland South.

The first of these is perhaps the best known. Planters in the uplands of Mississippi and Alabama pushed cotton production out of the bottom-lands and onto the slopes. Upland acreage in cotton expanded rapidly between 1880 and 1910. Although many upland planters understood the erosional liabilities of steep slopes and the value of planting them according to the methods of "horizontaling"—the practice of planting rows along rather than across the contour—the latter practice made little headway. Planting on the contour was, in fact, a difficult feat, requiring among other things a sharp eye, fairly sophisticated instruments, and some understanding of surveying and engineering principles. Lacking some or all of the technical prerequisites for proper "horizontaling," most planters did the best they could to prevent soil erosion. Some tried to approximate the practices of contouring while others experimented with terracing. Many others, regrettably, planted their rows straight across the contour.[24]

Although steep slopes and poor row alignment contributed to accelerated soil erosion in the uplands, these sources of soil loss do not tell the whole story. Of equal, if not larger, significance is the erosional contribution attributable to the wide spacing of plants in the row and in the drill. Certainly planters spent a great deal of time talking about plant spacing. Everyone seems to have had an opinion on the optimal distances between cotton plants in the row and in the drill. While the precise spacing of plants was a matter of continuing controversy, most antebellum planters agreed with the conventional wisdom that called for planting cotton thick on poor land and thin on fertile land. To be sure, a few astute planters such as Martin Philips of central Mississippi voiced a doubt or two about this "rule of thumb," but for the majority it was gospel. On fertile land, they planted "thin," meaning that cotton plants were spaced widely with the intervals ranging from four to five feet in the row and one and a half to two feet in the drill. On infertile land, they planted "thick," meaning that the plants were spaced more closely, with the intervals collapsing to as little as two to three feet in the row and a foot or so in the drill.[25]

The introduction of commercial fertilizers and the assumption of soil parity, however, altered the antebellum rules of thumb. If fertilizers largely canceled out differences in natural soil fertility, it logically followed that planters would plant "thin" on fertilized marginal upland soils. Planting wider rows in the uplands thus had an impeccable logic in its own right; but what made that logic ineluctable was the fact that wider rows also lent themselves to new and faster methods of cultivation. The practice of planting thin proved especially convenient for maneuvering mule-drawn shovel plows and scrapers of forty to fifty inches in width.[26]

The planters' decision to plant "thin" was logical, convenient, and, lamentably, misguided when conducted on erodible upland soils. Erosion rates accelerated dramatically. The nub of the problem was that wide plant spacing delayed canopy closure (when the leaves of the cotton plants covered the intervening soil) until late in the season, if at all. Closure on "thin" plantings did not take place until September or October, well after the midsummer maxima in precipitation and runoff when soils were most vulnerable to surface washing and gullying.

It is unlikely that nineteenth-century cotton planters appreciated this nexus between row spacing, canopy closure, and erosion, but contemporary agronomists have cleared up any doubt that might remain. In a controlled study of contemporary cotton-management practices in Mississippi, agronomists have documented the critical erosional role of variable row spacing and canopy closure. When row width was increased from twenty inches to forty inches and then to sixty inches, sediment yields increased by 80 percent and 136.5 percent, respectively. These dramatic increases in sediment yields, in turn, seem to have been a function of canopy closure. Closure on the narrow rows occurred in early July, on rows of medium width in early August, and on wide rows in late September or early October. Early canopy closure thus impeded erosion by intercepting raindrops and dissipating their erosional energy. But if early closure prevented splash and rill erosion, it had little impact on runoff, which increased by only 1.4 percent and 8.9 percent as rows were widened.[27]

This contemporary agricultural experiment is especially apt for the environmental history of the cotton belt. It convincingly demonstrates that planting "thin," today or in the past, results in a linear increase in the rate of erosion. Moreover, this experiment conducted on lands of modest slope invites the speculation of even higher erosion rates when cotton is planted "thin" on the steeper slopes of the hilly uplands in Mississippi, Alabama, and Georgia which were brought into cultivation in the 1870s and 1880s. The historical relevance of this experiment requires, however, a proviso. While erosion rates based on contemporary methods are directly transferable to the postbellum agrarian system based on commercial fertilizers, they apply less readily to antebellum crop rotation. Antebellum agrarian practices retarded erosion first by affording a protective canopy of cowpeas one year in three, and second by facilitating higher rates of water infiltration and lower rates of surface runoff through improvements in soil structure and soil drainage attributable to the practice of plowing under cowpeas. Soil-building measures inherent in the crop rotation system thus served as a effective counter-poise to soil erosion associated with planting "thin."

If, as the antebellum case suggests, planting "thin" was not invariably an invitation to accelerated erosion, then we need to recast our interpretation of postbellum agrarian practices. The planters' decisions to plant thin on fertilized upland soils does not get at the heart of the problem of accelerated erosion. Their mistake, more accurately, was in borrowing a "rule of thumb" designed for and appropriate to one agrarian system (crop rotation) and thoughtlessly applying it to another (fertilizers). The result of thin planting—when conducted in the absence of soil-building cow-peas, on steep slopes, and with chronically deficient fertilizers—was accelerated erosion in the cotton belt, in general, and in its uplands, in particular.

This new agrarian system, with its reliance on deficient fertilizers, widely spaced rows, faster cultivators, marginal upland soils, and the assumption of soil parity via fertilizer, initiated a half-century of unparalleled destructive occupance. The effects were everywhere apparent, in the washing of topsoil, the gullying of the subsurface sands, the filling of channels and valley sidewalls with sediment, the widening of rivers and streams, the disruption of navigation, and the degradation of bottomlands by overbank flows of coarse sand.[28]

While the evidence of accelerated erosion is indisputable, the precise chronology of destructive occupance remains a matter of controversy. The prevailing view assigns culpability for accelerated erosion to the entire period of southern occupance. Soil exhaustion and erosion, in this view, are continuous; they commence with initial settlement, increase linearly through the Civil War, and turn exponential between the 1870s and 1930. Insofar as erosion rates change over time, their variation is regarded as quantitative rather than qualitative. I have argued the converse both here and elsewhere: namely, that (1) southern rates of soil exhaustion and soil erosion are specific to historically and spatially differentiated agrarian systems and (2) these systems vary cyclically between 1600 and the present. Historical variations in erosion rates are qualitative not quantitative; they reflect more nearly the dramatic changes in dynamic agroecological systems than the steadfastness of an unrestrained capitalism. Accelerated erosion in the cotton belt, I believe, is concentrated in two of these momentous cycles—between initial settlement and the 1830s and between 1880 and 1930, but not in between.[29]

If I am correct in my insistence on a more dynamic view of southern agroecological systems, then the documentary evidence cited above should be corroborated by the physical evidence of geomorphology. In an earlier study of Chesapeake agrarian systems and environmental change, I was able to point to precisely that kind of corroboration in the sediment chronology worked out by Grace Brush. Her evidence of sedimentation corresponded closely with the cyclical historical interpretation that I had proposed; namely, early spikes in sediment following initial settlement (1607–1670s), a long period of modest erosion and sedimentation (which I associate with the introduction of the land rotation system, 1680s–1770s), and a rapid acceleration of erosion after 1780 (the period of high agrarian reform, plows, and clean tillage). Something very similar emerges from the geomorphic record in the cotton belt.[30]

The historical argument for the cotton belt, to recapitulate, runs in three cycles: (1) accelerated soil erosion following initial occupance through the cycle of "vicious cultivation" (continuous cultivation followed by abandonment) which ended in the 1830s and 1840s; (2) decelerated soil erosion beginning with the introduction of the cotton–corn–cowpeas crop rotation system in the 1840s and ending in the 1870s and 1880s; and (3) accelerated erosion following the introduction of commercial fertilizers, faster cultivation methods, cotton specialization, and "thin" planting in the uplands in the 1870s and 1880s and lasting until the 1930s.

This cyclical interpretation of southern agrarian systems is given point by certain geomorphic evidence tucked away in the classic study of southern soil erosion conducted by Happ, Rittenhouse, and Dobson in the 1930s.[31] Although concerned mainly with identifying erosion and sedimentation rates subsequent to Euro-American settlement, the authors also reported the results of various borings in the Tobitubby and Hurricane valleys in the uplands of north central Mississippi near the town of Oxford. These results appear in a series of tables that list the proportion of coarse materials at varying depths in the bore columns of six different sites. This figure is very useful since it serves as an indicator of the nature and extent of erosion processes: high proportions of coarse material imply accelerated erosion of the subsoil and, in all probability, gullying; low proportions of coarse material imply more moderate rates of erosion associated with surface wash and the transport of fine sediments from the topsoil.

Insofar as mechanical analysis of sediment is an appropriate indicator of erosion processes, the borings of Happ, Rittenhouse, and Dobson suggest that the erosional history of the uplands after 1800 was more nearly cyclical than linear. Accelerated erosion, as measured by high loads of coarse materials, occurs in two phases: immediately after Euro-American settlement (40 to 50 percent coarse material at depths of sixty to eighty inches) and just before the test borings in the 1930s (greater than 50 percent coarse material at depths between twenty to thirty inches and the top of the column). Put another way, the record suggests a smaller episode, a spike if you will, of erosion immediately after settlement; a low-slung saddle of modest erosion (less than 40 percent, and usually less than 25 percent coarse material at depths between twenty to thirty and sixty to seventy inches); and a long episode (a slug) of accelerated erosion in the years immediately prior to the 1930s.[32]

Although these three erosional phases cannot be dated with precision by mechanical sediment analysis alone, their correlation with the macrohistorical interpretation is remarkably good. In their sequencing and columnar apportionment, the geomorphic evidence of three erosional phases comports nicely with the cyclical alternations in cotton-belt agrarian systems and planter management strategies. The early spike corresponds with the initial occupance of Euro-Americans and their practices of continuous cotton cultivation, soil exhaustion, and land abandonment (what I have called elsewhere linear shifting cultivation or, for good reason, "vicious cultivation"). The low-saddle of erosion corresponds with the phase of constructive occupance associated with the innovation and diffusion of an agrarian system based on the crop rotation of cotton, corn, and cowpeas and its botanic solution to the problem of soil fertility maintenance. And the large erosional slug at the top of the bores corresponds with the introduction of commercial fertilizers, wide row spacing, faster rates of cultivation, and occupance of marginal uplands. These factors, rather than climatically induced increases in runoff, seem to be the principal causes of accelerated erosion.[33] This correspondence between independent bodies of evidence, geomorphic and historical, is encouraging indeed. It corroborates certain provisional hypotheses on the macrohistorical alternations in agroecological systems as it stimulates ensuing investigations aimed at a more precise sediment chronology based on chemistry (phosphates, for example), pollen, or half-lives.

As this chapter on the cyclical alternations of southern environmental history draws to a close, it seems fitting to look beyond the half-century of destructive occupance after 1880 and toward the more benign occupance of the ensuing half-century. A variety of evidence suggests that environmental abuse did not continue into the 1930s. Indeed, the turning point from destructive to constructive occupance seems to have occurred somewhat earlier. In many upland areas ravaged by fertilizers and cotton specialization, cotton acreage and output seem to have peaked just before or during World War I.[34] The pace of accelerated erosion also seems to have slackened about the same time, judging from the sediment cores. Although the deposition of coarse materials in the lower reaches of upland streams continues right up to the dates of the borings in the mid-1930s, deposition in their upper reaches shifts abruptly from coarse to finer materials on the eve of the borings. The geomorphic interpretation of these depositional patterns is unambiguous: in the headwaters, subsoil gullying had been sharply reduced if not eliminated by the mid-1930s; in the lower reaches of upland streams, coarse materials eroded at an earlier date were still in transit through the system. Stored temporarily as colluvial deposits, these materials awaited one of two eventual fates— flushing out of the fluvial system or deposition as alluvium by overbank flows.[35]

The reasons for the ending of this cycle of accelerated erosion and the beginning of the next are hardly mysterious. Among the factors that came into play are the general slowdown of economic activity that accompanied the downswing in the long wave in the capitalist economy, the withdrawal from production of marginal lands in the upland headwaters (the area containing soils most susceptible to erosion), and the *rediscovery and reimplementation* of traditional southern conservationist practices that ranged from crop rotation to terracing to contour plowing or "horizontaling." A new agrarian system was aborning in the 1930s, but it was a system incapable of sustaining the numbers accommodated by its predecessors. As planters and croppers abandoned their farms and joined in the general exodus from the cotton belt, they were replaced by trees and pasture. Once again, as it had on no less than five previous occasions, a new face spread across the rural South. On this occasion, as twice before, there seems to be the hint of a smile on the southern visage.

Out of the Abyss

Students of southern environmental history from Carl Sauer to Stanley Trimble have pressed the region's cyclical history into a linear mold, a mold in which destructive occupance begins with Euro-American settlement and persists until the 1930s (and sometimes down to the present). This macrohistorical model invites misgivings on more than a few particulars. In the first place, this linear model of unrelieved environmental abuse under a capitalist agrarian system is refuted by an ample body of historical and geomorphic evidence. Southern agrarian systems were, in fact, more dynamic. The evidence for the cotton belt alone suggests at least three alternating phases of destructive and constructive land occupance (and perhaps four if we go beyond 1930). Agroecological systems in the cotton belt were destructive before 1840, constructive between the 1840s and 1870s, and destructive from the 1880s through the 1920s.

In the second instance, the linear interpretation of environmental history obscures the role of agency in shaping the southern landscape. In its

portrayal of southern planters as one-dimensional and historically invari-
ant soil abusers, the linear model too readily papers over the planters'
propensity for recurrent agrarian innovation, environmental sensitivity,
and ecological wisdom as well as unintended folly. Southern planters
were not fools; they understood all too well that their livelihood depended on the fertility and productivity of the soil. Even in cases when the
planters' innovations led them into the abyss of destructive occupance,
their actions were not merely the product of a mindless pursuit of profit.

More often than not their path into the abyss was paved with good
environmental intentions. That was clearly the case in the cycle of destructive occupance which unfolded after 1880. Planters, croppers, experts from state agricultural agencies, and the agents of fertilizer companies genuinely believed that an agrarian system based on commercial
fertilizers and cotton would maximize profits while maintaining soil
fertility. It is inconceivable that any of them would have proceeded along
this path had they envisioned the ecological and social costs of gullied
lands and social peonage.

None of this, I might note, has very much to do with capitalism. Planters who had effectively maintained soil fertility through botanic crop
rotations between 1840 and 1880 were as capitalist as those who before
and after them wreaked havoc on the southern landscape. The truth of the
matter (and the irony) is that southerners after the Civil War had suc-
cumbed at last to the blandishments of agrarian modernity (of science
and capital intensity "northern style," as it were), replete with fertilizers,
faster cultivators, widely space rows, and a host of unintended environmental consequences. In a region where planters pursued profit from the
beginning, capitalism is largely irrelevant for differentiating alternative-
ly wise and foolish environmental behaviors. The critical determinant of
their environmental behavior, I submit, resides in the dialectic of agrarian systems and its alternation of innovations predicated on practice and
science—the former of which proved the wisest for southern soils and
landscapes.

The generally benign cycles of land occupance in the Chesapeake region
between 1680 and 1780 and the cotton belt between 1840 and 1880 serve
as a reminder that the pursuit of agrarian profit and ecological wisdom
are not incompatible. Southerners, accordingly, can point to a legacy,
albeit a punctuated one, of wise usage of the land; ecological wisdom did
not arise phoenix-like with the Soil Conservation Service and the New
Deal or with the environmental movement of the 1960s and 1970s. On
the contrary, a tradition of constructive resource usage is deeply rooted
in southern history, in the trials and errors of a cyclical macrohistory—
should we care to see it. Tempering our condescension for things south-

ern (and perhaps as well our contempt for things capitalist) might permit us to do precisely that. Thus braced by the insights of multiculturalism, we may begin to grasp why southerners to a person find offense in being labeled as miners, robbers, and killers of the soil. One might just as soon call them dumb—which they assuredly were not.

Acknowledgments

In doing this chapter, I have benefited immensely from conversations with and sources provided by Richard Kesel, a geomorphologist with remarkable historical sensibilities. My thanks extend also to the 1991 entering class of Louisiana State University graduate students who assisted in gathering much of the data on which this chapter is based.

Notes

1. The indictment of unrestrained capitalism is more or less explicit in Donald Worster, "The Vulnerable Earth: Toward a Planetary History," in *The Ends of the Earth: Perspectives on Modern Environmental History*, Donald Worster, ed. (Cambridge: Cambridge University Press, 1989), 3–20; Garrett Hardin, "The Tragedy of the Commons," *Science* 162 (December 13, 1968): 243–48; Stanley W. Trimble, "Perspectives on the History of Soil Erosion Control in the Eastern United States," *Agricultural History* 59 (1985): 162–80; Carl O. Sauer, *Land and Life: A Selection from the Writings of Carl Ortwin Sauer*, John Leighly, ed. (Berkeley: University of California Press, 1963).

2. For the alternative view, see Arthur F. McEvoy, "Toward an Interactive Theory of Nature and Culture: Ecology, Production, and Cognition in the California Fishing Industry," in *The Ends of the Earth*, 211–29; Carville Earle, "The Myth of the Southern Soil Miner: Macrohistory, Agricultural Innovation, and Environmental Change," in *The Ends of the Earth*, 175–210. See also various essays in *The Earth as Transformed by Human Action: Global and Regional Changes in the Biosphere over the Past 300 Years*, B.L. Turner II, William C. Clark, Robert W. Kates, John F. Richards, Jessica T. Mathews, and William B. Meyers, eds. (Cambridge: Cambridge University Press and Clark University, 1990), esp. Michael Chisholm's "The Increasing Separation of Production and Consumption," 87–101 and Carolyn Merchant's "The Realm of Social Relations: Production, Reproduction, and Gender in Environmental Transformation," 673–84.

3. For this harsh critique of southern agrarians, see Trimble, "Perspectives on the History of Soil Erosion Control," 162–80; Warren C. Scoville, "Did Colonial Farmers Waste Our Land?" *The Southern Economic Journal* 20 (1953): 175–81, and sources cited therein.

4. Trimble, "Perspectives on the History of Soil Erosion Control," 162–80;

for the legacy of plantation slavery, see Eugene D. Genovese, *The Political Economy of Slavery: Studies in Economy and Society of the Slave South* (New York: Vintage Books, 1967), 85–105. These arguments have been widely adopted by both historians and economic historians.

5. Carville Earle, *The Evolution of a Tidewater Settlement System: All Hallow's Parish, Maryland, 1650–1783,* Research Paper No. 170 (Chicago: University of Chicago Department of Geography Research Papers, 1975), 24–30; Earle, "The Myth of the Southern Soil Miner," 194–98; Edward C. Papenfuse, Jr., "Planter Behavior and Economic Opportunity in a Staple Economy," *Agricultural History* 46 (1972): 297–311; Lois Green Carr, Russell R. Menard, and Lorena S. Walsh, *Robert Cole's World: Agriculture and Society in Early Maryland* (Chapel Hill: University of North Carolina Press, 1991), 34–43, 55–71.

6. Earle, *The Evolution of a Tidewater Settlement System*; see also the travel narratives cited in Avery O. Craven, *Soil Exhaustion as a Factor in the Agricultural History of Virginia and Maryland, 1606–1860*, University of Illinois Studies in the Social Sciences, XIII, No. 1 (Urbana: University of Illinois Press, 1926).

7. Earle, *The Evolution of a Tidewater Settlement System*, 24–30; Papenfuse, "Planter Behavior and Economic Opportunity," 297–311.

8. The nature of post-Revolutionary agrarian reform and its consequences are recounted in Curtis P. Nettles, *The Emergence of a National Economy, 1775–1815* (New York: Harper & Row, 1962); Earle, "The Myth of the Southern Soil Miner," 198–200; for evidence of selective diffusion, see Lorena S. Walsh, "Land, Landlord, and Leaseholder: Estate Management in Southern Maryland, 1642–1820," *Agricultural History* 59 (1985): 373–96.

9. The environmental consequences of agrarian reform are evident in Henry M. Miller, "Transforming a 'Splendid and Delightsome Land': Colonists and Ecological Change in the Chesapeake, 1607–1820," *Journal of the Washington Academy of Science* 76 (1986): 173–87; Craven, *Soil Exhaustion as a Factor in the Agricultural History of Virginia and Maryland*; Louis C. Gottschalk, "Effects of Soil Erosion on Navigation in Upper Chesapeake Bay," *Geographical Review* 35 (1945): 219–38; Grace S. Brush, "Geology and Paleoecology of Chesapeake Bay: A Long-term Monitoring Tool for Management," *Journal of the Washington Academy of Science* 76 (1986): 146–60. For the ideological consequences of destructive occupance, as exemplified by Fitzhugh and Helper, see Eugene D. Genovese, *The World the Slaveholder's Made: Two Essays in Interpretation* (New York: Random House, 1969), 118–224 and Hinton Rowan Helper, *The Impending Crisis of the South: How to Meet It* (New York: A.B. Burdick, 1860).

10. Thomas Perkins Abernathy, *The Formative Period in Alabama, 1815–1828* (Montgomery, Ala.: 1928); W.J. Cash, *The Mind of the South* (New York: Random House, 1941). On frontier expansion, see Carville Earle and Changyong Cao, "Rates of Frontier Expansion in American History, 1650–1890," in *GIS and the Social Sciences: A Handbook*, Leonard Hochberg, Carville Earle, and David Miller, eds. (Basil Blackwell, forthcoming). It is worth noting that the expansion of the southern frontier slowed down dramatically after 1840. See ibid. and

Roger L. Ransom, *Conflict and Compromise: The Political Economy of Slavery, Emancipation, and the American Civil War* (Cambridge: Cambridge University Press, 1989), 53–60. The slower pace of frontier expansion after 1840 owes much, if not all, to the rise of a new agrarian system capable of maintaining soil fertility.

11.   Earle, "The Myth of the Southern Soil Miner," 201–4; Earle, "The Price of Precocity: Technical Choice and Ecological Constraint in the Cotton South, 1840–1890," *Agricultural History* 66 (forthcoming, 1992); John Hebron Moore, *The Emergence of the Cotton Kingdom in the Old Southwest: Mississippi, 1770–1860* (Baton Rouge: Louisiana State University Press, 1988), 334–36; idem, *Agriculture in Ante-Bellum Mississippi* (New York: Bookman Associates, 1958), 54–55, 59–60, 123–27, 174–76.

12.   On the customary acreage ratios of cotton to corn after 1840, see Lewis C. Gray, *History of Agriculture in the Southern United States to 1860*, 2 vols. (Gloucester, Mass.: Peter Smith, 1958), 707–8; Moore, *Agriculture in Ante-Bellum Mississippi*, 111–12; Ulrich Bonnell Phillips, *Life and Labor in the Old South* (New York: Grosset & Dunlap, 1929), 288; Martin Philips, *Southern Cultivator* 4 (1846): 78–79; idem, *Diary of a Mississippi Planter, January 1, 1840 to April 1863*, Franklin L. Riley, ed. (np: nd). The impact of crop rotation on subsistence production is evident in Sam B. Hilliard, *Hog Meat and Hoecake: Food Supply in the Old South, 1840–1860* (Carbondale: Southern Illinois University Press, 1972).

13.   U.S. Census Office, Tenth Census [1880], *Statistics of the Population of the United States at the Tenth Census (June 1, 1880)* (Washington, D.C.: Government Printing Office, 1883). U.S. Census Office, *Report on the Production of Agriculture in the United States at the Tenth Census* (June 1, 1880) (Washington, D.C.: Government Printing Office, 1883). U.S. Census Office [1890], *Report on the Population of the United States at the Eleventh Census: 1890*, 2 parts (Washington, D.C.: Government Printing Office, 1895, 1897). U.S. Census Office, *Reports on the Statistics of Agriculture in the United States* (Washington, D.C.: Government Printing Office, 1895). U.S. Census Office, Twelfth Census [1900], *Census Reports: Agriculture*, 2 parts (Washington, D.C.: Government Printing Office, 1902). U.S. Census Office, *Thirteenth Census of the United States . . . 1910, Agriculture* (Washington, D.C.: Government Printing Office, 1913).

14.   James W. Markham, *The Fertilizer Industry* (Nashville, Tenn.: Vanderbilt University Press, 1958), 33–35; William L. Rowland, *Report on the Manufacture of Chemical Products and Salt* (Washington, D.C.: Government Printing Office, 1883), 17–69. On fertilizer and yields, see *Report of the Georgia State Commissioner of Agriculture* (Athens: 1874), 74; Earle, "The Price of Precocity."

15.   The figures cited are compiled from publications of the U.S. Census Office listed in note 13. The lead role of Georgia and South Carolina in this diffusion process is noted in Peter Temin, "Patterns of Cotton Agriculture in Post-Bellum Georgia," *Journal of Economic History* 43 (1983): 661–74. See also David Weiman, "The Economic Emancipation of the Non-Slaveholding Class:

Upcountry Farmers in the Georgia Cotton Economy," *Journal of Economic History* 45 (1985): 71–93.

16. The fortuitous match between phosphate-based fertilizers, spring precipitation maxima, and soil chemistry proved misleading in the long run. See Roy L. Donahue, *Soils: An Introduction to Soils and Plant Growth*, 2nd ed. (Englewood Cliffs, N.J.: Prentice-Hall, 1965), 201, 294; O.J. Kelley, "Requirement and Availability of Soil Water," *Advance in Agronomy* 6 (1954): 67–94. On seasonal precipitation patterns in the nineteenth century, see E.H. Wahl and T.L. Lawson, "The Climate of the Mid-Nineteenth Century United States Compared to the Current Normals," *Monthly Weather Review* 98 (1970): 259–65.

17. See Census Office sources cited in note 13. On fertilizer deficiencies, see Earle, "The Price of Precocity" and the sources cited therein.

18. On fertilizer expenditures, see Census Office sources cited in note 13; also, Roger L. Ransom and Richard Sutch, *One Kind of Freedom: The Economic Consequences of Emancipation* (Cambridge: Cambridge University Press, 1978), 188–90; Rosser H. Taylor, "Fertilizers and Farming in the Southeast, 1840–1900," *North Carolina Historical Review* 30 (1953): 305–28. For cotton prices, see ibid., 165–68, 191–93; Stephen J. DeCanio, *Agriculture in the Postbellum South: The Economics of Production and Supply* (Cambridge: MIT Press, 1974), 105–106.

19. For elaboration, see Earle, "The Southern Soil Miner," 205–8; idem, "The Price of Precocity."

20. Earle, "The Southern Soil Miner."

21. On rates of cultivation, see Gray, *History of Agriculture in the Southern United States* 2, 701–702; Paul W. Gates, *The Farmer's Age: Agriculture 1815–1860* (New York: Harper & Row, 1960), 136; Phillips, *Life and Labor in the Old South*, 278–80; Moore, *The Emergence of the Cotton Kingdom*, 42, 50; idem, *Agriculture in Ante-Bellum Mississippi*, 172, where the claim is made that horse- or mule-drawn cultivators reduced hoe work by 50 percent. Willard Range, *A Century of Georgia Agriculture, 1850–1950* (Athens: University of Georgia Press, 1954), 81, 159.

22. See the Census Office sources cited in note 13. Ransom and Sutch, *One Kind of Freedom*, 189.

23. On the environment of the uplands, see Eugene W. Hilgard, *Report on the Geology and Agriculture of the State of Mississippi* (Jackson, Miss.: E. Barksdale, 1860), esp. 293–95; Stafford C. Happ, Gordon Rittenhouse, and G.A. Dobson, *Some Principles of Accelerated Stream and Valley Sedimentation*, U.S. Department of Agriculture Technical Bulletin No. 695 (May 1946): 1–53. On upland expansion of cotton, see Sunji Ouchi, "Possible Effects of Soil Erosion on Land Use Change in Northern Mississippi, USA," *Geographical Reports of Tokyo Metropolitan University*, No. 21 (1986): 133–43.

24. According to Willard Range, "many [Georgians] seemed to believe that fertilizers did away with the need for proper tillage, rotation, cover crops, composting, terracing, and other essentials. Soil analysis was ignored by all but a few." And herein lies the logic that undergirded the revolutionary notion of fertilizers and soil parity. Range, *A Century of Georgia Agriculture*, 122–23. On

horizontaling and its difficulty, see Moore, *Agriculture in Ante-Bellum Missis-sippi*, 44–45, 177–78; Hilgard, *Report on the Geology and Agriculture of the State of Mississippi*, 293–95. "Hillside washes" on more steeply sloping land, though apparent in some uplands by 1860, was more conspicuous after the Civil War; ibid., 293. Happ, Rittenhouse, and Dobson, *Some Principles of Accelerated Stream and Valley Sedimentation*, 1–10. See also Stanley W. Trimble, "Cultur-ally Accelerated Sedimentation on the Middle Georgia Piedmont," (Master's Thesis, University of Georgia, 1969).

25.   Major E.G. Wall, *Wall's Manual of Agriculture for the Southern United States* (Memphis, Tenn.: Southwestern Publishing Company, 1870), 89–90. Moore, *Agriculture in Ante-Bellum Mississippi*, 116–17. For a sampling of opinion on plant spacing, see *Southern Crops as Grown and Described by Successful Farmers and Published from Time to Time*, comp. by G.F. Hunnicutt (Atlanta, Ga.: Cultivator Publishing Company, 1908), 30, 33, 37, 39, 44–45, 47–48.

26.   In 1906, a correspondent to the Southern Cultivator reported "several parties this year trying seven or eight-foot rows. This is too wide." Quoted in *Southern Crops*, 51. On cultivators, see ibid., 30, 34; Range, *A Century of Georgia Agriculture*, 81, 159; and Moore, *The Emergence of the Cotton Kingdom*, 37–56. Wide row spacing and fertilizers were also recommended as a preventative against boll weevil infestation. See Douglas Helms, "Revision and Reversion: Changing Cultural Control Practices for the Cotton Boll Weevil," *Agricultural History* 54 (1980): 108–25.

27.   D.G. Coursey, "Runoff, Erosion, and Crop Yield Simulation for Land Use Management," *Transactions of the American Society for Agricultural En-gineers* 23 (1980): 379–86. See also, C.E. Murphree, C.K. Mutchler, and L.L. McDowell, "Sediment Yields from a Mississippi Delta Watershed," *Proceedings of the Third Federal Interagency Sedimentation Conference* (1976): 1-99 to 1-109.

28.   Happ, Rittenhouse, and Dobson, *Some Principles of Accelerated Stream and Valley Sedimentation*, 1–61; J.D. Sinclair, "Studies of Soil Erosion in Mis-sissippi," *Journal of Forestry* 29 (1931): 533–40.

29.   Geomorphologists, generally speaking, have assumed that southern crop-management practices were unchanging from the time of initial settlement to the 1930s. Their estimates of soil erosion, accordingly, project a uniform rate over this entire period. In fact, management practices and erosion rates exhibit dra-matic swings during the course of Euro-American occupance. See, for example, Happ, Rittenhouse, and Dobson, *Some Principles of Accelerated Stream and Valley Sedimentation*; S.A. Schumm, M.D. Harvey, and C.C. Watson, *Incised Channels, Morphology, Dynamics, and Control* (Littleton, Colo.: Water Resources Publications, 1984).

30.   Brush, "Geology and Paleoecology of Chesapeake Bay," 146–60.

31.   Happ, Rittenhouse, and Dobson, *Some Principles of Accelerated Stream and Valley Sedimentation*, esp. the results of the test borings reported in the appendix.

32. Happ, Rittenhouse, and Dobson, *Some Principles of Accelerated Stream and Valley Sedimentation.*

33. Runoff does not appear to have been responsible for accelerated erosion between 1880 and 1930, judging from water-budget analyses of climatic records for Memphis, Tennessee. Moisture surpluses—a surrogate for increased runoff potential—occurred between 1890 and 1905 and not again until the 1950s and 1970s. Runoff in the epoch of accelerated erosion (1890–1930) thus appears to have been relatively high during the first fifteen years and low in the ensuing twenty-five years—a chronology that fits poorly with the erosional slug noted above. Moreover, what evidence we have from earlier climatic records suggest that moisture surpluses and runoff from the mid-1840s—a period of modest erosion—were not dissimilar to those from the period 1890–1905—a period of accelerated erosion. See Robert A. Muller and James E. Willis, "Climatic Variability in the Lower Mississippi River Valley," in *Man and Environment in the Lower Mississippi Valley*, ed. by Sam B. Hilliard, Geoscience and Man, Vol. XIX (Baton Rouge: Louisiana State University School of Geoscience, 1978), 55–63; Marion B. Fairchild, "Climate and Cotton: An Analysis of the Climate at Baton Rouge, Louisiana and the Cotton Regime from 1843–1846," unpublished ms., 1989.

34. Ouchi, "Possible Effects of Soil Erosion and Land Use Change," 136–42. See also Merle Prunty, Jr., "Recent Quantitative Changes in the Cotton Regions of the Southern States," *Economic Geography* 27 (1951): 189–208; John Fraser Hart, "The Demise of King Cotton," *Annals of the Association of American Geographers* 67 (1977): 307–22. Gilbert C. Fite, *Cotton Fields No More: Southern Agriculture, 1865–1980* (Lexington: University of Kentucky Press, 1984), 91–162.

35. Happ, Rittenhouse, and Dobson, *Some Principles of Accelerated Stream and Valley Sedimentation*, 22–53.

5

Mining and Landscape Transformation

Richard V. Francaviglia

> Man puts his hand to the flinty rock,
> and overturns mountains by the roots.
> He cuts out channels in the rocks,
> and his eye sees every precious thing.
> He binds up the streams so that they do
> not trickle, and the thing that is hid
> he brings forth to light.[1]

Although written several thousand years ago, these verses from the Book of Job describe an activity that continues to transform the face of the earth. Mining, the process by which treasures locked in the earth are "won" by, requires both brain and brawn, that is, knowledge as well as physical effort. The consequences of mining activity are quite visible in the landscape: the overturned mountains, channels, and dams described as early as biblical times are familiar surface consequences of mining even today. To the historical geographer, the resulting topography left in the wake of mining is evidence that sheds light on the behavior of mining enterprises and the cultures in which they operate.

How does mining shape the landscape? What types of features result from mining? This chapter will answer these questions by presenting a basic classification system of mining-related topography. Furthermore, as historical geographers we are concerned with the element of time, and so we will also answer another important question: How have mining landscapes evolved, or changed, over time?

Historically, mining's early impacts were quite localized and determined by how much rock could be removed by hand tools. Nevertheless, these early mining activities created a distinctive type of topography that brands mining country: holes of extraction in the form of small open pits, or tunnel-like mine shafts, are flanked by piles of waste debris that may choke or redirect stream channels and accelerate erosion. Yet, one axiom of mining is that man moves far more material than the ore that is sought, and furthermore, that even the ore must be reduced to obtain the valuable metals sought. As mining technologies developed, the scale of pits, shafts, and especially debris piles vastly increased. All have left marks on the land.

The Classification of Mining Landscapes

Looked at systematically, mining landscapes often contain four kinds of topographic features that result from the specific processes used to extract, mill, concentrate, smelt and refine metals:[2]

1. Primary Extractive (that is, subtractive features, such as pits, stopes, tunnels, and shafts).

2. Secondary Accretionary (additive) features such as mine dumps and gob and overburden piles that result from the physical or structural breakdown of mined material.

3. Tertiary Accretionary (additive) features, namely the wastes of chemical concentrating processes, for example, "tailings" in the proper use of the term.

4. Quaternary Accretionary (additive) features, such as cinder and slag piles, resulting from the complete restructuring of materials through heat, which is to say the smelting, fluxing, and/or refinement of ores.

Using a geomorphological approach, such landscape features can be classified according to their physical properties (Fig. 5-1). Whether any particular mining-related landscape will possess all four types of features depends on the kind of ore mined and the technology of the miners.

Some Native American peoples conducted mining operations on a small scale (leaving primary extractive features at archaeological sites in places like Michigan's Upper Peninsula). When the Spanish in the New World successfully mined and processed silver and gold ores, they left a greater number of residual features, including some quaternary accretionary features such as slag piles. The mining legacy of the United States is closely tied to the British Industrial Revolution in that its technology was transported to the Eastern Seaboard around 1800. Generally, the technology was very eclectic, having been borrowed from many sources—including Spain, Saxony, and Mexico, and it was improved as the nation expanded in size and encountered new ore bodies. Therefore, it can be said that in the last two hundred years the mining landscapes of the United States were created with the westward move of Euro-American culture. By the mid-nineteenth century, Americans were rapidly

Category	Type Feature	Composition	Morphology
Primary Extractive	Open pit	Bedrock	Vertical walls internal drainage
	Shaft, stope	Bedrock	Tunnel to reach or remove ore
Secondary Accretionary	Ore dump	Shattered but unaltered rock (mineralized) cobble-size or smaller (<256 mm)	Piles of rock, dumped close to the minehead, often the color of the ore body
	Overburden pile	Shattered but unaltered rock unmineralized) variable in size (100 to 400 mm)	Piles of rock, boulders, and/or detritus-rubble the color of the "cap" or the bedrock
	Leach dump	Shattered rock of low-grade mineralization variable in size (64 to >256 mm)	Steep-sided with cells or ponds on top surface; trace color of mineralization
Tertiary Accretionary	Tailings	Pulverized fine-grained material deposited after chemical/slurry processing (2 mm or less)	Steep-sided, occasionally terraced and often eroded; pale/pastel-colored
Quaternary Accretionary	Slag dump	Vitrified, compacted, or consolidated material resulting from fluxing (size variable)	Dark/multicolored piles; unconsolidated material often used as fill

Figure 5-1. Classification system of metals mining-related topographic features. (After Richard Francaviglia, "The Ultimate Artifact," 1988.)

developing new mining technologies to meet the challenges of extract-
ing, milling, and smelting ores from Michigan to California, and these
have left a full-blown landscape legacy of all four types of features.
Through an increasingly sophisticated and aggressive sequential process,
the bonanzas were mined first, and then newer industrial/metallurgical
technologies were applied to gather up that which was missed in the first
round(s) of exploitation. The president of the Homestake Mining Company summarized the major changes in technology that have shaped the
landscape of America's mining districts as follows:

> An amazing, rapid succession of mineral districts of first rank in the world
> was found as the westward exploration of the continent progressed. Then,
> a half century or so later, as the richer ores were running out, deposits of
> far lower grade but with even greater gross value were profitably exploited
> as the base of immense enterprises by application of new methods of mining
> and by concentration on scales that dwarfed any such activities in the
> past.[3]

The demand for mineral products was spurred by a rapidly growing
population that consumed more natural materials as a consumer-oriented
society was created; which is to say that our mining landscapes are a
reflection of our growing affluence as a nation. Especially since 1890,
the landscape changes brought about by mining have increased dramatically in scale and impact. The topographic changes that resulted from
the adoption of new technologies have been nothing short of phenomenal: Certain mining districts have primary extractive features—the huge
open-pit mines where early mining towns once stood or secondary and
tertiary accretionary features, such as huge overburden piles and tailings
ponds, covering the sites of others. In the cases of mining districts that
have developed over decades, these changes may completely reorder the
geography as earlier mines, and even entire "historic" communities, are
obliterated in response to the increasing scale of mining activities. As
geographer Benjamin Richason put it, the landscapes associated with
open-pit mining are an "example of man and his machine as the greatest
erosive force on earth today."[4] Visually, mining's erosive impact produc-
es some of the most stark and dramatic landscapes on earth.

Thus, although there is a timeless quality to man's digging holes into
the earth and dumping mining wastes upon the surface, by using the
geomorphological model one can see that mining landscapes are really
assemblages of artifacts derived from a powerful and rapidly evolving
industry that reshapes the land by restructuring mineralized areas.

Landscape Effects of Mining

There are two major types of mining—underground and surface mining—both of which affect the earth's surface through extraction and deposition. The localized or concentrated underground mining operations honeycombed the ore body and left in their wake ore dumps and waste piles—as well as "tailings" resulting from the pulverization and solution recovering of metals. These can be seen in most of the underground hard-rock mining districts today (Fig. 5-2). From the iron mines of New York and Tennessee, to the copper mines of Michigan's Upper Peninsula, to the precious-metals mining districts of the West, the American landscape is dotted with the surface evidence of underground metals-mining activity. Many of these developed in the mid- to late-nineteenth century, although their underground mining activity often continued well into the twentieth century. Such historic mining landscapes are "islands" of intensely modified land where the "scars" of mining are confined to the areas immediately surrounding the underground mines.

These localized mining landscapes are developed on a smaller scale than their twentieth-century surface-mined counterparts—the open-pit

Figure 5-2. The landscape of a typical hard-rock underground mining district is characterized by localized topographical disturbance. Here, at Virginia City, Nevada, conical ore dumps and tailings veneer the landscape. (Photo by Richard Francaviglia, 1978.)

Figure 5-3. Open-pit mining creates awesome topography. Here, the Rouchleau Pit near Virginia, Minnesota, has been excavated nearly 500 feet into the countryside, and huge waste rock dumps lie near by. (Photo by Richard Francaviglia, 1990.)

metals mines that are part of a long tradition of surface mining. The traveler driving into a mining district where open-pit mining has been conducted is likely to be shocked by the scale of activities; the size, shape, and even the coloration of the man-made topography is overwhelming (Fig. 5-3). The focus of most attention—the open-pit mine itself— is awe inspiring. Open-pit mines are among the most spectacular man-made features on earth. They may be more than 1,000 feet deep and several miles across, their shape and size dependent on the configuration of the ore body and the techniques of extraction.

In Minnesota's Iron Ranges, huge open-pit mines punctuate the landscape. As seen on topographic maps, they are deep depressions that mark the penetration of the hematite iron-ore body by man and machine. The largest open-pit iron mine is found near Hibbing; it occupies about 13,000 acres and is more than 400 feet deep. Open-pit mining began in about 1890 in Minnesota, a function of new technology, such as the steam shovel, and low-cost steam-powered railroad transportation.

In the West, beginning in about 1910, copper mining began to be carried out on a large scale as low-grade-ore extraction removed entire mountains of low-grade porphyry ores. The topographic map of Bingham

Canyon, Utah (Fig. 5-4), provides a good example of an open-pit mine. Like most large, open-pit mines, Bingham Pit consists of a deep, scooped-out depression surrounded by a series of benches about fifty feet high,

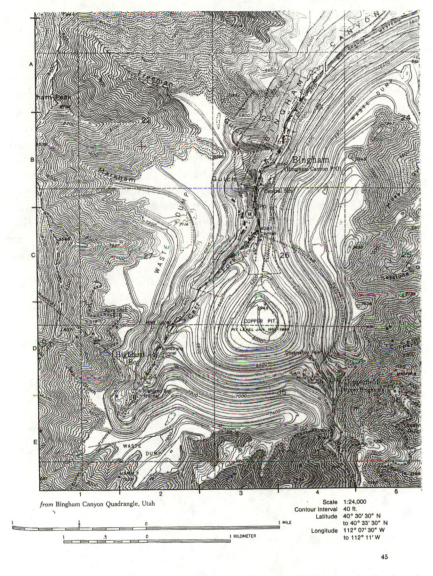

from Bingham Canyon Quadrangle, Utah

Scale 1:24,000
Contour Interval 40 ft.
Latitude 40° 30' 30" N
to 40° 33' 30" N
Longitude 112° 07' 30" W
to 112° 11' W

1 MILE

1 KILOMETER

45

Figure 5-4. Topographic map of Bingham Canyon, Utah, reveals the bowl-shaped depression created by open-pit mining. Note that overburden and lower grade waste materials of accretion are dumped near by to reduce transportation costs.

a classic landscape of subtraction. Railway lines or roads run along these benches, permitting the removal of ore and waste rock. The pit is more than two miles in diameter and over 1,500 feet in depth—the largest open-pit copper mine in the world.

Since most open-pit mines involve the exploitation of low-grade ores, much waste rock must be removed, and all of this material has to be put somewhere. Topographic maps also show major areas of deposition or accretion: the overburden, or waste rock, consists of coarse material scraped or blasted away from the barren (nonmineralized) zone that covered the ore body. This overburden may consist of boulder-size fragments of rock, most of which were hauled to the edge of the pit and dumped in huge ridges. In Minnesota, the Iron Ranges are characterized by a series of red, steep-sided hills that slowly become covered by trees. In the case of western copper mines, the material to be leached (or piled up so that water can be passed through it to further remove concentrations of copper) is usually configured into huge "leach dumps"—impressive, stark, accretionary topographic features consisting of a rather heterogeneous mixture of rubble and coarse, shattered porphyry rock (Fig. 5-5). At the top of leach dumps one finds shallow ponds, or cells, into which acidic water is pumped. By percolating through the leach dump,

Figure 5-5. A leach dump located near the open-pit copper mine at Ely, Nevada, is a local topographical landmark and is one of the features associated with large-scale copper mining in the West. (Photo by Richard Francaviglia, 1989.)

this water becomes rich in copper, which is then precipitated, or deposited, in metallic form on scrap iron. In some copper-mining districts, leach dumps are among the most impressive accretionary features in the landscape.

In copper-mining districts, we often find another very impressive accretionary topographic feature, the tailings ponds, or tailings dams. Here, "tail water" (a mixture of pulverized, slimy, nonmetallic wastes from which virtually all metals have been removed) is piped from the copper concentrator and dumped into huge ponds to evaporate. These tailings dams consist of terraces about twenty feet high; each successive terrace indicates the front of an earlier dam. In the arid and semiarid West, these tailings are landmarks; their light-colored, symmetrical terraces are a distinctive feature found in the West from Montana to Arizona (Fig. 5-6).

In the Tri-State lead- and zinc-mining district of Missouri–Kansas–Oklahoma, one finds huge piles of "chat" (the sandy wastes from the concentrating process that tower above the landscape). These are local

Figure 5-6. Tailings are one of the most distinctive topographic features associated with ore processing. These eroded tailings dams consist of terraces about 40 feet in height, behind which thick solutions of waste rock settled and evaporated. The posts in the foreground mark the site of a proposed development that was eclipsed by the dumping of these accretionary mine tailings from about 1920 to the 1970s. (Photo by Richard Francaviglia, 1981).

Figure 5-7. A spectacular chat pile looms behind the Federal Mill complex at Flat River, Missouri, in this 1950s photograph. Composed of fine tailings left over from lead and zinc ore processing, these are distinctive topographic features in the Tri-State mining district. (Photo courtesy of the Missouri Mines Historic State Park.)

landmarks, and their steep-sided, conical shape define the area (Fig. 5-7). In coal mining areas, one finds characteristic "gob" piles or "culm banks" that loom behind communities, creating localized topography that helps to define the geography of any particular mining district. These accretionary features consist of the slate and other waste rock that is separated from the coal and piled onto the land.

In most metals-mining districts, one finds another very important manmade topographic feature: namely, those quaternary accretionary landforms called slag piles, or slag heaps, that result when ores are smelted. In many cases, they outlast the smelters themselves and remain as dark, steep-sided hills, or tablelands. Sometimes deeply eroded, these vitrified, cindery wastelands are common at smelter sites. Slag is usually deposited as molten dross, or waste, from the smelter, and can be identified by its glassy consistency, which testifies to the high temperatures involved in its creation. In some places, such as Anaconda (Montana), Clifton (Arizona), and Eureka (Nevada), slag dumps are prominent landscape features underscoring the visual desolation that results from large-scale mining.

In mining country, then, the man-made topographic features, such as open-pit mines, ore dumps, or slag piles, are diagnostic: they reveal the type of processes that created them (extractive or accretionary), and their overall form, or morphology (conical, tabular, irregular), helps define the visual geography of the mining district. Some of the more spectacular features may be incised hundreds of feet into the landscape or tower hundreds of feet above it to form landmarks. Each of these topographic features in a mining district is the result of specific processes. They do not result by accident, and they are surely one of the most distinctive aspects of the site—the topographic framework in which all activity is developed. However, the challenge to historical geographers goes beyond simply describing the landscape we see today to determining how, and why, it has been shaped by man through time.

The Sequential Development of Mining Landscapes

Transformation—a technologically driven change in structure or physical appearance—is one of the constants of the historical geography of mining districts.[5] With improvements in technology, the transformation occurs on a larger scale, culminating in mining-related topographic features occupying square miles instead of acres. This means that surface mining may obliterate (or bury) earlier evidence of mining as its impact spreads across the landscape. In mining districts, large-scale man-made topography is episodic, resulting from technological change that usually occurs in an orderly progression, each successive stage normally being larger in scale than the one immediately preceding it.

The landscape impacts of these transformations allow a mining engineer to tell the age of a district. All mines, and the mining districts in which they occur, have a life cycle. Geographer Homer Aschmann outlined the four inevitable stages in the development of a mine: (1) prospecting and exploration, (2) investment and development, (3) stable operation, and (4) decline.[6] During the life history of a mine, the geographic impacts of stages of development veneer the landscape's topographic artifacts. Just as these are not random features in space (bearing a close relationship to the geological features), they are also not random through time: each is a result of technological processes introduced at some point in history.

In the case of the Warren mining district[7] and the Clifton–Morenci district[8] in Arizona, for example, historical geographers determined that each economic phase of mining activity produced distinctive landforms that are an integral part of the "image" of each district at any particular time. By employing historical maps, historical photographs, corporate/ oral histories, archaeological techniques, and an analysis of the current landscape features, it is possible to illustrate sequentially the topographic changes that have occurred in a mining district. This spatial approach is important because "each episode of mining activity that takes place potentially destroys part or all of existing archaeological sites."[9] Mining historian Otis Young, in describing the decline of Nevada's Comstock mining district, noted that new cyanidation processes created new mining activity that transformed the landscape:

> The tailing heaps of the original mills were fastened upon, run through the vats, and pumped away. Therefore, although the original waste dumps are still visible in place, the tailing heaps which were once found below them are gone.[10]

These topographic changes that Young described in Virginia City–Gold Hill are common elsewhere, for mining interests are constantly evaluating all materials, not just natural ores, for their mineral content. Thus, older tailings and dumps may be "worked," actually reprocessed, in order to reclaim minerals left by earlier, less efficient, processes. These activities create new landscape features, but in so doing may obliterate older features. Few mining district landscapes offer simple, unbroken linear chronologies. The fact that many have been reworked, or scavenged, at different times helps to make their interpretation more challenging and more interesting.

The features associated with specific mining processes, such as tailings and leach dumps, can be best interpreted and evaluated if they are differentiated both spatially and chronologically, that is, in space and time. Despite their spatial and chronological complexity, the large-scale topographic changes affecting mining districts occur in an evolutionary manner, and can, for convenience, be treated in time-dated sequences. The series of several "time exposures" for the Warren mining district are maps that illustrate the major land-use patterns in several critical "watershed" years (Fig. 5-8).[11] These time exposures, or "freeze frames," exemplify how technology had shaped the landscape up to particular points in time: 1885, 1912, 1931, and 1974. They include all major developments from the early hard-rock mining activities in the early 1880s to the closure of the open-pit mines in the mid-1970s.

The topographic change that occurs in a mining district is really a reflection of the changes in both the quality of the ores mined and the techniques used in their processing. It is the job of the mining engineer-metallurgist to separate in the most efficient manner the metal from the impurities—a function of technology that has markedly improved over the last century.

As time progresses, lower and lower grade ores are mined. In the case of copper, for example, the percentage of what constitutes a paying ore has dropped; in the late 1800s, only ore averaging at least 25 percent copper was mined; by about 1915, lower-grade deposits of less than 5 percent copper were developed; and by the 1940s, the percentage had dropped to about 2 percent. This means that more than 98 percent of the ore deposit is waste material in the more recent mining operations. Mining such low-grade deposits required large machinery and sophisticated ore-treatment technology. Flotation (the counterintuitive process by which ores are pulverized and their heavier metallic constituents separated as they float on top of the liquid and are collected on minute bubbles of oil) revolutionized the mining industry after about 1900. It also revolution-ized the landscape.

Likewise, the percentage of other metals in ores has dropped with improvements in processing technology. At one time only high-grade ores (about 60 percent iron, or virtually pure hematite) could be shipped from the Lake Superior region to the steel mills of Ohio and Pennsylvania. Beneficiation (the process by which impurities are removed from a low-grade iron ore to permit its economical shipment and smelting) has encouraged the mining of lower-grade ores in the Lake Superior region, giving a new lease on life to the open-pit mining technology that has transformed the region's landscapes since about 1900. The resulting processed ore, called taconite, can be shipped great distances.

Just as any individual mine may have a life cycle, so, too, does a district. Its life cycle is expressed in the landscape. If we were to study sequential maps for many districts, an overall pattern of landscape evolution might emerge. Many would seem to fit into a predictable, or at any rate orderly, sequence, as outlined below:

1. *Exploration:* The prospecting phase in which areas showing "col-or," or promise, are opened; initial probings reveal information about the extent of the ore body; and, a rapidly changing localized mining topog-raphy begins to take shape.

2. *Initiation:* After the quality of the ore and the general parameters of the ore body are understood, the investment of capital and energy is applied to the site and successful exploitation results. The richest ores are mined because they must justify the high expenses of shipping them to smelters. Waste dumps are typically rich and located adjacent to the mines. Most of the features associated with exploration are obliterated during this period, which may last about fifteen years in the typical mining

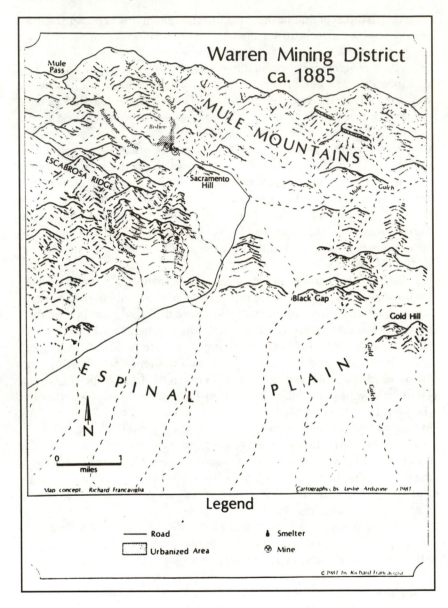

Figure 5-8 (a, b, c, d). A series of maps showing the evolution of land use and mining-related topography in Arizona's Warren mining district reveals an increasing scale of operations—and resulting landscape modification—in over nearly a century. (Source: Richard Francaviglia, "Copper Mining and Landscape Evolution," 1982.)

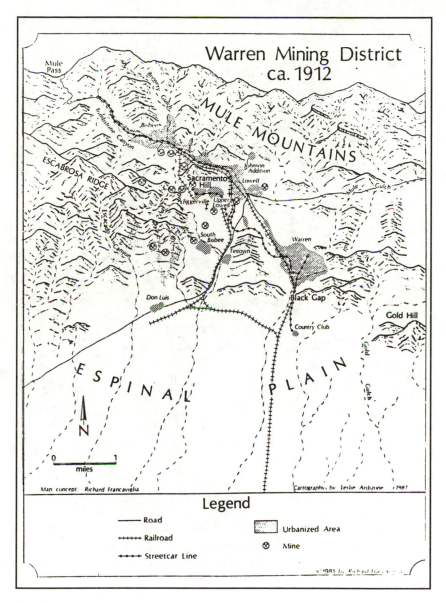

Figure 5-8b.

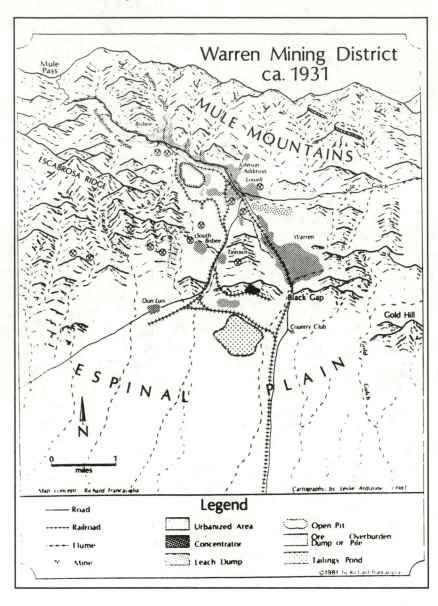

Figure 5-8c.

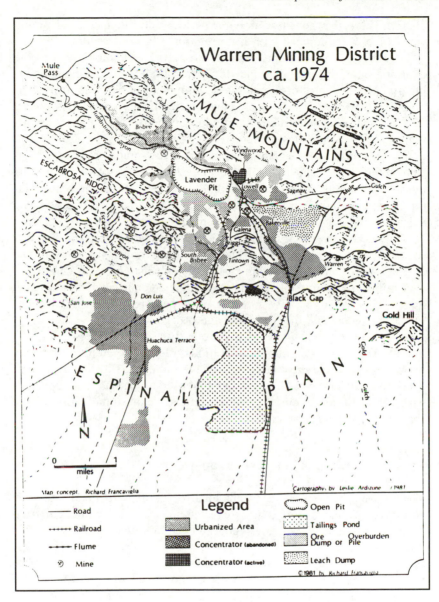

Figure 5-8d.

district. This is the "bonanza," or boom period of development, and mining wastes are often dumped with little regard to future activities.

3. *Diversification:* Improvements in mining technology lead to the exploitation of different or somewhat lower grade ores. Efficient smelting and processing of ores, and the development of concentration technologies suited to specific ores, characterize operations in this phase. The landscape becomes increasingly dominated by waste piles and tailings. This phase may last twenty-five years.

4. *Intensification:* Development of large, low-grade ore bodies adjacent to the richer deposits exploited in earlier stages occurs during this phase. The method most often selected to develop the ore body is open-pit, or surface, mining which depends upon the availability of large-scale earth moving equipment and technologies that reduce the costs of concentrating. Massive reworking of the landscape occurs, and detritus (overburden) or waste materials such as tailings may cover thousands of acres. Tailings and dumps from earlier periods may be reworked. Solution-mining (leaching) operations are conducted on leach dumps or leach heaps. This type of activity may last forty, perhaps fifty, years, depending on the economy, the ore body, and other conditions.

5. *Cessation:* Exhaustion of the ore body and/or rising costs of production bring an end to mining operations. Major corporate investments are liquidated. Mine shaft pumps cease operation, thus flooding the mines. The economic processes in the development of topography are superseded by the natural factors of erosion/attrition or the stabilization of the topography through reclamation.

Attitudes Toward Mining Landscapes

The impacts of these changes are local or perhaps regional, but they result from "outside" forces being exerted on a particular mining district. That helps to explain why the topography of mining districts has such a "familiar" look from place to place. Similarities result in places as distant as Arizona, Montana, and Chile because mining companies operate worldwide and respond to worldwide economic conditions. The mining engineers who transformed the landscape were part of a fraternity that traveled widely and maintained close contact with technological developments by visiting other properties, reading mining and metallurgical journals, and attending conferences. Just as the price of metals/minerals helps determine the speed with which change will occur, the technological subculture of mining engineers helps to determine its actual form. Mining engineers often view their handiwork as functional if not actually beautiful—a manifestation of technology and landscape design that symbolizes the power of man to increase the productivity of the earth. Some say mining improves otherwise "unproductive" land.[12]

The landscape features in a mining district become its topographic badge of identity. They affect places as different as Eureka, Utah, where conical mine dumps and localized tailings brand the landscape as the handiwork of underground miners; Mormon Bar, California, where the aggressive activity of placer miners left a distinctive landscape; Eveleth, Minnesota, where one sees that "most conspicuous disturbance of the surface," to quote a mining engineer, the cookie-cutter topography associated with open-pit mining. An industrial archaeologist tells us that large-scale "earthworks" of all kinds require vast expenditures of human effort, are a measure of a civilization's ability to organize human activity, "and produce both intended and unintended consequences for social and natural systems."[13]

Of all the topographic features associated with mining, none have captured the imagination more than the "desolation" left by the open-pit mining described earlier in this chapter. These are overpowering landscapes, for the transformation from nature to artifact (some might say wilderness to wasteland) is complete where such mining has been practiced. Novelists have provided us some insightful looks at mining-related topography. Consider, for example, how the development of an open-pit iron mine in Minnesota is described by Phil Stong in *The Iron Mountain*. He writes that Mr. Sturges, who oversees the explosives used to blast the iron ore,

> always liked to reflect on the fact that thousands of years of nature had done less to this deposit of ferric oxide than a few thousand tons of explosives that he had planted in strategic places at one time or another. When he had left the Range, almost in childhood, this pit had been a tentative and unremarkable little hole hardly big enough to bury all the pyramids. Now the ellipse was two miles long and half as wide; the cancer had bitten about a thousand feet deep, and the waste dump was bigger than the mountain had been. The difference was accounted for by the enormous pit—the mountain inverted and enlarged, and shipped away.[14]

An official 1959 United States Steel company report on Minnesota's awesome Hull–Rust–Mahoning Open Pit at Hibbing stated that this was "the largest open pit mine in the world, being approximately three miles long and over a mile wide at its greatest width," and that 35,106,296 cubic yards of material had been stripped from the pit.[15] Geographer John Webb's definitive dissertation on the Iron Ranges[16] revealed the phenomenal extent of the pits and dumps which physically—and perhaps psychologically—define the edges of settlement, and even control the directions of community growth and development. Webb's land use maps of the Iron Range communities, of which Hibbing, Minnesota, serves as a good example, reveal the spatial extent and proximity to settlement of such huge topographic features (Fig. 5-9). The Iron Ranges exemplify some of the most awesome earth moving undertaken by mankind; their legacy is a series of canyons rimmed by huge accretionary dumps that run diagonally across northeastern Minnesota for nearly ninety miles.

This landscape took almost eighty years to create, and its development occurred in stages. Each stage was largely a function of the economy, with mines booming during periods of war and/or prosperity. With the passage of time, these open-pit mines came to be considered part of the scenery, and the harshness of the landscape was somewhat mitigated by vegetation that was either deliberately planted to "soften" the scene or which tenaciously reestablished itself on all but the steepest slopes. Residents of the Iron Ranges came to develop a strange affection for the open-pit mines, most of which had been abandoned by the 1970s. Enthusiastic travel/tourism efforts actually led to comparisons of the resulting mining landscape with that of natural features: the Hibbing Chamber of Commerce termed the huge Hull–Rust–Mahoning pit the "Man-Made Grand Canyon,"[17] and much of the tourism-related literature proudly described the awesome impact of technology in creating these new landscapes that were an inevitable result of "progress."

We see from these descriptions that it is not only the resulting topography, but the actual process by which it is created, that excites interest. Within their lifetimes, people can experience change that might take eons of geological time, or as geographer Benjamin Richason put it, "within three-quarters of a century, man has accomplished what nature would have taken hundreds of thousands of years to do."[18] Although all mining-related topography reminds us that a resource is disappearing for good, no place reminds us of this more than an open-pit mine, for it takes the original landscape with it.

Most open-pit mines have turnouts, or viewpoints, where travelers can gaze into the pit and read almost incomprehensible statistics while huge machines are dwarfed in the bowl-shaped, terraced canyon–landscape below. These are popular places. Even abandoned open pits, such as the Berkeley Pit just east of Butte, Montana, attract visitors. Here, one sees the terraces slowly collapse, and the pit filled with an imperceptibly rising emerald-green lake whose beauty is exceeded only by its toxicity. In northern Minnesota, the abandoned open-pit mines have filled with water, and commercial salmon have begun to be raised in these "lakes"; slowly, these abandoned mines are becoming scenic resources.

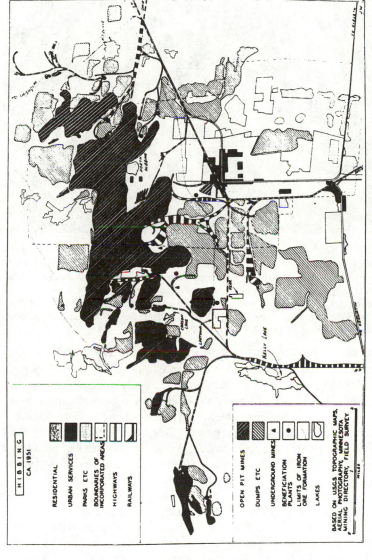

Figure 5-9. Geographer John Webb's 1958 study of Minnesota's Iron Ranges demonstrated that the distinctive topography created by mining affects the distribution and character of settlements. A map of Hibbing shows the complex interrelationships between mining topography and settlement.

Figure 5-10. Natural or man-made topography? The topographic works of man, such as this tailings pile near Ruth, Nevada, often emulate natural topography of arid and semi-arid areas. Whereas such works are considered functionally beautiful by mining engineers, and nightmares of environmental abuse by conservationists, the general public often considers them to be more or less natural "badlands" in the context of the surrounding desert landscapes. (Photo by Richard Francaviglia, 1989.)

This combination—the effects of time and physical processes in creating the landscape—is exactly what people appreciate when they look into the Grand Canyon. The scenery is remarkably similar: an exciting but reassuring landscape of nearly vertical cliffs stratified into a series of benches much like the canyonlands of the Southwest. Conservationists may reject the idea that mining landscapes are "beautiful," but they do so not on aesthetic grounds but rather in light of real or imagined impacts to the natural environment, or attitudes toward the mining industry that created such "wastelands." Looking objectively at mining-related topography, we can see that it *does* mock natural features: The visual parallels between tailings dams and the large truncated alluvial fans in the Southwest are fascinating, as are the barren, eroded mine dumps that resemble "badlands" topography (Fig. 5-10). Discussions with residents and travelers in the West reveal that many cannot tell the difference between "natural" and "man-made" topography. In the public mind, mining-related topography may fit so well into a stereotypic visual image of rugged, denuded "western" landscapes that it seems "natural."

The Persistence of Mining Landscapes

However grand their scale, nature begins to reclaim even the most ambitious topographic works of miners shortly after they are "completed," that is, abandoned. Attrition is a factor in the way a mining landscape looks, reminding us that mining landscapes, like all topography, are further transformed by sedimentation, erosion, and revegetation. From their inception, mining-related topographic features are exposed to, and become part of, the "natural" environment. Historian Phil Notarianni characterized this interrelationship for the Tintic mining district in Utah by noting that "years of mining have parched the land, leaving twisted cedars and hardened conical mine dumps, weathered with age, yet monumental remnants of days past."[19]

Whereas the original design of the man-made topography of a mining district is attributable to technology and economy, its persistence after the cessation of mining is a result of weathering under various climatic regimes. In well-watered (humid) forested areas, the legacy of mining may be harder to detect as brush and trees return after mining activity ceases. In deserts, however, the topographic features created by mines may last for centuries. The scars of mining activity dating back nearly three millennia are reportedly still visible in the desert regions peripheral to the Mediterranean Sea. Some of our mining landscapes in the arid West probably will be visible for at least that long. Even in the coal fields of northeastern Pennsylvania, the landscape is marked by huge culm banks that remain distinctive years after abandonment, prompting a student of the area's cultural landscape to conclude that "what we see in the hard coal valleys is that it is far harder to end a landscape than to start or despoil one."[20]

The British call landscapes despoiled by all types of industry, including mining, "derelict lands,"[21] but we have no similar term in the United States. In many ways, our mining landscapes are both a startling commentary on our attitudes toward nature and an honest expression of our belief in material wealth and our faith in technology. For more than a century, the mining industry has fought to keep the permissive 1872 Mining Law in place. Only where mining's impact is so extensive, as in the late-nineteenth-century hydraulic-placer mining that disrupted entire river systems in California, do we find strict laws governing mining.

Nevertheless, conservation appears to be an important factor in what happens to mining lands. With the rise of a strong publicly supported conservation ethic in the mid-1960s, demands have been placed on mining companies to reclaim mined landscapes. Such reclamation efforts tend to reduce erosion, mitigate air and water pollution, and return the land to productive uses such as grazing or agriculture. But they also obliterate many historic mining-related landscapes that have been created as a direct result of the management philosophies and policies of mining companies. Despite conservation efforts, however, many mining-related landscapes go unreclaimed, as such efforts increase the cost (and complexity) of mining. The United States is dotted with thousands of unreclaimed "orphan" mines of the type recently described by two environmental analysts.[22]

It is not surprising that mining-related topography—if not reworked by mining interests or "reclaimed" through conservation efforts—may be the most long-lasting, and therefore ultimately the most important, of the vestiges of human activity in a mining district. It is likely to long outlast other above-ground features such as settlements, structures, and transportation systems. Thus, mining-related topography is more than unpleasant scenery, for it may be the only remaining tangible record of the major activity that once flourished in a particular place. Because it is so long-lasting and has such an impact on other features, the man-made topography may serve as the "ultimate artifact" in describing the historical geography of mining districts.

Acknowledgments

The author wishes to thank the miners and scholars who provided information and inspiration for this chapter, including Warren Witry of the Missouri Mines Historic State Park; Phil Notarianni of the Utah Historical Society; John Webb of the State University of New York at Albany; Arnold Alanen of the University of Wisconsin at Madison; Donald Hardesty of the University of Nevada, Reno; Homer Aschmann of the University of California at Riverside; and Ed Lehner of Bisbee, Arizona. Elaine Porchett of the Ohio Historical Society and Kirsten Dennis of the University of Texas at Arlington helped with the typing and editing of the original manuscript.

Notes

1. The Book of Job, Chapter 28, verses 9 through 11, *The Holy Bible*.
2. Richard V. Francaviglia, "The Ultimate Artifact: Interpreting and Evaluating the Man-Made Topography of Historic Mining Districts." Paper presented at the annual meeting of the Society for Historical Archaeology, Reno, Nevada, January 16, 1988; for a general geomorphic classification of landscapes of exca-

vation, refer to Andrew Goudie, *Human Impact on the Natural Environment* (Cambridge: MIT Press, 1990), 204–11.

3. Donald H. McLaughlin, "Man's Selective Attack on Ores and Minerals," *Man's Role in Changing the Face of the Earth*, William Thomas, ed. (Chicago: University of Chicago Press, 1956), 855.

4. Benjamin Richason, *Atlas of Cultural Features: A Study of Man's Imprint on the Land* (Northbrook, Ill.: Hubbard Press, 1972), 46. Note: Although agriculture may have a more extensive, large-scale impact on soil erosion, mining creates the most heavily eroded localized landscapes.

5. Richard V. Francaviglia, *Hard Places: Reading the Landscape of America's Historic Mining Districts* (Iowa City: University of Iowa Press, 1991).

6. Homer Aschmann, "The Natural History of a Mine," *Economic Geography*, 46:2 (April 1970): 171–90.

7. Richard V. Francaviglia, "Copper Mining and Landscape Evolution: A Century of Change in Arizona's Warren Mining District" *Journal of Arizona History* 23:2 (Autumn 1982): 267–98.

8. Udo Zindel, "Landscape Evolution in the Clifton-Morenci Mining District, Arizona, 1972–1986" (Unpublished Master's Thesis, Arizona State University, 1987).

9. Donald Hardesty, "Industrial Archaeology on the American Mining Frontier: Suggestions for a Research Agenda" *Journal of New World Archaeology* 6:4 (1986): 51.

10. Otis E. Young, *Western Mining: An Informal Account of Precious Metals Prospecting, Placering, Lode Mining, and Milling on the American Frontier from Spanish Times to 1893* (Norman: University of Oklahoma Press, 1970), 265.

11. Richard V. Francaviglia, "Time Exposures: The Evolving Landscape of an Arizona Copper Mining District," in *Mineral Resource Development: Geopolitics, Economics, and Policy*, Harley Johansen, Olen P. Matthews, and Gundars Rudzitis, eds. (Boulder, Colo.: Westview Press, 1987).

12. Examples of the mining engineers literature include *Mining and Scientific Press*, published weekly in San Francisco, California, from 1860 to 1922 and bulletins issued by the U.S. Bureau of Mines. For an example of a metallurgical engineering text see Carl Schnabel, *Handbook of Metallurgy*, 3rd. ed. (London: Macmillan, 1921).

13. Jeffrey L. Brown "Earthworks and Industrial Archaeology," *IA: The Journal of the Society for Industrial Archaeology* 6:1 (1980): 1.

14. Phil Stong, *The Iron Mountain* (New York: Farrar & Rinehart, 1942), 52–53.

15. Lake Superior and Canadian Iron Ore Properties Operated by Pickands Mather & Co. Report dated August, 1959, 15–16.

16. John W. Webb, "An Urban Geography of the Minnesota Iron Ranges," (Ph.D. Dissertation, University of Minnesota, April 1958).

17. *The Hull-Rust Mine, The Man-Made Grand Canyon of the North* (Hibbing, Minn.: Hibbing Chamber of Commerce, n.d.).

18. Richason, *Atlas of Cultural Features*, 44.

19.   Philip F. Notarianni, *Faith, Hope, & Prosperity: The Tintic Mining District* (Eureka, Utah: Tintic Historical Society, 1982), 13.

20.   Ben Marsh, "Continuity and Decline in the Anthracite Towns of Northeastern Pennsylvania," *Annals of the Association of American Geographers*, 77:3 (September 1987), 351.

21.   Kenneth Wallwork, *Derelict Land: Origins and Prospects of a Land-Use Problem* (London: David and Charles, 1974).

22.   Leisa M. Huyck and John P. Reganold, "Environmental Policies and Issues Surrounding Holden Mine Tailings: A Case Study of an Orphan Mine," *Environmental Impact Assessment Review* 9 (1989): 97–123.

6

American Indian Reservations: Controlling Separate Space, Creating Separate Environments

Martha L. Henderson

American Indian reservations are separate spaces on the American landscape. They are separated from other public and private lands in the United States by treaty or executive order for functional purposes identified during European and, later, United States advances into North America. Primarily created to segregate native groups from European colonists and later American settlers, reservations have become distinct environmental and social settings.

The United States federal government controlled social and material wealth on reservations, including natural resources, as part of the trust relationship established between native groups and the government. That trust relationship also established a reservation-management process that placed the federal government in the role of mediator and benefactor of Indian populations.[1] The relationship has been redefined by congressional acts and regulations over time. In this context, modern reservation landscapes are the results of federal policy and congressional act implementation, demands by non-Indians, economic conditions both on and off reservations, and culturally specific goals of native groups.

Not all American Indian reservations have been equally modified by these forces, but each reservation landscape includes evidence of the interaction between American Indians and dominant American society. Interaction between the two entities is evident in land-use patterns, resource-development patterns, residence patterns, and concepts of place. This chapter examines resource-development patterns on the Mescalero Apache Reservation by measuring federal policy implementation, demands on resources by non-Indians, and development of commercial activity with respect to the Mescalero Apache forest reserve. Analysis of

115

the interaction between the federal government and Indian and non-Indian users of the forest reserve indicates that reservations, once outwardly controlled spaces, are becoming increasingly separate and inwardly controlled environments on the American landscape.

American Indian Trust Forests

Forests of North America were important resource areas for various Native American groups. They served as habitats for wildlife, provided significant plant resources, and formed buffers between neighboring and often competing native groups. American Indians developed methods of managing forest environments to ensure a specific type and level of resource production, modifying the forest landscape in the process. Analysis of native management practices and methods of forest management indicate that American Indians were effective in modifying forests to meet specific agricultural and subsistence goals.[2]

With European and, later, Euro-American demands on forest reserves, American Indians entered into competition for forested lands. Europeans promoted goals of resin and timber production and agricultural clearing. Their redefinition of forest-management practices replaced native practices and systematically reduced forests in size and species diversity.[3] Indians in the eastern United States and Canada lost in their attempt to continue a lifestyle based on Indian forest-management goals as colonization progressed westward. Native response to the change in forest management and other social and environmental changes brought about by European settlement included westward migration or social disintegration.[4]

American Indian groups in the western United States who traditionally occupied forestlands encountered American settlers during a later period of federal policy. Euro-American westward movement in the nineteenth century was accompanied by federal policies that established large "treatied" areas, sometimes including forests. Later, however, treatied lands were reapportioned either through the sale of unallotted land or the renegotiation of treaties. The result of the reapportionment process was a net loss of Indian lands, including forest reserves.[5]

Today there are 104 forested reservations in the United States (Fig. 6-1). Nearly 90 percent of the reservation forestlands are located in the northern and western regions of the country excluding Alaska, although commercial forests, containing marketable products, exist on nearly all of the forested reservations.[6] The choice to develop forest resources and the methods employed to harvest timber on reservations is the point at which implementation of U.S. federal policy, non-Indian demands,

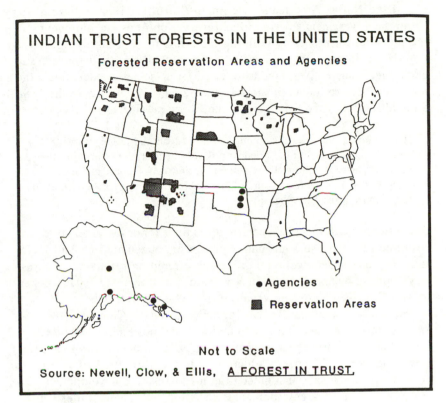

INDIAN TRUST FORESTS IN THE UNITED STATES

Forested Reservation Areas and Agencies

● Agencies

■ Reservation Areas

Not to Scale

Source: Newell, Clow, & Ellis, A FOREST IN TRUST.

Figure 6-1.

economic conditions, and American Indian culture interact to create separate spaces on the map of the American environmental landscape.

Historical analysis of forestry on American Indian reservations provides evidence of this interaction and its cumulative impacts. From the historical record it becomes clear that (1) federal policies shaped the health and productivity (both commercial and noncommercial) of trust forests as the government used forests to promote assimilation programs of the federal government; (2) Indian and non-Indian populations competed for commercial forest benefits such as capital accumulation and jobs; and (3) there has been considerable variation in the degree to which American Indians participated or are currently involved in the management of the trust forest.

Development of Trust Forest Resources

The presence of forestlands within reservation boundaries strongly influenced the Native American/government/Euro-American relationship. From the government's perspective, reservation forest development had the potential for providing building materials for a primarily houseless population in apparent need of structures, facilities, and fences, and encouraging the native population to adopt a "socially redeeming" and economically profitable, in short a "civilizing," way of life. In the 1888 Annual Report of the Secretary of the Interior, William F. Vilas stated:

> If the Indians had the right to cut and sell (dead and fallen) timber, . . . so as to secure to them the greatest possible benefits for improving their condition and promoting the civilization and self-support methods . . . they will thereby acquire some of the habits of industry so essential to their future prosperity.[7]

Some treaties thus included specific provisions for development of forest resources. In response, some native groups organized political and social units of governance, while other groups offered no resistance to forest development by non-Indians. In any event, forest removal usually began as soon, or even before, reservation treaties were ratified.[8]

The earliest American Indian logging started on Chippewa reservations in Minnesota and Wisconsin under guidelines established by Chippewa Indian Agents. The agents also supervised timber cutting on Chippewa allotments. Timber production led to construction of facilities, revenue from the sale of lumber to non-Indians, and development of a Euro-American work environment in the Chippewa communities.[9] However, in 1885, the government opened Chippewa reservations to non-Indian cutting. Access by non-natives to Chippewa timber stands initiated harvesting for profitability, not necessity, educational purposes, or capital accumulation by the Chippewa. This dramatically reduced the timber stock on the Chippewa lands in northern Wisconsin by 50 percent between 1885 and 1888.[10]

Non-Indian logging enhanced timber production and revenues for non-Indians, but directly violated trust responsibility of the federal government. In 1889, a Senate select committee investigated non-Indian logging in Wisconsin. The committee concluded that the Indians had lost a major resource and had not been adequately reimbursed. All logging was halted. The Chippewa situation initiated a series of discussions about reservation forests in light of the trust relationship between American Indians and the U.S. government.[11]

Suspension of all logging on the Chippewa reservations and allotted lands highlighted several new problems for federal administrators and the Indian population. First, the federal order to suspend timber harvesting denied some American Indians their only source of cash revenue and access to building supplies. Second, proper administration of timber contracts required personnel and management programs, none of which were authorized by the federal government. Third, while some traditional native groups did not want their forest reserves used for commercial purposes, other Indian leaders demanded that the forests be opened to logging companies in order to provide employment and allow young Indian men to earn a living and remain on the reservations. Finally, professional forest managers, new on the American environmental scene in the 1890s, recommended that timber harvesting progress to ensure a healthy forest stock. This confusing web of problems created vigorous controversy about the management of the trust forests.

Resolution came in 1889 with Congressional passage of the "Dead and Down Act," which sanctioned recovery of fallen timber for commercial purposes.[12] An 1888 amendment to section 5388 of the Revised Statutes (1878), which protected specific public lands from trespass, authorized Indian Agents to stop trespass by non-Indian loggers and in some cases initiate court proceedings against logging companies.[13] The Dead and Down Act and the revision to the trespass statute created opportunities for American Indians to achieve economic value from the forest trust. However, the ideal of Indian logging and retention of revenue was not achieved. Non-Indian loggers harvested greater than contracted volumes on Minnesota Chippewa reservations.[14] While these sawmill operations on reservations once again provided employment for Indian workers, they did little to enhance opportunities for Indian-owned logging operations.

The Allotment Act of 1887, by which eastern Indians received parcels of land, did not redistribute the majority of western reservation lands, primarily because the lands could not physically provide for an agricultural economy. Some western reservations such as the Colville, Spokane, Yakima, Warm Springs, Fort Apache, San Carlos, Navajo, Jicarilla, and Mescalero Apache instead maintained extensive trust forests. The forests attracted the attention of Indian agents who viewed them as grazing lands as well as the only sources of revenue for tribal members. Without allotment, reservation territory remained intact, a situation that made timber production and grazing more profitable and easier to administer.

Neglect of the trust relationship over forest-management issues in the north stimulated western American Indian leaders and reservation agents to request more careful management of western trust forests. The growing conservation movement in the United States also turned its attention to the needs of Indian forest management. As a result, the Indian Service developed a professional forestry branch to manage trust forests. J.P. Kinney, the first forester of the Indian Service, became an advocate of timber management as a source of Indian revenue and a means of assimilating Indians into the larger American society. Kinney's role as forester of the Indian Service included reservation visits to assess the extent of the forest reserve as well as an administrative capacity in Washington, D.C.

The Forestry Branch of the Indian Service, later renamed the Division of Forestry of the Bureau of Indian Affairs (BIA), was charged with the responsibility of developing and maintaining the trust forests while at the same time generating revenue for livestock expansion, jobs, and needed forest products for reservation populations. The forestry division spent minimal amounts of time monitoring other forest-management goals such as restocking, fire fighting, disease control, development of watershed-management units, and outdoor recreation facilities such as occurred on U.S. Forest Service lands. Generally, the BIA forestry unit facilitated timber removal. The perceived benefits of timber removal included revenue generation for the tribes, jobs in the woods for individual Indians, and associated benefits such as road and railroad construction across otherwise inaccessible reservation areas. In supporting timber harvesting and achieving associated economic and social goals, the BIA believed it was upholding the trust relationship.

Timber harvesting as managed by the BIA also maintained a set of social and economic conditions on reservations. Management of the forest reserve continued to be in the hands of the government. Indian people had only a consulting role. Timber contracts were sold to non-Indian logging companies because very few American Indians could accumulate the capital necessary to create a logging company. Furthermore, reservation sawmills were small and often capable of producing only limited amounts of lumber needed by the reservation population. Hence, commercial lumber processing took place beyond reservation boundaries at mills built by non-Indians. This situation limited Indian employment opportunities and transferred potential revenues to non-Indians. Consequently, non-Indians received benefits from the timber reserve, again a violation of the trust relationship despite BIA claims to the contrary.

Management of the American Indian forest reserve also sharply reflects three distinct changes in overall federal Indian policy since the 1887 Allotment Act. Each new phase of federal management included goals and objectives for developing reservation resources. In 1934, federal Indian policy reversed its assimilation agenda with the Indian Reorganization Act (IRA) and initiated tribal organization, funding of economic development projects, and organized social programs that enhanced American Indian culture. Forest resources, particularly those on western reservations, were largely developed via the 1934 policy. After 1952 the federal government reversed its policy of cultural pluralism and began a policy of reservation termination. Some forested reservations, such as the Klamath Reservation in Oregon and the Menominee Reservation in Wisconsin, were terminated, leaving each tribe without their primary economic base.[15] On the other hand, since 1975 all reservations have been managed by a policy of self-determination that allows American Indian participation in administering the trust relationship, including forest-management decision making. This has coincided with legally enforced scientific management absent during earlier phases. One example is the 1978 Cooperative Forestry Assistance Act, which funded disease and insect control on trust forests.[16] Reservation landscapes reflect these three periods of Indian policy and resource-development initiatives.

The Mescalero Apache Trust Forest

The historical pattern of American Indian forest development and the implementation of federal policy on reservations is evident in the case analysis of a single reservation's forest resource-development process. The Mescalero Apache Reservation in south-central New Mexico illustrates the implementation of federal policy and competing demands for forest resources. After its creation by executive order in 1883, patterns of resource use have evolved with changes in federal policies and a movement from federal management goals to a tribal orientation of forest resource management.

The Mescalero Apache Reservation occupies the core of the Sacramento Mountains of New Mexico (Fig. 6-2). Relatively high elevations provide adequate moisture to support an extensive stand of ponderosa pine on the higher slopes and pinyon–juniper stands on the lower flanks of the mountains. It is estimated that 50 percent of the 470,280-acre reservation is forested.[17]

The forest reserve is historically well known to the Mescalero Apache population and includes their most sacred area, Sierra Blanca, as well as other resource sites the group frequented prior to Spanish intrusion into the American Southwest. Traditional forest uses by the Mescalero Apache included hunting, gathering, and religious activities in the forested areas. The group also utilized grassland and desert resources within reservation boundaries on a seasonal basis.[18]

The anthropologist Henry Basehart has described the Mescalero Apache as having a resource-holding capacity that emphasizes community rather than individual development. Basehart observed that they used resources

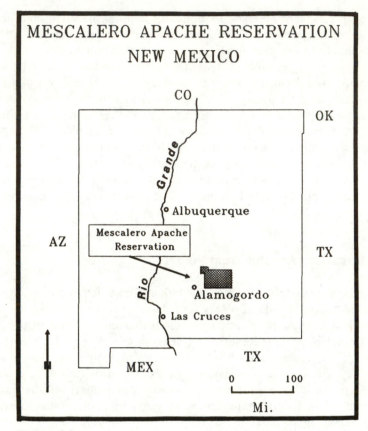

Figure 6-2.

such as water, food, and shelter materials conservatively and shared them within and among the tribal bands rather than consuming them immediately upon discovery or at a rate that denied others survival. The Mescalero Apache traditionally were aware of long-term community needs and allowed resource-bearing sites to recover from intense usage.[19]

Although the 1887 Allotment Act did not affect their reservation, Theodore Roosevelt in 1909 temporarily assigned the forest reserve to the Alamo National Forest. Roosevelt believed that reservations created by executive order could be terminated and reassigned to other public land managers such as the U.S. Forest Service. A 1910 ruling by the Attorney General denied the President's power and restored the reserved forest lands to the Mescalero Apache.[20]

Indian agents from 1907 to 1934 consistently identified reservation forests as the most likely resource for generating desperately needed revenues. They promoted a cooperative agreement between the Indian

Service and the Forest Service to develop the forest resources. However, the agreement created bureaucratic disputes between the two agencies that slowed resource and revenue development. Timber and lumber production on the Mescalero Apache Reservation during the early stage was limited to housing needs on the reservation. Small, temporary sawmills served nearby residential areas.

In 1919 the BIA received its first application for commercial harvest of Mescalero Apache timber. They denied the application, but in 1920 awarded a bid by the Cloudcroft Lumber and Land Company. News of imminent logging operations along the Tularosa River and adjacent lands caused recreationists from El Paso to demand conservation efforts along the river and associated watershed. The BIA agreed to 300-foot corridors along the river. Thus the Mescalero Apache timber became a resource issue between opposing non-Indian interest groups. The logging operation did not produce a profit for the company, however, and timber was harvested at a slow rate until 1941.

The BIA organized a second timber sale in 1920 but canceled it due to mismanagement of the resource. Then in 1925 Tularosa Tie and Lumber Company, a division of Hines Lumber Company of Chicago, signed a third contract. This contract also proved unprofitable, and it was later sold to the Tularosa Lumber Company, a locally owned sawmill.[21] These attempts at commercial sale of reservation timber were stalled by market conditions, lack of administrative process, and the lack of adequate transportation systems.

Mescalero Apache Forest Management After 1934

The Indian Reorganization Act of 1934 (IRA) provided the Mescalero Apache with political and financial means to develop their own forest reserve. The IRA reinforced traditional methods of resource management and provided mechanisms for development of commercial forest resources. The act specifically stated: "The Secretary of the Interior is directed to make rules and regulations for the operation and management of Indian forestry units on the principle of sustained-yield management."[22] Given the extent of timbered lands, tribal ownership of the forest, and a tribal management style that reinforced resource management by group rather than individual, the Mescalero Apache were one of the first native groups to organize as a tribe and take advantage of federal financial and technical assistance.

In addition, BIA administrators singled out the Mescalero Apache to develop their commercial forest resources. They provided low-interest loans to be used to increase and improve the reservation's road system, evaluate the forest's capability to produce timber, and initiate forest management. Civilian Conservation Corps (CCC) programs also funded and supported forest management. Improvements included a road network, a reservation-wide telephone system, two fire lookouts, and brush removal. The latter increased fire protection and accessibility in the forest. CCC funding continued until 1942 when wartime priorities discontinued the program. During its ten-year existence, the CCC spent $900,000 on the Mescalero Apache Reservation, the majority going to forest and rangeland improvements.[23]

Mescalero Apache logging began in 1936 with an agreement between the BIA, the tribe, and an Alamogordo, New Mexico, sawmill. The agreement stipulated that logs cut by Indians would be milled at the Alamogordo site. The mill paid the BIA for the logs. The BIA turned the profits over to the tribe who, in turn, applied them for credit on lumber from the mill. The lumber was used to construct homes on the reservation.

In 1942, tribal members Bernard and Andrew Little proposed to subcontract logging units from the tribe. BIA officials welcomed the Indian subcontractors and, after a lengthy discussion, drew up a contract allowing the Littles to log tribal timber for the BIA. The Littles carried on logging during World War II until equipment and labor shortages closed down their enterprise.[24]

The war years created a fast-paced market for lumber operations all over the Southwest. Most of the region's lumber supplied construction projects in California. It was a promising development, and demand for Mescalero lumber remained high through the war. However, the reservation suffered from labor shortages as most men went to Los Angeles to work in wartime factories. Without the needed labor force, lumbering slowed, and tribal revenues decreased. After the war, in 1946, the Tribal Council planned to resume and even expand operations. They requested that the BIA study the feasibility of opening a larger sawmill on the reservation. The study was delayed, reportedly because the number of sales offered by the BIA declined and tribal interest in a sawmill waned until the mid-1950s.[25]

Mescalero Apache Forest During the Termination Period

The BIA encouraged tribal administration of forest-related enterprises in accordance with the 1952 termination policy. The agency initiated a forest resource-development plan that would allow the tribe to become economically self-sufficient. The development plan provided for the training of tribal members to be professional foresters, for the full-time employment of Indians in the forestry branch of the BIA, for the development of a Christmas tree enterprise, and for identification of the need to attract a pulp mill and charcoal kiln to the reservation. Tribal leaders, eager to adapt federal policy to meet tribal economic needs, welcomed this emphasis on employment and development of a forest-products industry on the reservation.

The focus of both tribal and BIA goals was the outright sale of the forest reserve. Contracts for timber and salvage sales and Christmas tree harvesting from the reserve were offered between 1950 and 1970. With an improved road system, the entire forest reserve was dedicated to timber stand improvement and timber harvesting. Forest-management activities in the early 1960s included the removal of mistletoe-infected trees and timber-stand improvements using Indian labor, planting stock, and cooperative research projects with the U.S. Forest Service. In 1963, the tribe used $97,000 of public work funds to reduce forest fire hazards and to construct visitor facilities, fire detection lookouts, and forest roads.[26]

The BIA maintained an active role by establishing management and harvest goals, administering contracts, and determining the rate of tribal revenue generation. Management plans based on inventory data specified removal of salvage and commercial timber in accordance with sustained-yield forest-management prescriptions. Presale work on salvage and commercial timber sales included aerial photography, topographic mapping, and field surveys by BIA personnel. They also determined stumpage and timber appraisal values.

Two major timber sales occurred in the late 1960s. The BIA proposed the sales, which the tribe supported as long-term forest-management tools, sources of employment, and for enduring economic stability for the reservation population. Non-Indian contractors secured the final contracts but were instructed to work with the tribe on all matters of employment and forest-management issues. The BIA's role was to monitor the contractors and protect the forest reserve. As the sales progressed the three parties encountered disagreements over management styles, logging activities on the ground, and the amount of generated revenue. These disagreements later led the tribe to legally challenge BIA forest administrators and secure greater control of the valuable timber resource.

Self-Determination on the Mescalero Apache Reservation

In 1975 the federal Indian policy once again shifted, this time from termination to self-determination. The Mescalero Apache Tribe quickly responded by initiating several changes in forest management. Overall, the new direction in tribal decision making allowed the Mescalero Apache to push for more intensive forest management to increase forest revenues and at the same time protect the resource base. Pressure from the tribe to increase productivity while protecting the forest reserve resulted in tribal law suits against the BIA and contractors after 1970. This newest direction also led to the initiation of a forest inventory and a series of management plans in the 1960s which were completed in 1989. These two planning steps, which hastened forest productivity by intensive management and tribal revenue, indicate the tribe's increasing involvement in resource-management decision making and adaptive use of federal policy to meet tribal goals.

The two major sales made during the 1960s ended in tribal litigation against the BIA. In the first lawsuit the tribe alleged that the BIA had misjudged the value of salvage timber in a timber sale, failed to enforce minimal cutting requirements, and failed to charge adequate rates for stumpage in burn areas within the sale. As a result, the tribe contended that it was losing income and interest on current and future sales. The U.S. Solicitor General settled the case by requiring the contractor, White Sands Forest Products, to pay the Mescalero Apache $266,362.55 in stumpage fees and an additional $67,635.40 in interest. The BIA was instructed to increase the profit margin on reservation timber, decrease the cost of salvage removal in the sale, and increase allowances for road construction and reforestation.[27]

In 1979 the tribe sued the BIA for mismanagement of the second sale. Once again, the tribe contended that the BIA had not enforced forest-protection regulations and had allowed the sale contractor to destroy present and future timber resources. The suit focused on tribal income lost in a forest fire believed to have been started by improper operation and maintenance of a slash burner by the contractor. The tribe contended that fire suppression had cost the tribe $1,095,352 plus damages to the watershed and forage resources. The suit was eventually dropped because of insufficient evidence. Despite these problems with the contractor, the tribe requested that logging operations continue rather than lose immediate revenue.[28]

The contractor, in turn, failed to improve slash-piling and forest-improvement work despite the earlier conflict with the tribe and the BIA. Here the tribe's complicated relationship with non-Indian loggers is fully evident. The tribe, hoping to ensure income, entered into negotiations with this unsatisfactory contractor and the BIA. The BIA did not believe the contractor could meet requirements and refused to participate in the negotiations. As a result, the tribe sued the BIA for faulty supervision of the original sale and negligent administration of the trust responsibility. Wendell Chino, president of the Mescalero Apache Tribal Council, listed damages incurred by the tribe as (1) stumpage payment deficient

$105,866.37, (2) remaining uncut timber worth $2,912,859, (3) cost of slash disposal estimated at $157,490.04, and (4) cost of erosion control estimated at $16,392.28. With addition of interest on the lost value, the final loss to the Mescalero Apache was set at $3,535,467.33.[29]

The tribe admitted partial responsibility for some of the problems with the contractor, but laid much of the blame on the contractor. The BIA assumed some responsibility for mismanagement by not enforcing forest-protection regulations. The sale was terminated in 1978, with all parties losing monetary and/or administrative benefits. The Mescalero Apache lost income from the sale, Indian employment opportunities, protection of the forest reserve, and maximization of future tribal funds.

In 1978 the tribe attempted to overcome the problems of management and relations with non-Indians by contracting with George Banzhaf and Company to develop a forest management plan based upon a 1978 BIA forest inventory. The plan included three documents: a timber stand management plan, a series of map overlays, and a market-opportunities assessment. However, after review, both the tribe and the BIA rejected the documents as a management plan on the basis that the inventory data were not satisfactorily used in the planning process.[30]

The Mescalero Apache continued their efforts to enhance timber production by working on a forest-management plan in cooperation with the BIA. That plan, based on estimated timber volume and forest conditions, recommends uneven age management in all areas of commercial timber and aggressive harvesting in certain areas where disease and fire-control methods are necessary to protect the forest. Uneven age management, as opposed to clear-cutting and even age management, removes harvestable trees within a stand while allowing younger trees to mature. This harvest method maintains a forest canopy over time and reproduces a forest with the original size, density, and species characteristics as the premanaged forest.[31]

The Mescalero Apache expanded their enterprises in the fall of 1987 with the opening of a tribally owned Apache Timber Products Company sawmill. Following a six-year economic feasibility study, the mill was constructed on U.S. 70 just south of Mescalero. The mill was built at a cost of $6 million, secured as grants from the Economic Development Administration, the Administration for Native Americans, and a $4.5 million loan from the BIA. Once built, the long-awaited sawmill was capable of processing a volume of 18,700,000 logs annually, generating an annual payroll of $750,000.[32] Unfortunately, a fire destroyed the sawmill in 1990. It was rebuilt and was scheduled to reopen in 1992. The tribe continued to sell timber to an Alamogordo mill during the reconstruction period.[33]

Patterns of the Developing Mescalero Trust Forest

Historically, the Eastern Apache maintained the extensive pine forest for
basic survival and spiritual needs. The anthropologist Basehart described
the Eastern Apache use behavior as reflecting the group's long-term vested
interest in forest resources. Changes in use patterns occurred with implementation of the U.S. government's Indian policies, interpretation of the
trust relationship, and response to market pressures. Today, the Mescalero Apache plan to manage the forest reserve consistent with traditional
patterns for both commercial and noncommercial long-term uses. Resource development to meet these interests is evident in the location,
areal extent, and frequency of timber sales and in timber harvest volumes.

   The locations of timber contracts demonstrate the periodic shifts in
policy and desired returns from the forest reserve (Fig. 6-3). Timber
contracts prior to 1934, during the Allotment Act, were located in the
southwest portion of the reservation near mill and lumber markets. Profit
margins depended upon the ability to get the logs to the mill and then
to the market at the lowest cost. The Indian Service sold timber with

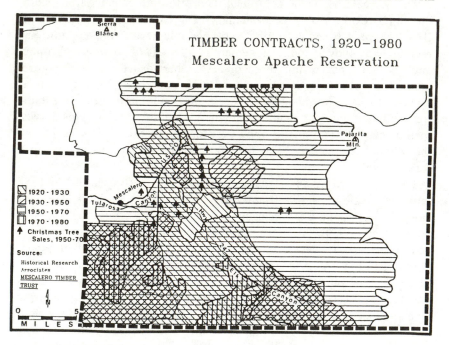

Figure 6-3.

little input from the Mescalero Apache. Consequently the location of the sales depended solely upon non-Indian markets and did not reflect the interests of the Indians, except tribal revenue.

After 1934, with the initiation of the IRA, the number of timber contracts expanded to more locations within the reservation. Opening the timber reserve created a road system, offered employment for Mescalero Apache, and in one case allowed the organization of a tribal salvage company. The IRA increased Mescalero Apache commercial use of the forest reserve and initiated Indian-oriented benefits from the expansion.

The dispersal of timber contracts reached its greatest areal extent during the policy of termination in the 1950s and 1960s. Tribal interest in economic development and revenue returns was supported by the federal push for termination of the trust responsibility. The entire upland pine portion of the forest reserve was opened for salvage harvesting to eradicate mistletoe, to increase tribal revenue, and to develop recreational uses (Fig. 6-4).

Salvage sales increased timber harvesting to a rate that left forest stocking levels dangerously low. Without careful consideration of long-term forest-management goals, the tribe was on the verge of losing its primary resource base. Forest planning, an emerging science during the

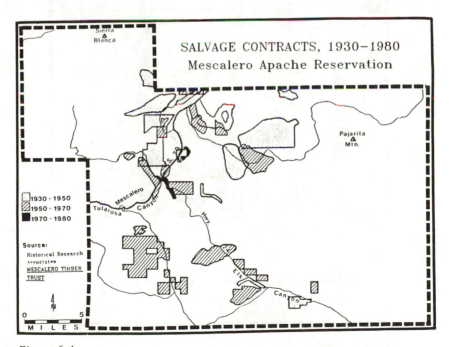

Figure 6-4.

1970s, and the advent of the Self-Determinatin Act modified timber harvesting rates and methods. The Mescalero Apache, with assistance from the BIA, slowed timber harvesting in the 1980s while they assessed long-term management goals.

Timber-sale frequency also reflects changes in federal policy (Fig. 6-5). Over a quarter of total timber sales occurred before 1940 and after 1955, while the remaining three-quarters took place during the Indian Reorganization Act and the early termination period, when Indian self-sufficiency programs were at their peak. In addition, the quality and age of Mescalero Apache timber was attractive to World War II suppliers and

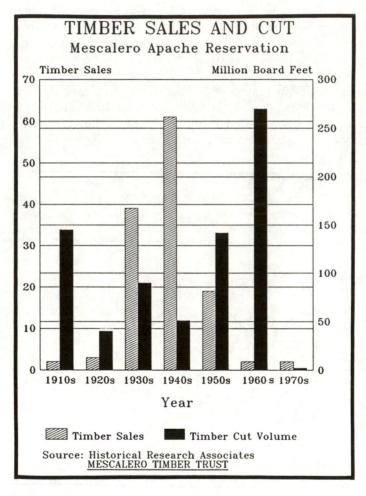

Figure 6-5.

postwar builders. Harvesting old-growth and young timber also alleviated disease pressure and increased wildfire protection within the forest reserve. Following the timber boom of 1940–1955, the frequency of sales decreased due to a slower market and federal bureaucratic processes such as planning programs, the establishment of timber values, and the development of a tribal sawmill.

Finally, timber volume data indicate that federal policy, market conditions, and forest health were key elements in trust forest use (Fig. 6-5). J.P. Kinney's push to harvest old-growth timber is evident in the 1919 sale of 144 million board feet. This harvest volume was not equaled until 1964, when the tribe cut 142 million board feet, taking a more active role in revenue generation. Volumes cut between the two benchmarks represent timber-protection practices, including partial-cut harvesting for disease and fire prevention.

While a cutting cycle can be extrapolated by comparing the sale and volume data, other factors must be taken into account before such an evaluation can be made. For example, the Mescalero Apache forest reserve was threatened by an infestation of dwarf mistletoe during the 1940s and 1950s. Timber harvesting to eradicate the fungus plus wartime demands increased the volume cut of all ages of timber during the time period. Due to Mescalero Apache cash-flow problems, they sold timber during a 1964 timber recession. The market conditions and the fungus infestation indicate that other forces determine when, where, and how much Mescalero Apache timber is put on the market.

Federal policy, increasing demands by the tribe for professional management of the forest trust, and the lumber market appear to be the strongest elements in timber harvest decision making. While locational and economic data demonstrate the changes in forestland use and economic outputs over time, the transformation in decision-making roles and responsibilities is equally important in exploiting the Mescalero Apache trust forest.

The Mescalero Experience: Summary

At the turn of the century, the Indian Service totally managed Mescalero Apache forest resources. It sold timber to non-Indians in order to provide goods and services on the reservation. During the IRA, the BIA managed the forest reserve, administered timber contracts with non-Indian logging companies, and assisted in developing a reservation infrastructure with the assistance of CCC enrollees. However, only one Apache logging company operated during the period of highest timber harvesting, and no permanent sawmills were constructed on the reservation.

During the 1950s and 1960s, non-Indian contractors remained the principal buyers of timber. The Tribal Council strove to expand use of the forest reserve for revenue generation and Indian employment. Achievement of these goals, however, was limited, in part due to BIA mismanagement. Tribal lawsuits against the BIA for mismanagement and neglect of its trust responsibilities dominated the late 1970s and early 1980s.

Most recently, modern interpretation of the trust responsibility with administration of the Self-Determination Act has placed the Tribal Council in the lead role of decision making. The tribe is currently focusing its management methods on long-term forest growth with uneven age management. Uneven age management as a long-term goal marked an important step in Mescalero Apache redefinition of their trust forest with emphasis on the traditional resource holding capacity. The tribe is deliberately choosing a harvest method that protects trust forest resources for present and future users. In so doing, the reservation will be defined by separate management goals that are unique to the forests surrounding the reservation. The same forest type surrounds the reservation and is managed by the U.S. Forest Service. The U.S. Forest Service established its management goals based on national economic needs, forest protection, and resource enhancement. Clear-cutting and even age management are more common in the national forest. Trust forest management will create environmental space defined by constant growth and harvesting. The difference in the two management goals creates a visible boundary between trust forest space and national forest space in south-central New Mexico.

Conclusion

The example of the Mescalero Apache trust forest illustrates a transformation in resource-development patterns on American Indian reservations. Resource development has historically been controlled by the federal government as a means of promoting assimilation. Reservation forests were initially managed by the federal government to serve non-Indian objectives of house construction, employment, and revenue accumulation. Indian agents discouraged traditional Indian use patterns.

Agents also played a significant role in applying the trust relationship to reservation forests. Inconsistent interpretation of the trust relationship by some Indian agents allowed non-Indians access to American Indian trust forests resulting, in the case of the Chippewa reservations, in the depletion of the virgin timber resources by 50 percent with very little compensation to the native inhabitants.

The Bureau of Indian Affairs also interpreted the trust relationship in ways that allowed non-Indians to benefit from the forest reserve. Generally, the BIA focused on timber harvesting and revenue accumulation, not on forest management or economic development for long-term tribal benefits. The BIA expended little effort on encouraging the development of Indian-owned forest-based companies. The agency administered timber contracts much the same way as did other public forest managers of the time by creating a process that allowed commercial foresters to develop public resources.

Various interpretations of the trust relationship have occurred in federal Indian policies. During the modern era of self-determination, resource development is more directly linked to American Indian goals rather than to non-Indian agendas. Tribes have become more sophisticated in establishing resource development goals that include culturally preferred management practices. At the same time all tribes are considering ways to increase revenue, including resource development programs.

Because reservations were created and administered by a separate set of federal acts and regulations, resource development and environmental protection may occur in different ways on reservations than they do in non-Indian development projects. Administered within a framework of self-determination, eventual elimination of the trust relationship, and increasing sovereignty, American Indian reservations will become even more distinct from neighboring non-Indian environments. American Indian reservations will continue to be separate spaces on the American landscape.

Notes

1. Francis Paul Prucha, *The Great Father: The United States Government and the American Indians*, Vol. 1 (Lincoln: University of Nebraska Press, 1984), xviii.

2. Ralph Brown, *Historical Geography of the United States* (New York: Harcourt, Brace, 1948), 13–19; and Michael Williams, *Americans and Their Forests: A Historical Geography* (New York: Cambridge University Press, 1989), 22–49.

3. Williams, *Americans and their Forests*, 111–49.

4. Francis Jennings, *The Invasion of America: Indians, Colonialism, and the Cant of Conquest* (New York: W.W. Norton, 1975), 15–31.

5. Kirke Kickingbird and Karen Ducheneaux, *One Hundred Million Acres* (New York: Macmillan, 1973), 14–50.

6. Alan S. Newell, Richmond L. Clow, and Richard N. Ellis, *A Forest in

Trust: Three Quarters of a Century of Indian Forestry, 1910–1986. Prepared for the Bureau of Indian Affairs. (Washington, D.C.: Government Printing Office, 1986), 1–16.

7.   William F. Vilas to Congress, November 24, 1888, Annual Report of the Secretary of the Interior, (January 1889) 50th Cong., 2d sess., H. Doc. 1, 68.

8.   Newell et al., *A Forest in Trust*, 1–16.

9.   J.P. Kinney, *Indian Forest and Range: A History of the Administration and Conservation of the Redman's Heritage* (Washington, D.C.: Forestry Enterprises, 1950), 11–27.

10.   Newell et al., *A Forest in Trust*, 1–21.

11.   Kinney, *Indian Forest and Range*, 25.

12.   U.S. Statutes at Large, 50th Cong., 2d sess., 1889, 673.

13.   U.S. Statutes at Large, 50th Cong., 1st sess., 1888, 166.

14.   Newell et al., *A Forest in Trust*, 1–32.

15.   Kickingbird and Ducheneaux, *One Hundred Million Acres*, 141–78.

16.   U.S. Statutes at Large, 95th Cong., 1st sess., 1978, 365.

17.   U.S. Department of Agriculture, Soil Conservation Service, *Soil Survey of Mescalero–Apache Area, New Mexico*, 1976, 39.

18.   Morris E. Opler and Catherine H. Opler, "Mescalero Apache History in the Southwest," *New Mexico Historical Review* 25 (January 1950): 1.

19.   Henry Basehart, "The Resources Holding Corporation Among the Mescalero Apache," *Southwestern Journal of Anthropology* 28 (Autumn 1967): 277.

20.   J.P. Kinney, *A Continent Lost–A Civilization Won* (Baltimore: Johns Hopkins Press, 1937), 277–78.

21.   Kinney, *Indian Forest and Range*, 151–53.

22.   U.S. Statutes at Large, 73d Cong., 2d sess., 1934, 984.

23.   Historical Research Associates, *The Mescalero Timber Trust: A History of Forest Management on the Mescalero Indian Reservation, New Mexico.* Prepared for the Bureau of Indian Affairs. (Missoula: Mountain Moving Press, 1981), 124. This document is the only public record of Mescalero Apache forest history and timber transactions. The tribe has proprietary rights to the primary data, thus requiring the author to rely on the historical document.

24.   Ibid., 145.

25.   Ibid., 151–52.

26.   Ibid., 203.

27.   Ibid., 235.

28.   Ibid., 237.

29.   Ibid., 242.

30.   Ibid., 256.

31.   David M. Smith, *The Practice of Silviculture,* 8th ed. (New York: John Wiley & Sons, 1986), 332.

32.   Franke, Jarrell, "Apache Sawmill Opening Marked," *The Ruidoso News*, August 24, 1987.

33.   Steve Haglund, Albuquerque Area Forester, Bureau of Indian Affairs, telephone interview, January 3, 1992.

**Part Three
Management and Environmental Change**

7

Laws of Nature: Wildlife Management Legislation in Virginia

David S. Hardin

In *The History and Present State of Virginia*, first published in 1705, Robert Beverley admonished Virginians for the deterioration of the natural riches of their colony. Romantically describing what he imagined to be the idyllic lifestyle of Virginia's Indians before the English arrived, Beverley wrote that "none of the Toils of Husbandry were exercised by this happy People" and that "without the Curse of Industry, their Diversions alone, and not their Labour," supplied them with the necessities of life. The English colonists, on the other hand, had made only "some of these Native Pleasures more scarce, by an inordinate and unseasonable Use of them; hardly making Improvements equivalent to that Damage." He concluded by correcting himself: the changes in Virginia from the "original State of Nature" found by the English at the outset of settlement had given way to a new environment created by "the Alterations, I can't call them Improvements, they have made at this Day."[1]

Only a precious handful of modern researchers have shared Beverley's concern with the changes in Virginia's environment during the colonial period. Among those, most focused on the Virginians' thoughtless and destructive *control over* the natural world; exhaustion and ruination of nature has been a consistent theme in discussions of the human/environmental interface in colonial Virginia.[2] The image of Virginians as despoilers arose from the supposition that settlers were simply too busy surviving to be afforded the luxury of an awareness or appreciation of nature. However, as Beverley demonstrated, some Virginians were aware of and became increasingly concerned with their environment over time. Recent studies have shifted toward a more balanced treatment of the interrelationship. Virginians are now seen as *participants within* the colony's natural system, subject to its vagaries, increasing their knowledge in order to adapt, and promoting changes—both positive and negative.[3] When an obvious need arose, they responded and met their challenges with surprising intelligence and ingenuity.

Throughout the colonial period, Virginians witnessed many environmental changes. Usually those changes were self-induced—whether inadvertently or deliberately—through the processes of economic development. More often than not, agriculture, the most invasive activity of that time, initiated the most important environmental changes. Many animal species were caught up in the process of alteration and response. Settlers encountering wild species left them much to themselves unless their presence or absence affected the colonial economy. Economically valuable native species or those unable to adapt to environmental change became scarce, while native species capable of exploiting change or those that were economically unimportant proliferated. It was change in the relative numbers of favored species and "pest" species that drew the attention of colonial lawmakers and inspired imaginative and sometimes bold legislative initiatives.

Animal populations in colonial Virginia were influenced by both direct and indirect human actions. Direct actions included activities such as hunting, fishing, and the fur trade, and they caused declines in animal populations. Indirect actions, however, were more subtle and much less obvious in their workings. They included agriculture, forestry, and mining and tended to modify habitats rather than directly target animal species. Virginians were sophisticated enough to know that overexploitation could exterminate animal species, and they undertook measures to preserve and increase certain animal populations; however, they failed to recognize the significance of the impacts of indirect alterations. Compounding that ignorance was the fact that habitat modification could either cause decreases *or* increases in animal populations. It was in the context of complex environmental relationships that Virginians strove to craft legislation for the management of the native wildlife.

Wildlife management involves "making decisions and taking action to manipulate wild animal populations and their environments."[4] It is chiefly concerned with stabilizing and increasing rare or desirable species and decreasing populations of harmful animals.[5] The oldest tools of wildlife management are wildlife management laws, which have a long history in the Anglo-Saxon world.[6] The primary goal was to create a balance between animal populations and habitats to allow the annual harvesting of the excess numbers by hunting and fishing.[7] In England, laws also sought to eliminate predators and pests, encourage weaponry skills, grant special privileges to elites, protect animal ranges, and conserve habitats.[8] In Virginia, those traditions were carried on, albeit in a limited form: legislation there focused on sustaining favored animal populations and eliminating harmful species.

The purpose of this chapter is to examine the legislation created in colonial Virginia to either suppress or encourage wildlife. Very little material has survived from the colonial period that directly reveals Virginians' expressed attitudes toward their environment. However, examination of the largest single collection of documents relating to wildlife management, Hening's *Statutes at Large*,[9] offers an invaluable glimpse at the prevailing problems Virginians faced and the solutions they engineered. The laws of Virginia from 1619 to 1776 were examined for their environmental content. Individual acts were abstracted and categorized according to the species and approaches involved. Temporal, spatial, and thematic patterns were then observed. Particular attention is paid to the legislation designed to encourage fish and deer and eradicate crows, squirrels, and wolves. Each section will consist of a brief description of the animals involved, a discussion of the changes in each animal's population, the legislation related to them, and an evaluation of the effectiveness of that legislation.

Fish

At the outset of colonial settlement fish were an important resource in Virginia. East of the Blue Ridge, both commercial and frontier subsistence fishing depended on spring spawning runs by anadromous fish, or fish that were born in freshwater, matured in saltwater, and returned to freshwater to spawn.[10] Several anadromous fish species, such as sturgeon, bass, and perch, used Virginia waters, but the most important by far were the members of the herring family.[11] Beginning in late February and early March, the branch herring or alewife (*Pomolobus pseudoharengus*) headed into the rivers and streams, followed by the shad or American shad (*Alosa sapidissma*) in late March, and finally by the glut herring or May herring (*Pomolobus aestivalis*) in April and May.[12] The spawning runs were impressive. In 1705, Robert Beverley wrote that "Herrings come up in such abundance into their Brooks and Foards [sic], to spawn, that it is almost impossible to ride through, without treading on them."[13] To William Byrd II, it was "unbelievable, indeed, indescribable, as also incomprehensible, what quantity is found there."[14] The most important spawning areas were the Rappahannock and James rivers and their tributaries, where fish moved up the Piedmont as far as the Blue Ridge to spawn.[15]

Anywhere that fish could be found in the numerous waterways in

Virginia they were caught for home consumption and for export. An examination of the *Virginia Gazette* reveals the extent of the fisheries in the colony (Fig. 7-1).[16] Because fisheries were valuable, farms and plantations occasionally used them as selling points. Advertisements and other articles usually named either the watercourse or the county in which the fishing grounds were located. During the colonial period, the *Gazette*

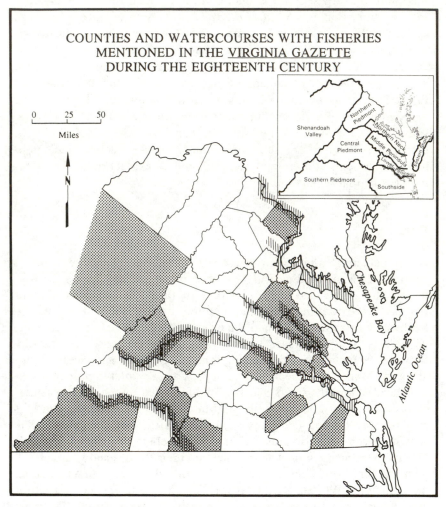

Figure 7-1. The watercourses from north to south are the Potomac River, Aquia Creek, Mattaponi River, Pamunkey River, James River, and Roanoke River. (Source: Lester J. Cappon and Stella Duff, *Virginia Gazette Index, 1736–1780* and the *Virginia Gazette*, microfilm, Virginia State Library and Archives, Richmond, Virginia.)

mentioned six watercourses and fifteen counties. Seven of the fifteen counties were on the Piedmont and one—Augusta—was in the Shenandoah Valley. The fisheries in the Shenandoah Valley and in the three Southside counties of Charlotte, Mecklenburg, and Pittsylvania reinforce the notion that areas several hundred miles from the sea (in this case on the Shenandoah and Roanoke rivers, respectively) could maintain valuable fisheries.

Fish were caught by many methods during the colonial period, including striking with clubs, harpooning, and snagging with hooks ("gigging"), but the most common devices were weirs (traps), seines, dragnets, and hook and line.[17] Although fish and seafood formed an integral part of the diets of Virginians from the outset, most of the catch was for domestic, household consumption. Large-scale commercial exploitation of fish was the exception. Nonetheless, by the end of the eighteenth century the spawning runs had begun to dwindle. That decline resulted less from overfishing than from the alteration of streams on the Piedmont by dams and by siltation from agricultural runoff.[18]

Colonial legislators designed laws to prevent wasteful fishing practices and to preserve the spawning runs; the earliest measure came in 1680 and dealt with fishing methods in the lower Rappahannock River.[19] A popular practice was to spear, snag, and strike fish (collectively known as "gigging") as they swam upstream. While this method was efficient for killing, many fish could not be retrieved and were left to rot in the water. Gigging was particularly offensive in the warm summer months, as thousands of fish carcasses often fouled the many bays and stream mouths on the Rappahannock.[20] In order to prevent the waste of fish and the stench that gigging caused, residents in Gloucester, Lancaster, and Middlesex counties petitioned for a ban on the practice between March and November, the principal spawning period (Fig. 7-2).[21]

By the 1750s, the economy of some portions of Virginia changed from tobacco to mixed farming, creating an increased demand for grain milling facilities and leading to concerted efforts to preserve the spawning runs. On the Piedmont, where tobacco held less sway in agricultural production and where tributaries were of manageable size, mills and mill dams were erected with great frequency.[22] Increases in grain production and export after the 1740s accelerated the process of mill dam construction, permanently altering the nature of watercourses throughout the Piedmont.

The first areas to feel the effects of the problem were in the headwaters of the Rappahannock River and along rivers in southside Virginia, two early focuses of Piedmont settlement. In 1759, residents in Orange and Culpeper counties—where grains were integral to the mixed farming

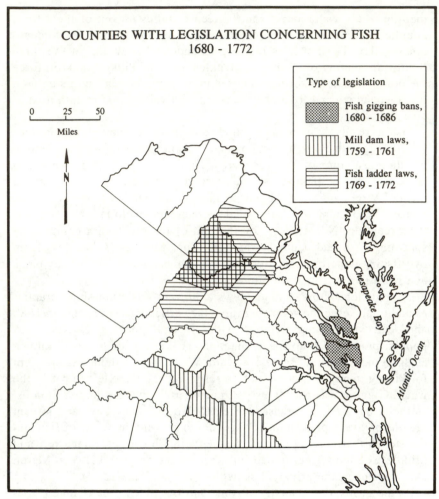

COUNTIES WITH LEGISLATION CONCERNING FISH
1680 - 1772

Type of legislation

Fish gigging bans,
1680 - 1686

Mill dam laws,
1759 - 1761

Fish ladder laws,
1769 - 1772

0   25   50
Miles

N

Chesapeake Bay

Atlantic Ocean

Figure 7-2. (Source: William W. Hening, *The Statutes at Large*, 1969.)

economy—complained to the assembly that spawning runs had declined in the Rappahannock's south branch, the Rapidan River. The resulting legislation required mill owners to make ten-foot-wide openings in their mill dams to accommodate the passage of migrating fish.[23] Two years later, legislators renewed the laws and extended them to include the portions of the Meherrin, Nottoway, and Appomattox rivers running through the Southside counties of Brunswick, Lunenburg, and Prince Edward—another important grain-producing area.[24]

These mill dam laws, however, proved inefficient, and legislators crafted new measures to rectify the inadequacies. The solution was to specify the nature of the opening created in the mill dams. Rather than simple ten-foot-wide openings, the new openings, or "fish slopes," were to be more akin to modern fish ladders. The specifications—laid out in 1762 and improved in 1772—were to make the slopes

> ten feet wide, tightly built, and planked up the sides, so as to confine the water from spreading off the said slope, two feet in depth at least, and the length of every such slope shall be four times the perpendicular height, with basins therein, at eight feet distance from their passage up the said slope, and shall be fixed in the dam eighteen inches below the common height of the water, and contiguous to the deepest part of the river.[25]

The new fish slope requirements were first used on the Rivanna and Hedgeman rivers in Albemarle and Fauquier counties. The slopes, which could be closed with gates, were to remain open during the shad and herring runs from the beginning of March until the end of May. Owners of existing fish slopes had to meet the new specifications, remove other impediments, including stone hedges, seines, and dragnets, and refrain from erecting new ones. The fish ladder laws proved so effective that the colonial legislature soon replaced the older mill dam laws applying to the Rapidan River and extended their territorial reach to the rest of the Rappahannock River down to Tidewater.[26]

By the 1770s Maryland's suffering fisheries forced the colony to take drastic measures to amend the situation.[27] Ultimately, however, none of the imaginative mill dam legislation created during the colonial period could forestall the decline of the spawning runs in the Piedmont waterways. Even though Virginia had been more prudent in taking action to preserve the fish runs, by the time fish slope laws became widespread there, nearly a half-century of mill dam construction had left the annual spawning cycles of the herring and shad permanently disrupted.

In conjunction with obstructions, another unseen factor was at play: agricultural runoff. Sedimentation in waterways and the attendant choking of channels became more common as plows came into greater use on the steep slopes and clayey soils of the Piedmont. There is no evidence that Virginians realized what was happening to their waters, and there was certainly no legislation designed to deal with the problem. In the lower portions of the rivers, commercial exploitation of the spawning runs using more efficient fishing methods increased toward the end of the century. Unable to use their spawning beds and intercepted before they could even reach the many small tributaries in the Piedmont, the great runs of fish that had once plied the waterways near the mountains disappeared.

Deer

The Virginia white-tailed deer (*Odocoileus virginianus virginianus*) was one of thirty subspecies of white-tailed deer in North America and ranged from the line of the Ohio and Potomac rivers to the Gulf of Mexico and from the Atlantic Ocean to the Mississippi River.[28] It was the principal meat supply for Indians and early frontier settlers alike. In addition, it provided numerous materials such as tallow for soap and candles, hides for clothing, shelter, and export, and bones for tools.[29] In Virginia, deer populations were largest where oak–hickory and oak–pine forests predominated. They favored open forests and forest margins where low-growing vegetation and grasses were more abundant.[30] At the time of European contact, overall deer populations in Virginia were stable, although deer were more common on the eastern edge of the Piedmont—the boundary between major Indian groups—than in Tidewater, where they suffered from overexploitation. The greatest concentrations occurred in the Shenandoah Valley and the Trans-Allegheny West (now West Virginia).[31] Europeans introduced conditions that brought about fluctuations in the deer population. Removal of Indians and predators and the opening and conversion of hardwood forests allowed populations to rise, while the introduction of competing livestock, economic exploitation, and the use of firearms caused declines.

Legislation concerning deer moved from an initial interest in establishing colonists' right to hunt deer to action designed to preserve dwindling populations. The very right to hunt on unseated lands was first established in 1632 so that "the inhabitants may be trained in the use of their armes, the Indians Kept from our plantations, and the wolves and other vermine destroyed."[32] More importantly, however, the act recognized that the abundant resources of Virginia allowed the colonists to enjoy rights they had not known in England. Restrictive poaching laws—designed to reserve game for royalty and the landed gentry—did not translate into the reality of Virginia.[33] In 1640, laws positively established the right to hunt deer.[34]

Legislation during the remainder of the seventeenth century began to reflect concerns with changes in the deer population. By 1643, the number of deer had declined enough to encourage the assembly to modify the right to hunt deer by giving exclusive gaming rights to landowners on their own lands.[35] By the 1690s, the scarcity of deer in eastern Virginia led to restrictions on deer hunting in general.

Cognizant of declines in deer numbers, legislators in 1699 attempted to control the hunting practices that were to blame. Citing the indiscriminate killing of weak bucks and pregnant does in late winter and spring,

"An Act prohibiting the unseasonable killing of Deer" established a closed season between February 1 and July 31.[36] Although fines were heavy, violations occurred and the act did not bring about the desired effect of arresting the slaughter. Therefore, in 1705, the closed season was extended to include the months of January and August.[37]

The closed-season legislation succeeded in gradually stabilizing deer populations at low levels in the longer-settled Tidewater counties. For a time, the stabilization of deer populations was aided by two conflicting processes: forest clearance and expanding fields created greater amounts of the forest/open land boundaries preferred by deer, promoting population growth; at the same time, increasing human pressure for food kept deer populations in check. Eventually, however, the pressure of expanding human numbers overwhelmed the natural increase of deer populations, and numbers declined in the east.[38]

In 1738, the first "Act, for the better preservation of the breed of Deer" was passed.[39] It acknowledged that previous legislation had not been as effective as hoped. The act targeted three practices in particular: (1) killing deer for skins and leaving the carcasses; (2) allowing hounds to run loose; and (3) fire hunting. It established a restricted hunting season (August 1 to November 30 for mature deer, October 1 to December 31 for young deer), although it provided exemptions, regardless of season, if deer threatened crops or if they were intended for food on the frontier.[40] The new act also established fines for possessing "red" or fresh deer skins out of season.[41] Hounds, commonly in the habit of running in semiwild packs and killing deer, were not to be allowed to run loose. Finally, legislation also outlawed fire hunting, the practice of encircling game in a ring of fire.[42]

The assembly amended the act of 1738 twice. In 1761 stronger regulations prevented settlers in counties west of the Blue Ridge from leaving deer carcasses in the forests and selling the skins in Philadelphia. Such actions deprived the colony of revenues from the duty on skins and attracted wolves and "other noxious beasts."[43] An amendment in 1772 recognized the still greater problem of "idle people making a practice, in severe frozen weather, and deep snows, to destroy deer, in great numbers, with dogs." In fact, such large numbers of deer were killed in the winter of 1771–72 that the supply of "that wholesome and agreeable food" was almost eliminated, and a moratorium was placed on the killing of wild deer until 1776.[44]

Ultimately, the legislation could not stem the decline of deer. Growing human population densities throughout Virginia heralded the ultimate collapse in the number of deer. Another contributing factor—and one overlooked by the legislation—was the fact that there was never a moratorium against the killing of female deer. Fur trade statistics from 1763 to 1773 reveal that over 61 percent of exported deer skins came from does.[45] That imbalance probably resulted from the fact that doe skins were softer than buck skins and brought a higher price at market. With the breeding animals under the stress of such exploitation, it is little wonder that deer were incapable of replenishing their numbers.

As deer disappeared throughout the colony, they became less important in the daily lives of colonial settlers. Beef and pork replaced venison in the diet of Virginians as each area of the colony established a stable mixed-farming economy.[46] Deer hunting in eastern Virginia became less a matter of survival than of sport, and deer populations stabilized at very low levels. To ensure that he and his friends would have enough deer to hunt, George Mason fenced off his plantation on Mason Neck in Fairfax County and stocked it with deer.[47] It is unlikely that any legislation could have prevented the virtual elimination of deer in the heavily populated necks of Virginia. Without legislation designed specifically to maintain deer populations over the long term, significant deer populations could be maintained only where human numbers were low, such as the Dismal Swamp and the western mountains.

Crows and Squirrels

The common crow (*Corvus brachyrhynchos*) lived throughout eastern North America.[48] Although not particularly numerous until the arrival of Europeans, it adapted quickly to the opening of the forests and the introduction of small grains and other agricultural products.[49] Crows became especially numerous around corn fields, where flocks were capable of causing severe damage.[50] However, they played an unnoticed role in aiding farmers because part of their diet consisted of insects that proved harmful to crops.[51] Although crows were occasionally killed for food during the colonial period, they were viewed primarily as pests to be eradicated.[52]

Squirrels were more important as a food source, but also became nuisances. There were two species of tree squirrels in Virginia, the gray squirrel (*Sciurus carolinensis*) and the fox squirrel (*Sciurus niger*). Both were most common in mast-rich hardwood forests, but the gray squirrel preferred forest interiors while the fox squirrel preferred open stands and forest margins. The larger of the two, fox squirrels were also the most likely to travel long distances to invade farmers' fields.[53] With each squirrel consuming as much as two pounds of food per week, large numbers of these rodents could strip bare small isolated fields in a short time.[54] More inclined to feed on agricultural products, the fox squirrel benefited most from forest clearance and the expansion of grain fields, although gray squirrels also adapted quickly to the environmental changes wrought by Virginians.[55]

The numbers of crows and squirrels undoubtedly had declined during the seventeenth and early eighteenth centuries as tobacco planters leveled the hardwood forests. However, once grain production increased in the colony, a domesticated food supply replaced what had been lost. Much to the dismay of farmers, crow and squirrel populations exploded.

The Eastern Shore experienced the earliest problems with marauding crows and squirrels because it had been the first region to switch to a grain-based economy. By the 1720s, the two Eastern Shore counties, Accomack and Northampton, had largely abandoned tobacco in favor of wheat, corn, and oat production for export. Not surprisingly then, they were the first to agitate for laws to control crows and squirrels. In 1727, crows and squirrels caused so much damage to the corn crop that colonists passed a law the following year requiring each tither to produce six crow heads or squirrel scalps to the county court.[56] Similar acts were necessary in 1734 and 1742 and included counties in the Northern Neck—another early grain-producing area (Fig. 7-3). Each act lasted for three years and required three and four heads or scalps per tither, respectively.[57]

The only act that applied to all the counties in Virginia was "An Act for destroying Crows and Squirrels," passed in 1748.[58] The act called for each tither to produce six crow heads or squirrel scalps annually for the years 1749 and 1750. A minimal penalty of one pound of tobacco for each missing item was set. The 1748 act provides a significant contrast between grain- and tobacco-producing counties. Twenty-four of the counties in existence in 1749 and 1750 have county court records that have survived and that record the number of scalps missing from the county levy. Colonywide, almost 69 percent of the tithers complied with the law, bringing in a total of 379,903 scalps. Compliance levels ranged from 95 percent in grain-growing Accomack County to 20 percent in tobacco-dominated York County (Fig. 7-4).[59] High compliance rates in the face of insignificant fines suggest that colonists were glad to be rid of the troublesome pests, especially where grain was important to the local economy.

The final set of acts for the eradication of crows and squirrels clearly reflected the growing importance of the small-grain economy. Again, after major damage to corn crops by large numbers of crows and squirrels, the assembly enacted legislation calling for their elimination. In 1769, tithers were required to bring in five heads or scalps in Accomack

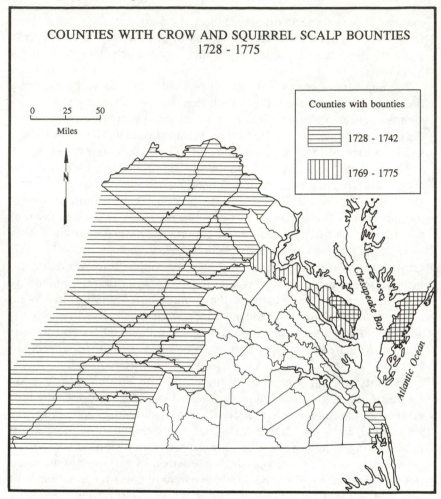

COUNTIES WITH CROW AND SQUIRREL SCALP BOUNTIES
1728 - 1775

Figure 7-3. (Source: William W. Hening, *The Statutes at Large*, 1969.)

and Northumberland counties in eastern Virginia, in all the Piedmont counties along the Blue Ridge, and in the Valley Province. After its initial three years the legislation dropped Northumberland and all the Piedmont counties, while adding Botetourt and Princess Anne counties (see Fig. 7-3).[60]

Laws to eliminate crows and squirrels were effective immediate responses to depredations but offered dubious value in the long run. Legislation, enacted for short periods, garnered quick (if not lasting) results. Indeed, colonists killed at least 778,432 crows and squirrels between 1728 and 1775 as a result of the laws, and compliance averaged about

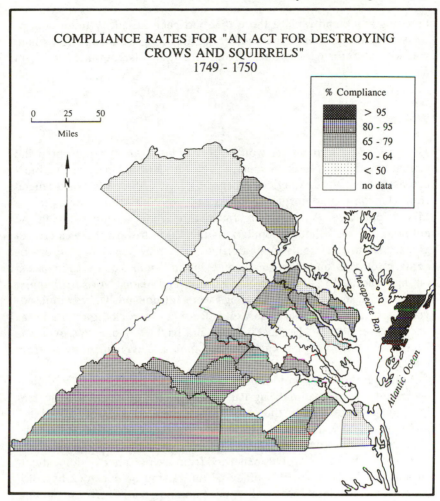

Figure 7-4. (Source: County Court Order Books, microfilm, Virginia State Library and Archives, Richmond, Virginia.)

80 percent.[61] In the areas where grains were vital to the economy, farmers adhered most closely to the regulations. Planters in other areas may have viewed the laws as a nuisance that distracted them from the important tasks of agriculture, but they also met the requirements of the legislation at a greater rate than the penalties justified.

Even in the face of eager participation by colonists, it is easy to imagine why the legislation consistently failed and had to be reapplied. Squirrels were prolific breeders and, left unmolested after the termination of each act, quickly replenished their numbers. Crows migrated across colonial boundaries and could enter Virginia at will to reestablish a breeding stock and replace those that had been killed. Without continuous pressure on their large numbers and as long as enough forestland was available for nesting sites, crows and squirrels continued to haunt Virginia's fields.

Wolves

The gray or eastern timber wolf (*Canis lupus lycaon*) represented the primary predator of large mammals in eastern North America. The most extensive of all North American subspecies, the eastern timber wolf ranged from Hudson Bay to northern Florida and from the Atlantic coast to the Mississippi River. Wolves were found throughout Virginia during the colonial period, although populations increased toward the western regions.[62] Hunting as individuals during the summer, they preyed on rodents, birds, fish, and other small game, but in winter they roved in packs, taking larger wild game such as deer, elk, and bison. Not surprisingly, when cattle, sheep, horses, and hogs were introduced, wolves took advantage of that food source as well.[63] Running in packs, they made (as one observer noted) "the most hideous and frightful Noise that ever was heard," but they were not known to kill men and even shied away from them.[64]

Although they were not bloodthirsty man-killers, wolves nonetheless presented a dire threat to the agricultural economy of Virginia. In sparsely populated portions of the colony, the "pernicious vermine wolves" posed a persistent problem.[65] Shadowing the deer population at first, the number of wolves declined along with deer, their primary prey species. Unlike deer, however, wolves benefited from the presence of domesticated animals. Wolves severely hindered the raising of livestock by colonists.[66] The complaint that "wolves have and do greatly increase in number, and that frequent spoyle and distruction, in every part of this country, is by them made upon hogs, sheep, and cattle" was not an idle one.[67] After initially decreasing as settlement expanded, wolf populations stabilized and sometimes increased. Without the introduction of livestock—an integral component of Virginia's frontier and mixed-farming economies—wolves would have declined to an even smaller number. Open-range livestock replaced and improved their food supply, and wolves exploited the situation. The only constraints on the wolf population, therefore, became forest depletion or loss of cover and outright extermination programs.

Virginians established the first reward for killing wolves in 1632[68] and the first wolf-scalp bounty was set at 100 pounds of tobacco in 1646.[69]

Despite these measures, by 1658 wolves had "multiplied and increased exceedingly," and county courts were authorized to increase the bounty as they saw fit and to allow Indians to receive wolf-scalp bounties as well.[70] They did so in 1662 and 1691 when bounties posted increases.[71] By 1705, wolf-scalp bounties stood at 300 pounds of tobacco for killing by using pits or snares, 200 pounds by gun or other method, and 100 pounds for each scalp brought in by an Indian.[72]

Although bounties remained in effect through the first quarter of the eighteenth century, their levels fluctuated and did not present enough incentive to kill wolves. A complete overhaul of the wolf-scalp bounty system came in "An act for lessening the Reward for Killing young Wolves; and for preventing Frauds in obtaining Certificates for Wolves-Heads" in 1732.[73] Legislators recognized that high bounties for all wolves sometimes encouraged creative interpretations of the law's intent. The primary transgression arose from the fact that the reward for young wolves was as high as that for the mature animals; the result was that people were induced to "spare the breeding wolves, for the advantage of taking their future increase."[74] Creation of a variable bounty that paid half as much for immature wolves as for adults eliminated the incentive to kill wolf cubs but spare the mother. Those wishing to receive a wolf bounty were required to swear an oath that included the statement, "I have not wittingly or willingly spared the life of any bitch wolf in my power to kill."[75]

The revised legislation successfully hastened the extinction of wolves in Tidewater and parts of the eastern Piedmont. With the threat of depredation receding, in 1748 bounties once again were reduced to 100 pounds of tobacco for an old wolf and fifty pounds for a young wolf.[76] Closer to the mountains, where open-range herding and deer skinning remained important, wolves continued to pose a threat. In 1765, the assembly was forced to target specific counties for increases in the wolf-scalp bounty.[77] It raised the bounties back to their pre-1748 levels in Loudoun, Prince William, Fauquier, Culpeper, and Buckingham counties on the Piedmont, in Frederick County in the Shenandoah Valley, and in Hampshire County in the Trans-Allegheny West.[78] The Assembly dropped Buckingham and Loudoun from the list after one year, but added Louisa on the Piedmont and Botetourt in the Valley four years later (Fig. 7-5).[79] Extended to the end of the colonial period, these increased bounties also became tied to deer-hunting regulations, so that anyone found guilty of leaving a skinned deer carcass in the forest would be ineligible to receive a wolf-scalp bounty.

The wolf-scalp bounty legislation successfully removed wolves from most of eastern Virginia by the end of the colonial period. The sheer

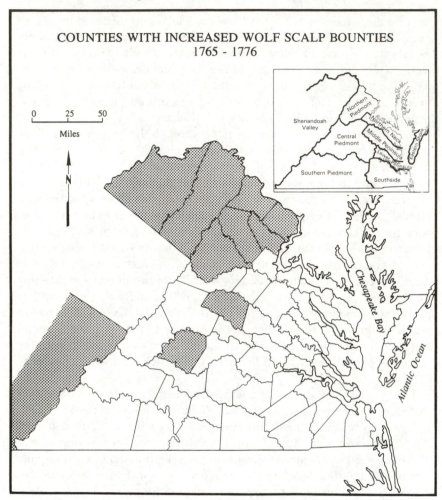

Figure 7-5. (Source: William W. Hening, *The Statutes at Large*, 1969.)

magnitude of the slaughter was impressive: at a minimum, colonists killed 17,571 wolves between 1645 and 1776.[80] Regionally, they took the greatest number of scalps in the Valley Province, the southern Piedmont, and the central Piedmont.

Of greater interest are the dates when counties recorded their last bounties. From that data it is possible to construct a map of wolf extinction in colonial Virginia (Fig. 7-6). No bounties were recorded on the Eastern Shore after 1676, and the last wolves had disappeared from the Lower Peninsula and the ends of the Middle Peninsula and the Northern Neck by 1719. By 1740, much of the rest of the Middle Peninsula and the Northern Neck was free of wolves. Wolves were extinct in almost all

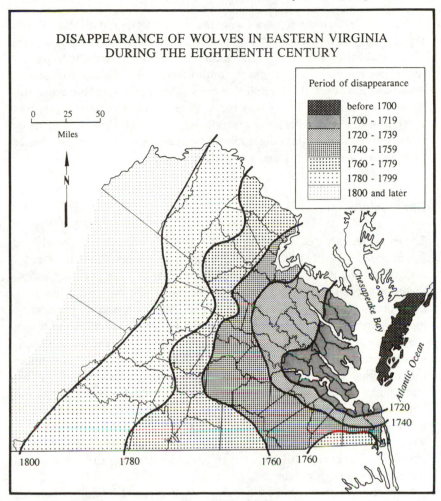

DISAPPEARANCE OF WOLVES IN EASTERN VIRGINIA
DURING THE EIGHTEENTH CENTURY

Figure 7-6. (Source: County Court Order Books, microfilm, Virginia State Library and Archives, Richmond, Virginia.)

of Tidewater by 1760. The exception was an area in Nansemond, Norfolk, and Princess Anne counties encompassed by the Dismal Swamp, where wolves found enough cover to survive until the 1760s. At the time of the Revolution, wolves had been eliminated from most of the northern and central Piedmont and the eastern half of the southern Piedmont. A wedge of counties along the Blue Ridge extending from Albemarle in the north to the North Carolina border in the south provided the last sanctuary for wolves in eastern Virginia. Bounties there were recorded well after the colonial period in Albemarle, Amherst, Bedford, Charlotte, and Pittsylvania Counties.

The wolf-extermination laws were the most efficient of all the wildlife legislation, and they clearly demonstrate the two most important aspects of an eradication program: create an incentive for individuals to participate and maintain the program continuously. By placing substantial bounties on wolves, the assembly made wolf scalps a valuable commodity worth going out of one's way for. Unlike crows and squirrels, wolves existed in fewer numbers and reproduced at a much slower rate, so by maintaining the bounties continuously, wolves were not given the chance to replace their numbers and repopulate areas.

Conclusions

The environmental record of Virginia's colonial legislature must be viewed in the broader context of wildlife-management history. The entire colonial period and the nineteenth century were part of a long era of natural-resource depletion in North America. The American conservation movement did not begin to jell until the late nineteenth century,[81] precluding the onset of programs for the preservation of species such as the bison, the passenger pigeon, and the Carolina parakeet. For the latter two, it was too late, but the bison represented a success story for the movement that heralded a new period of repopulation and replenishment of important animal species. The protective laws and predator/pest elimination legislation in colonial Virginia were typical of early wildlife-management strategies. Restocking, range protection, and habitat management were activities that occurred much later; true conservation and the beginnings of modern wildlife management did not appear in Virginia until the early twentieth century.[82]

Over time, it has become clear that conservation of wildlife depends on establishing its value to a particular society. Technological and scientific sophistication permit an appreciation of the complex interrelationships between animals and their environments, which in turn leads to a multidimensional valuation of wildlife. Wild animals can be seen as having economic, aesthetic, and biological value.[83] Colonial Virginians primarily used economic rationales for their valuations of and the attention they paid to wildlife. The economic valuation of animals led naturally enough to legislative initiatives for wildlife management, because close regulation of many aspects of economic life was a tradition in Virginia. The political economy of the colony was subject to oversight by both the assembly and the Crown; laws to influence the natural world simply became part of a larger body of legislation in colonial Virginia.

Wildlife-management regulations, then, can be seen as integral components in the legislative history of Virginia.

It can be said that environmental legislation in colonial Virginia was responsive to environmental issues primarily when the economy was threatened. That was understandable in an emerging capitalistic Atlantic realm. The irony was that the greatest catalyst for environmental change in Virginia was also its most important economic activity: agriculture. By clearing hardwood forests and replacing them with fields of tobacco, grains, and other crops, by damming the rivers and streams for mills, and by allowing topsoil to run off into watercourses, colonists dramatically altered habitats. Hunting and fishing—both for subsistence and commerce—also caused changes in animal populations. In essence, Virginians reworked the environment through both deliberate and inadvertent means, compelling animals to adjust. Those species capable of adapting to and exploiting change thrived, while those incapable of adapting or those of some economic value declined. Finally, it was decreases in desirable species and increases in undesirable species that elicited legislative response.

Even though legislative initiatives regarding animals did not always succeed, at least they demonstrated a greater awareness of environmental issues by colonial Virginians than scholars have traditionally suggested. The ultimate failure of preservation legislation and the relative success of extermination laws derives from the fact that the knowledge and sophistication necessary to manage sustained yields of certain species was greater than that required to simply eliminate others.[84] An understanding of wildlife population dynamics was largely beyond the capacity of colonial Virginians; they failed to recognize the impact on wildlife of habitat modifications. Deer and other animals that benefited from forest clearance and old-field successional patterns experienced population increases. The numbers of crows and squirrels grew with the expansion of grain production. Wolf populations increased because of the introduction of open-range livestock. The key to sustaining species was a complicated matter of recognizing and reducing the impact of activities that overwhelmed population increases. Eliminating species entailed destroying breeding populations and their annual increase.

Perhaps the most misguided chapter in the history of wildlife management in colonial Virginia was the decline in the annual fish-spawning runs. The assembly's failure to recognize the impact of indirect actions on habitats explains the demise of the fish runs throughout the colony. Even though fishery-management legislation was imaginative, it could not counteract the dire influence of habitat changes. Obstructions, farm runoff, and deforestation inexorably altered the nature of watercourses.

By crafting legislation to deal with dams, the assembly addressed only part of the problem, albeit the most obvious.

Legislation also failed to maintain sustainable deer populations. Although they benefited from the thinning of the hardwood forests, the creation of mixed successional environments, and the elimination of predators, deer populations decreased dramatically in Virginia over the course of the colonial period. The demands of subsistence and commercial hunting were the most significant drain on their numbers; the pressure of growing populations throughout the colony placed a high demand on their meat and the colonial fur trade sought them for their hides. In fact, significant deer populations survived only in the most isolated areas, while in most portions of Virginia, deer continued to decline.

Laws for the destruction of pest species such as crows and squirrels did not substantially reduce their numbers. Such pests became more numerous as a result of the introduction of domesticated food sources that ensured a high reproductive potential. Legislators did not appreciate the need for long-term management laws tailored to eliminate crows and squirrels, despite the fact that such animals were held in contempt and colonists would have gladly destroyed them. Limited legislation simply did not exert sufficient pressure on their populations to counteract growth.

The elimination of large predators in colonial Virginia represented the most successful—if unfortunate—effort in the management of wildlife. Most of the colony's large carnivores retreated before the encroachment of farms and plantations. Bears, cougars, lynxes, and foxes all were driven toward the western mountains and virtual extinction in eastern Virginia. For the most part, the extensive range requirements and limited numbers of individual predators worked to their disadvantage. Constricted wilderness and overhunting conspired to eliminate most of them. Wolves were the exception in that pattern, because they were able to exploit the introduction of the colonists' livestock. But concerted and consistent extermination programs, based on the creation of bounties and therefore an economic incentive, successfully led to the wolf's demise as well.

Acknowledgments

The author wishes to thank Donald Zeigler for editorial comments, John Vogt of the Iberian Publishing Company for permission to use two maps from Michael Doran's *Atlas of County Boundary Changes in Virginia, 1634–1895* (Athens, Ga.: Iberian Publishing Company, 1986) as base maps for the various figures in this chapter, and Conley Edwards of the Virginia State Library and Archives for his kind indulgence and encouragement during the researching of this chapter while under his supervision in 1990 and 1991.

Notes

1. Robert Beverley, *The History and Present State of Virginia* (Chapel Hill: University of North Carolina Press, 1947), 156. Beverley's comments reveal his unique perspective: unlike his brother-in-law William Byrd II, he considered himself a Virginian rather than an Englishman, going so far as to call himself an "Indian."

2. Examples include: Avery Odelle Craven, *Soil Exhaustion as a Factor in the Agricultural History of Virginia and Maryland, 1606–1860* (Urbana: University of Illinois, 1926); Joseph J. Shomon, "Vanished and Vanishing Virginia Animals," *Virginia Cavalcade* 9 (Winter 1959): 24–31; Stanley W. Trimble, *Man-Induced Soil Erosion on the Southern Piedmont* (Ackney, Iowa: Soil Conservation Society of America, 1974).

3. For examples, see Carville V. Earle, "Environment, Disease and Mortality in Early Virginia," *Journal of Historical Geography* 4 (October 1979): 365–390; Henry M. Miller, "Colonization and Subsistence Change on the 17th Century Chesapeake Frontier" (Ph.D. dissertation, Michigan State University, 1984); Timothy Silver, *A New Face on the Countryside: Indians, Colonists, and Slaves in South Atlantic Forests, 1500–1800* (New York: Cambridge University Press, 1990).

4. Daniel N. Lapedes, ed., *McGraw-Hill Encyclopedia of Environmental Science* (New York: McGraw-Hill, 1974), 682.

5. Ibid., 682.

6. Raymond F. Dasmann, *Environmental Conservation*, 2nd ed. (New York: John Wiley & Sons, 1968), 231.

7. L.C. McNemar et al., *Wildlife Restoration and Game Management in Virginia* (Falls Church, Va.: Falls Church Chapter, Isaac Walton League of America, 1938), 53.

8. An extended discussion of early wildlife-management legislation in England may be found in Thomas A. Lund, "British Wildlife Law Before the American Revolution: Lessons from the Past," *Michigan Law Review* 74 (November 1975): 50–62.

9. William W. Hening, *The Statutes at Large; Being a Collection of all the Laws of Virginia, from the First Session of the Legislature, in the Year 1619*, 13 vols. (Charlottesville: University Press of Virginia, 1969).

10. John Wharton, *The Bounty of the Chesapeake: Fishing in Colonial Virginia*, Jamestown 350th Anniversary Historical Booklet No. 13 (Williamsburg: Virginia 350th Anniversary Celebration Corporation, 1957), 42.

11. William H. Massman et al., *A Biological Survey of the Rappahannock River, Virginia*, Virginia Fisheries Laboratory Special Scientific Report No. 6 (Gloucester Point: Virginia Fisheries Laboratory, 1952), 31.

12. Edward C. Raney, "Freshwater Fishes," in *The James River Basin: Past,*

Present and Future, comp. James River Project Committee of the Virginia Academy of Science (Richmond: Virginia Academy of Science, 1950), 155.

13.   Beverley, *The History and Present State of Virginia*, 146.

14.   William Byrd II, *William Byrd's Natural History of Virginia or The Newly Discovered Eden* (Richmond, Va.: The Dietz Press, 1940), 78.

15.   William H. Massman and Robert S. Bailey, *The Shad in Virginia Waters* (Richmond: Virginia Commission of Game and Inland Fisheries, 1956), 2 and Wharton, *The Bounty of the Chesapeake*, 15.

16.   References were obtained from Lester J. Cappon and Stella Duff, *Virginia Gazette Index, 1736–1780* (Williamsburg, Va: Institute of Early American History and Culture, 1950). All entries related to fishing grounds and fisheries were examined in the *Virginia Gazette* (microfilm, Virginia State Library and Archives, Richmond, Virginia); duplicate entries were not included in the count.

17.   John C. Pearson, "The Fish and Fisheries of Colonial Virginia," *William and Mary Quarterly* Series 2, 22 (October 1942): 353–60.

18.   Marshall McDonald, *Report upon the Fisheries and Oyster Industries of Tidewater, Virginia: with recommendations of such legislation as is necessary to regulate the same and derive a revenue from them* (Richmond, Va.: R.F. Walker, Superintendent of Public Printing, 1880), 7.

19.   Hening, *The Statutes at Large*, 2: 487–88.

20.   Middlesex County Court Order, 4 March, 1677/8, as quoted in Pearson, "Fish and Fisheries," 280–81.

21.   Hening, *The Statutes at Large*, 3: 395.

22.   C.G. Holland, "Dams," *Quarterly Bulletin of the Archaeological Society of Virginia* 38 (June 1983): 105–6.

23.   Hening, *The Statutes at Large*, 7: 321–22.

24.   Ibid., 409–10.

25.   Ibid., 8: 582–83.

26.   Ibid., 592; 9: 579.

27.   Holland, "Dams," 86.

28.   Remington Kellogg, "What and Where are the Whitetails?" in *The Deer of North America*, Walter P. Taylor, ed. (Washington, D.C.: The Wildlife Management Institute, 1956), 32.

29.   Stanley P. Young, "The Deer, the Indians and the American Pioneers," in *The Deer of North America*, Walter P. Taylor, ed. (Washington, D.C.: The Wildlife Management Institute, 1956), 16.

30.   Richard H. Manville, *The Mammals of Shenandoah National Park*, Shenandoah History Association Bulletin No. 2 (Luray, Va.: Shenandoah Natural History Association, 1956), 56.

31.   Burd S. McGinnes and John H Reeves, "A Comparison of Pre-Historic Indian Killed Deer to Modern Deer," *Quarterly Bulletin of the Archaeological Society of Virginia* 12 (September 1957): 5 and Randolph E. Turner, "An Intertribal Deer Exploitation Buffer Zone for the Virginia Coastal Plain-Piedmont Region," *Quarterly Bulletin of the Archaeological Society of Virginia* 32 (March 1978): 42.

32.   Hening, *The Statutes at Large*, 1: 199.

33. William Nelson, *Manwood's Treatise of the Forest Laws* (London: G. Nutt, 1717), 215 and Thomas A. Lund, "British Wildlife Law," 72.

34. Hening, *The Statutes at Large*, 1: 228.

35. Ibid., 248.

36. Ibid., 3: 180.

37. Ibid., 462.

38. Henry M. Miller, "Colonization and Subsistence," 279.

39. Hening, *The Statutes at Large*, 5: 60–63.

40. Ibid., 61.

41. Ibid., 62.

42. Ibid., 63.

43. Ibid., 7: 412–13.

44. Ibid., 8: 592; George Mason to Alexander Henderson, February 17, 1771, in *The Papers of George Mason, 1725–1792*, Robert A. Rutland, ed. (Chapel Hill: University of North Carolina Press, 1970), I: 130–32.

45. Virginia, "Accounts and Duties on Skins and Furs, College of William and Mary, 1763–1773" (manuscript, Virginia State Library and Archives, Richmond). Although these statistics do not distinguish between deer killed in Virginia and those brought into the colony for export, they nonetheless reveal a distinct preference for doe skins.

46. Miller, "Colonization and Subsistence," 350.

47. Kate M. Rowland, *The Life of George Mason, 1725–1792* (New York: Russell & Russell, 1964), 98.

48. Harold H. Bailey, *The Birds of Virginia* (Lynchburg, Va.: J.P. Bell Company, 1913), 193.

49. John L. Bull and John Farrand, *The Audubon Society Field Guide to North American Birds*, Eastern Region (New York: Knopf, 1977), 565.

50. John Lawson, *History of North Carolina* (Richmond, Va.: Garrett and Massie, 1952), 146 and Bailey, *The Birds of Virginia*, 193.

51. William T. Hornaday, *Our Vanishing Wildlife: Its Extermination and Preservation* (New York: Charles Scribner's Sons, 1913), 222 and John J. Audubon, *Ornithological Biography* (Edinburgh: Adam & Charles Black, 1834), II: 318.

52. Crows had long been viewed as nuisances, as witnessed by laws during the reign of Henry VIII designed to "kill and utterly destroy all manner of Crows." Robert M. Alison, "The Earliest Traces of a Conservation Conscience," *Natural History* 90 (May 1981): 75 and Lund, "British Wildlife Law," 51.

53. John W. Bailey, *The Mammals of Virginia: An Account of the Furred Animals of Land and Sea Known to Exist in This Commonwealth with a List of Fossil Mammals from Virginia* (Richmond, Va.: Williams Printing Co., 1946), 198 and Dorcas MacClintock, *Squirrels of North America* (New York: Van Nostrand Reinhold Co., 1970), 130.

54. Ibid., 107.

55. Bob Gooch, *Squirrels and Squirrel Hunting* (Cambridge, Md.: Tidewater Publishers, 1972), 57–59.

56. Waverly K. Winfree, *The Laws of Virginia; Being a Supplement to*

Hening's The Statutes at Large, 1700–1750 (Richmond: The Virginia State Library, 1971), 323–25.

57. Hening, *The Statutes at Large*, 4: 446; 5: 203–4.

58. Winfree, *The Laws of Virginia*, 403–4.

59. These data were collected from the various county court records that have survived (microfilm, Virginia State Library and Archives, Richmond). The county levy recorded the number of "scalps wanting" each year. By multiplying the number of tithers by six, it is possible to determine the number of scalps required in each locality. The required number less the number wanting gives the total number of scalps brought in, which is divided by the total required to arrive at the compliance level. Below are the statistics that survive:

CROW AND SQUIRREL SCALPS RECORDED, 1749–1750

County	Number Killed	% Complying
Accomack	28,744	95.43
Amelia	26,677	83.63
Brunswick	38,798	69.18
Caroline	32,719	71.90
Charles City	13,478	70.88
Chesterfield	16,325	75.35
Cumberland	14,361	72.40
Essex	20,359	66.83
Fairfax	17,179	76.51
Frederick	13,032	64.97
Goochland	5,769	77.73
Isle of Wight	14,505	74.20
King George	14,139	67.54
Lancaster	12,677	66.63
Lunenburg	15,792	66.43
Middlesex	10,196	61.33
Norfolk	14,843	51.08
Northumberland	10,657	80.44
Orange	8,790	55.49
Richmond	17,937	74.68
Southampton	18,041	85.84
Spotsylvania	14,452	61.63
Westmoreland	18,431	61.88
York	5,109	20.90
TOTAL	403,010	68.87

60. Hening, *The Statutes at Large*, 8: 596–97.

61.   These figures are compiled from the county court records. The figure for total numbers killed is a low-end estimate because many county records have not survived. Below are the statistics drawn from the various acts:

CROW AND SQUIRREL SCALPS RECORDED, 1728–1775

Year of Act	Number Killed	% Complying
1728–1732	50,702	71.73
1735–1737	86,026	90.71
1743–1746	38,798	93.71
1749–1750	379,903	68.84
1770–1775	223,003	76.37
TOTAL	778,432	80.27

62.   David L. Mech, *The Wolf: The Ecology and Behavior of an Endangered Species* (Garden City, N.Y.: Natural History Press, 1970), 36.

63.   Mech, *The Wolf*, 173 and Bailey, *The Mammals of Virginia*, 160.

64.   John Clayton, *The Reverend John Clayton: A Parson with a Scientific Mind*, Edmund and Dorothy Berkeley, eds. (Charlottesville: University Press of Virginia, 1965), 110; Beverley, *The History and Present State of Virginia*, 154; Lawson, *History of North Carolina*, 122–23.

65.   Westmoreland County Court Order, October 31, 1688, transcribed in *William and Mary Quarterly* Ser. 1, 15 (1907): 186.

66.   Clayton, *The Reverend John Clayton*, 106 and Miller, "Colonization and Subsistence," 232, make the case that wolves were the reason for the relative absence of sheep on seventeenth-century plantations.

67.   Hening, *The Statutes at Large*, 3: 42.

68.   Ibid., 1: 99.

69.   Ibid., 328.

70.   Ibid., 456.

71.   Ibid., 2: 87; 3: 42–43.

72.   Ibid., 3: 282. At first, the head, scalp, or ears of a wolf were brought to a session of the county court and a notation of the bounty was recorded for later inclusion in the county levy at the end of the year. Later, the entire head or scalp was required as proof, because people would bring in parts of the same wolf to acquire several bounties. The sheriff was given the responsibility of disposing of the wolf heads as they were brought in, usually by burning them in a nearby bonfire or by burying them in a convenient pit. In any event, the proceedings could not have been pleasant, as the majority of wolf heads were brought in during the summer months.

73.   Hening, *The Statutes at Large*, 4: 353–54.

74. Ibid., 353.
75. Ibid., 354.
76. Ibid., 6: 152.
77. Ibid., 8: 147.
78. Ibid., 148.
79. Ibid., 200, 388–89.
80. That figure is drawn from the county court records. Each county was responsible for paying wolf-scalp bounties out of the county levy at the end of the year. In most cases, the individuals receiving bounties were named, and the age and method of capture were often noted as well. Again, only a minimum number of kills is mentioned because several counties do not have records. Below are statistics on the number of wolf-scalp bounties recorded in each region of Virginia:

WOLF SCALP BOUNTIES, 1645–1776

Eastern Shore	3
Northern Neck	1,378
Middle Peninsula	689
Lower Peninsula	176
Tidewater-Southside	2,070
Northern Piedmont	158
Central Piedmont	3,243
Southern Piedmont	4,539
Valley	4,927
TOTAL	17,183

81. Agricultural Education Service, Virginia State Department of Education, *Wildlife Conservation in Virginia* (Seattle, Wash.: Outdoor Empire Publishing, 1977), 9; Harmut Walter, "Impact of Human Activity on Wildlife," in *Sourcebook on the Environment: A Guide to the Literature*, Kenneth Hammond, George Macinko, and Edna Fairchild, eds. (Chicago: University of Chicago Press, 1978), 253.
82. McNemar, *Wildlife Restoration*, 3.
83. Roderick Nash, "American Environmental History: A New Teaching Frontier," *Pacific Historical Review* 41: 3 (August 1972): 367–68.
84. Lund, "British Wildlife Law," 51.

8

The Ark: A Tale of Two Rivers

Olen Paul Matthews

The Arkansas River[1] begins in mountainous central Colorado near Lead-ville and descends over 11,000 feet to the Mississippi. A drainage area of 160,650 square miles and a length of 1,450 miles make the Arkansas one of the major river systems of the West.[2] River flows vary seasonally, yearly, and spatially. In late spring and early summer the upper Arkansas at Canon City, where it exits the mountains, reaches its maximum flow. Winter flows may be one-tenth the summer maximum, and yearly flows may deviate by 50 percent of normal flows.[3] Even before much of the river was diverted for irrigation and municipal uses, the water crossing the dry plains diminished in quantity, sometimes disappearing. Larger average precipitation in the eastern half of the Arkansas basin re-creates the river, occasionally as a raging torrent. At Tulsa the Arkansas' flow has been measured at over 700,000 cubic feet per second during flood events.[4] Extremes are common, with rains during one thirty-six-hour period producing eighteen inches of moisture in central Oklahoma while other areas of the watershed average less than ten inches annually.[5]

The variations in river flow create a problematic natural system which influences the evolving "law of the river." On the upper Arkansas west of the river's great bend in Kansas, agriculture requires irrigation for reliable production. Downstream, navigation and flood control are more important. On both parts of the river instream flows become priority considerations as environmental needs and recreational uses increase. Not all uses of the Arkansas' waters are compatible. Management con-flicts increase when legal jurisdiction over the basin is split between the federal government and seven states (Arkansas, Colorado, Kansas, New Mexico, Missouri, Oklahoma, and Texas; Fig. 8-1). Sharing a mobile resource like water creates unique problems that the legal system must resolve.[6]

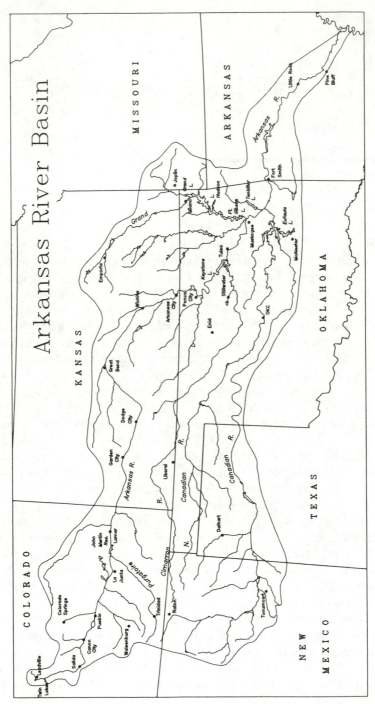

Figure 8-1.

The link between law, part of our political system, and the environment has been recognized by geographers[7] and includes three different research approaches: (1) legal impact analysis (prelaw and postlaw), (2) legal systems analysis, and (3) legal research on geographic issues.[8] The first two approaches use geographic methodology to understand law or the legal system. The impact of laws, before or after passage, have been evaluated by geographers, as well as elements of the legal system such as courts. Some geographic issues, such as federalism, can only be understood by understanding law. This chapter examines the postlaw impact on the Arkansas.

The legal system allocates rights among water users, promotes irrigation and navigation, controls floods, allows recreation on navigable rivers, prescribes water quality, and protects the environment. On the Arkansas the major issues are allocation between competing users in the basin's water-short western half and flood control and navigation in the eastern half. The jurisdictional problems surrounding a shared resource must be explored before examining allocation between individuals, allocation conflicts between states, and the federal government's role.

Power over Water: Jurisdictional Problems

Water is a transboundary resource creating a distinctive set of legal problems shared with other transboundary resources. Legal scholars generally recognize two types of issues: (1) overlapping jurisdiction with more than one political entity controlling the same space or resource and (2) mobile resources.[9] Conflicts occur because the environment is not a closed system operating within a single political unit and because federal systems allow more than one political unit to control the same thing. Rivers that cross state boundaries, like the Arkansas, fit into both categories. Water pollution or consumption has downstream impacts in other jurisdictions. Jurisdictional conflicts over mobile resources are inherently geographical, providing an excellent example of the problems federal political systems have in controlling the environment. Variations in power between jurisdictions controls how humans transform the transboundary environment.

Transboundary conflicts can be put in a more understandable context by using geographic scale and legal process. Generally, in the United States conflicts within and between scales occur with individuals, local governments, states, and the central government. In the West a local government's rights to use water are the same as the rights granted individuals and will be included with them. Also, conflict between central governments, which elsewhere poses serious legal questions, is not an issue, because the Arkansas is not an international river. Four different legal processes are used to resolve conflicts: (1) agreements, like inter-state compacts, treaties, or contracts, (2) judicial action, (3) legislation, and (4) administrative action.[10] All four can operate at the geographic scales described above. Control of water at different scales and by different legal processes is further complicated by the concept of water as both public and private property.

"Property" is popularly viewed as "things," especially tangible things like cars, land or clothing. A more sophisticated conception "understands property as *relations*. More precisely, property consists in certain relations, usually legal relations, among persons or other entities with respect to things."[11] These legal relations define property rights, creating both public and private rights.[12] In the century after U.S. independence, federal resource policy "was aimed almost exclusively at allowing private individuals, corporations, and states to appropriate the public domain and its various resources."[13] Property rights were defined as private rights by the primitive state and federal legal systems which kept peace between rival claimants.[14] In this century resource law shifted from resolving disputes over who benefits from private development associated with plentiful resources, to government control over scarce resources in the public's interest. Most resource law resolving conflicts between individuals developed at the state level, as reflected by the appropriation doctrine. More recently, both federal and state laws define a public-property interest in water.

A variety of rights associated with surface waters are recognized, as indicated in Table 8-1. These rights are defined by federal and state governments, with some rights being "public" and others "private." On the Arkansas, individual, state, and federal rights exist, creating a complex web of overlapping, complementary, and contradictory laws. A water right is a property right, but the exact meaning varies in time and place, with the four legal processes being used to resolve disputes.

State and Federal Power over Surface Water

During the 1800s the federal government ignored water law allowing states to experiment with different conflict-resolution systems.[15] Two major systems evolved, riparian rights and the appropriation doctrine. In the East the English common-law system of riparian rights was adopted with minor modifications.[16] The system was sufficient where plentiful water supplies reduced conflicts. This common-law judicial system needed

Table 8-1
Public and Private Water Rights

A. Private Rights
   1. Use and Consume Water
   2. Bed Ownership of Non-Navigable Streams
   3. Continuation of Stream Flow (Riparian-rights States Only)
   4. Waste Disposal
   5. Water Quality

B. Public Rights
   1. Free Commercial Navigation
   2. Bed Ownership of Navigable Streams
   3. Access for Fishing and Recreation
   4. Protection from Floods
   5. Instream Uses (Appropriation-doctrine States)
   6. Water Quality
   7. Environmental Protection
   8. Public Trust

little legislative modification or administrative backup until this century. Riparian rights are shared by all landowners adjacent to a river or stream. Under the English common-law system the river's natural flow continued undiminished, but state court decisions modified the common law to allow water to be taken from a stream if reasonable. To determine reasonableness the interests of all riparian owners are balanced. Because water may only be used on adjacent land and may not be taken from the watershed, the riparian doctrine is not very compatible with irrigation or large-scale municipal needs. Today, state legislation modifies the doctrine with administrative agencies being designated to manage water.[17]

Western irrigation, mineral development, and municipal use requires moving water long distances, often from one watershed to another. The English common-law system was inappropriate for these needs and thus resulted in the evolution of the appropriation doctrine, or, as sometimes called, the doctrine of prior appropriation. Western statutes, constitutions, and case law protect an individual's investment in developing a water right. This "first in time, first in right" priority system is the doctrine's core and is designed to simplify dispute resolution. A water right in most western states is established by intentionally diverting water and applying it to a beneficial use. In this century a permit has been added as a requirement. The meaning of intent, diversion, and beneficial use were frequently litigated. In the early days "beneficial uses" were narrowly focused on the traditional economic interests of that time: irrigation, mining, manufacturing, and domestic uses. Diversions usually required taking water out of the stream, limiting instream uses for environmental purposes.

Like the riparian rights doctrine, the appropriation doctrine defined and protected private rights. Both doctrines control consumptive uses of water. The riparian rights doctrine has some elements—continuous flow and water quality—which reflect a broader public interest, but these rights were private, enforceable only by riparian landowners. The appropriation doctrine gives any landowner a right to take unappropriated water, and traditionally environmental considerations were ignored. In his novel *Centennial*, Michener captures the spirit of the appropriator whose goal was to consume all the river's water before it could leave the state.[18] Today state statutes are beginning to recognize instream flows, provide access for fishing and recreation, and control environmental quality. The most extreme example is the public-trust doctrine as interpreted by California's courts. Under this concept, private rights established under the appropriation doctrine may be abrogated without compensation. The public's interest is superior because it preceded the private rights.[19]

State law facilitated development by individuals, but in the 1800s little state money was available to sponsor major public-works projects. In order to fund irrigation, farmers banded together to form mutual ditch companies, or corporations speculated on profit-making ventures. These "corporate" activities were authorized or controlled by state laws that favored private development over public needs. Although the public was ignored in the allocation process, the costs of the extremely large projects being proposed required some kind of public subsidy. Two significant changes occurred in this century. First, the federal government began substantially subsidizing irrigation, flood prevention, navigation, and power generation. Second, federal and state laws began recognizing environmental and recreational interests. In this century federal power has been used extensively to benefit both public and private rights.

Federal power derives from specific constitutional provisions granting Congress authority to regulate water resources. The major constitutional sources justifying the exercise of federal power are the commerce clause,[20] the compact clause,[21] and the property clause.[22] The federal or Indian[23] reserved rights doctrine creates a constitutionally based property right in water which supersedes state law. Created by the federal courts,[24] this doctrine reserves enough water on federal property and Indian lands to accomplish the purposes of the reservation. Only those state rights that precede the creation of a reservation will be superior to the reserved water right. This doctrine was applied only to Indian reservations at first,[25] but now the courts infer a federal water right in national monuments[26] and national forests.[27] Although politically unlikely, the property clause gives Congress power to appropriate all unappropriated waters on federal land. Congressional power over federal property is unlimited.[28]

Because water is considered an article of commerce, Congress has significant power over water not associated with federal or Indian property.[29] Congress has used this power to promote irrigation,[30] improve navigation,[31] prevent floods,[32] prescribe water-quality standards,[33] generate electricity,[34] protect fish and wildlife,[35] and preserve wild and scenic rivers.[36] Although many federal statutes contain language deferring to state law, the deference is political, aimed at appeasing western interests which consider private appropriation rights sacred. Congress can preempt state law, and conflicting state law cannot prevent the accomplishment of federal purposes.[37]

Congress must approve compacts between states, limiting state power to resolve conflicts through agreements.[38] Although compacts are the primary method used in interstate allocation, litigation in the Supreme Court[39] and congressional apportionment are possible.[40] Negotiated compacts are the preferred solution, but when negotiations fail, the Court uses the doctrine of equitable apportionment to allocate interstate waters. Even when compacts are negotiated, the Supreme Court may be asked to settle disagreements over compact interpretation.[41] Because few compacts have mandatory dispute-resolution mechanisms, individual states may veto proposed actions. Congressional approval makes compacts supreme over conflicting state law, and compacts may constrain interstate commerce, which state law cannot do alone.[42]

The complex mix of federal and state law creates a regulatory web along the Arkansas that is difficult to explain clearly. In the western half of the basin, shortages in water supply make allocation between competing uses the central focus. In the eastern half, too much water creates seasonal floods, and storage is necessary to allow navigation during parts of the year. Fierce competition over water results in a continuing dispute between Colorado and Kansas.[43] Recently, Texas and Oklahoma sued New Mexico over water in the Canadian River, an Arkansas tributary.[44] Solutions to shortages between states and among users within a single state include storing seasonal surplus water and bringing new water from outside the basin. In addition to allocation issues, the river has flood control, navigation, reclamation, recreation, and environmental issues which need integrated management rather than today's jurisdictionally split and issue-specific orientation. Federal and state laws all have an impact on the environment and therefore merit consideration. I have selected three subjects for detailed examination: allocation of rights under the appropriation doctrine, disputes between states, and federal development projects.

Appropriation Doctrine and Individual Development

The appropriation doctrine allows miners, irrigators, cities, and industries to spend large sums of money on diversion works with the security of knowing their investment will be protected. In the West, water development is more complicated than pumping water to land adjacent to a river. Although some small-scale flood irrigation occurs on hay land in the high mountain valleys, for the most part water has to be moved long distances. For example, one major irrigation system developed by Colorado irrigators is ninety-five miles long.[45] Growing cities and industries compete with irrigators for control of scarce water. To simplify things, only Kansas and Colorado will be discussed in this section.

In Colorado the appropriation doctrine has controlled water allocation from the beginning, but early Kansas law relied on the riparian-rights doctrine. By custom, irrigators in Western Kansas followed the appropriation doctrine, and eventually state law was modified to recognize the realities of irrigation practice.[46] Development in Colorado is similar to the structured process found in most appropriation states. The Kansas "customary" law operated in a relatively small area of the state without much impact on most state residents. As a result, the development process differed from the more structured Colorado approach.

In Colorado the major players in the water game were the companies organized by the irrigators, the cities along the base of the front range, especially Pueblo and Colorado Springs, and Colorado Fuel and Iron (C.F.&I.) a Pueblo steel maker. Irrigators diverted water far upstream from the land they wanted to irrigate in order to take advantage of gravity flow. These long ditches were a major investment requiring continuous upkeep. Floods on the Arkansas frequently destroyed headgates, caused sedimentation, and eroded banks. The urban and industrial users also needed expensive water-delivery systems and as time passed began diverting water from the Colorado River basin to secure the quantities needed.

Because of the costs, single irrigators, working alone, could not build and maintain water-delivery systems. By organizing into mutual-ditch companies, Colorado irrigators could secure the capital required for development. The landowners became shareholders with a vote in corporate management and an annual assessment to maintain the system.[47] The mutual-ditch companies were formed by agreement and generally created a small administrative structure to oversee daily operations. Without organized ditch companies the environmental impact along the Arkansas would have been much less. Because the appropriation doctrine allowed water to be used on nonriparian land, the companies could develop large blocks away from the river which would not have occurred in the riparian-rights system.

Not all ditch companies were the same with their nature controlled by priority date, location on the river, and quality of the land irrigated. James Sherow, in his recent book *Watering the Valley*, discussed at length three different Colorado systems: the Rocky Ford Ditch Company, the Fort Lyon Canal Company, and the Bessemer Irrigating Ditch Company.

One of the first companies organized was the Rocky Ford Ditch Company near the town of Rocky Ford, Colorado. An early priority date, the compact size of the district (8,000 acres), and good soils allowed the growth of sugar beets, cantaloupe, and other crops with heavy water requirements. Their secure water supply averaged sixty inches of water per year between 1895 and 1950.[48] The high-value crops that could be produced as a result provided this company's irrigators with a degree of stability and financial security unusual in the West. Rocky Ford cantaloupes are regionally famous.

The Fort Lyon Canal Company is at the other extreme. From the beginning the company was involved in litigation[49] and was plagued with natural disasters, poor financing, and bad management. Eventually, a ninety-five-mile-long canal provided irrigation water for 90,000 acres between La Junta and Lamar, Colorado. Their late priority date gives them a relatively weak water right which is countered by an aggressive management style. The company responds quickly to any perceived threat to the river's flow and is in frequent conflict with neighboring companies. Poorer soil and less-secure water rights resulted in the farmers' raising alfalfa and cereals. These crops have a lower economic return than the water-intensive crops grown by Rocky Ford.[50] Within the company, differences in management goals created factions that disagreed over canal repairs and improvement expenditures. In order to improve their chances of receiving water during times of shortage, this company constructed reservoirs.

The Bessemer Irrigating Ditch Company, downstream from Pueblo, supplies water for 50,000 acres.[51] The water right is more secure and in greater volume than the Fort Lyon system, allowing the production of higher value crops. The ditch supplying water for this company starts in the canyon upstream from Pueblo and flows through town. The rugged terrain required a complex delivery system which needed frequent repair. Also, the irrigators ditch was not always compatible with a growing Pueblo's needs. Bridges were needed for cars, the ditch was a safety hazard for swimmers, pollution from city streets contaminated the waters, and property owners sued for seepage damage.[52] All these factors led to high maintenance costs. Some handicaps were overcome by purchasing water from C.F.&I. which had surplus water in what today is called Turquoise Lake.[53]

Major irrigation developments impact the environment by reducing river flow, increasing sedimentation from field erosion, and increasing salinity. Native vegetation gave way to plowed land which in turn changed wildlife habitat. Along the Arkansas, cottonwoods began to grow in the river bed, and salt cedar, tolerant to increased salinity, spread. Reservoirs and diversion ditches fundamentally changed natural vegetation by increasing local soil moisture. Some changes have created greater species diversity but not all are positive.

Pueblo, at the confluence of Fountain Creek and the Arkansas River, was situated to take water directly from the river. With few irrigators competing for water above the city, supplies were adequate until drought in the 1930s pressured the city to secure its rights. In July 1934, the normal flow of 1,687 cubic feet per second was reduced to 81 cubic feet per second, and in March 1935, the river was dry.[54] A court decree awarded some rights with a priority dating back to 1874. Other rights were secured by purchasing farmer's rights and the Wurtz Ditch, which diverted water from the Colorado River watershed near Tennessee Pass.[55] City expansion meant a constantly increasing water demand. Additional water was made available by the completion of the Fryingpan–Arkansas Project in the 1960s.[56]

Colorado Springs, on the upper end of Fountain Creek, had to develop water supplies from the beginning. Although an eleven-mile-long canal north of Pike's Peak diverted water from Fountain Creek as early as 1872, additional supplies were needed within three years.[57] Between 1878 and 1908 Colorado Springs captured all available water on the south slope of Pike's Peak with a series of high elevation reservoirs, tunnels, and ditches. Some water came from outside the Fountain Creek watershed, a legal point challenged under the riparian-rights doctrine.[58] Disputes with neighboring Victor, thefts of water,[59] and attempts to appropriate a waterfall[60] enlivened Colorado Springs' water politics. Serious development was an ongoing process, but even with new supplies, shortages continued. In 1951 legal rights were secured on the Blue River, a tributary of the Colorado. As a result of the Fryingpan–Arkansas Project, water is now piped from the Arkansas near Pueblo.[61]

Water shortages were rare in Pueblo's early days, making this an ideal location for a steel mill. In 1881 C.F.&I.'s predecessor obtained water directly from the Arkansas and from artesian wells which filled a reservoir.[62] Water with an 1865 priority was purchased from a mutual ditch company in 1890. A cooperative agreement with the Bessemer Irrigating Ditch Company led to the construction of Sugar Loaf Reservoir (now Turquoise Lake) near Leadville.[63] Although C.F.&I. diverted considerable water, the company consumed only 17 percent. Unfortunately the return flow was untreated until the 1960s.[64]

Irrigators, cities, and industries all competed for an increasingly scarce commodity. Variations in seasonal and yearly supplies meant too much water occasionally and frequently too little. To enhance water available to them, the Fort Lyon Canal Company stored water. Their low priority date meant reductions in water use during even minor periods of shortage. C.F.&I. needed reservoirs to ensure a constant supply for steel making, and Colorado Springs could not get enough normal flow around Pike's Peak without storage. These three examples illustrate one solution available for resolving continuous water-shortage problems. Another way is to divert water from Colorado's western slope. Small projects were developed by Colorado Springs (Blue River) and Pueblo (Wurtz Ditch). One irrigation company developed a tunnel south of Independence Pass which takes water from Grizzly Reservoir into the Twin Lakes watershed. Western slope water is seen by many as the preferred solution to the Arkansas basin's shortages. The Fryingpan–Arkansas Project, financed with federal funds, is another example of transbasin diversions, but shortages still persist.

The major impacts from the urban and industrial users result from the removal of flowing water from the natural cycle, local changes associated with water storage and delivery systems, and deterioriation of water quality from discharges. The long-term impacts of diverting water across the continental divide from the Colorado basin are not yet known and may be insignificant when compared to the diversions further downstream on the Colorado. Constant increases in demand led to a continuous extension of acquisition systems. By the 1970s the freewheeling days where anything was fair ran into opposition from environmental groups backed by federal law.

Increased demands can be satisfied to an extent, without using Colorado River water. Existing rights, especially those with early priorities, can be purchased as some cities, industries, and irrigation companies have done. Purchasers may change the place of use or nature of use, but only if other appropriators are not harmed. Shortages may also be solved by conservation. Pueblo and Colorado Springs both rationed water during the 1930s drought and have taken other small steps in recent years. But for irrigators, the traditional means of diversion and use are protected, meaning unlined ditches exist and flood irrigation still occurs. Conservation could increase available water, but increasing the supply from the western slope and maximizing use before it reaches Kansas is the prevailing pattern.

In Kansas the historic need for irrigation was not as clear-cut as in Colorado. Eastern Kansas has sufficient natural moisture for a few crops, in all but the driest years. The early farmers in western Kansas were not convinced irrigation was necessary. In 1879 a property owner adjacent to an abandoned grist mill used water from the mill's ditch for irrigation. His bumper crop amazed the Garden City farm population, setting off a small boom in canal construction. By 1890 over 400 miles of canals had been constructed in western Kansas, at a cost of $3,000,000.[65] Still, many farmers felt dry-land farming could be successful and did not participate in the organization of mutual-ditch companies like those in Colorado.

Many of the ten irrigation company charters filed were little more than scams designed to take advantage of unwary investors. Here "the field was open for large-scale enterprises underwritten mostly by out-of-state capitalists unfamiliar with conditions in the Garden City area. Many financiers engaged in mere speculation."[66] Five Garden City companies managed to survive underfinancing, environmental disasters, and poor management. Wheat and sorghum did not need irrigation every year, but sugar beets require water at specific times during the season which nature did not always provide. When a sugar beet plant moved to Garden City, many comatose ditch companies became active again. Farmers eventually converted several companies into mutual-ditch companies, like in Colorado, but the main change was to groundwater. Shallow wells eight to twenty feet in depth could provide sufficient water for the very small farms advocated by some irrigationists.[67] Beginning with windmills, farmers eventually converted to gasoline- and electric-powered pumps. After 1910 the sugar beet "company largely guided development of irrigation in the area."[68] In spite of all attempts, irrigation from the Arkansas River and groundwater could not supply all farmers. Fortunately for some, irrigation was looked on as a supplement to rainfall.

As a result, the environmental impact of irrigation law in Kansas was much less than the impact in Colorado. Short water supplies and a weak water-rights system encouraged disputes between Kansas irrigators.[69] Although elements of the appropriation doctrine were followed by the farmers, the riparian-rights doctrine continued in Kansas until 1945.[70] Laws passed before 1900 did authorize irrigation canals, but the Kansas Supreme Court held previously established riparian rights as superior to appropriation rights.[71] With the status of the appropriation doctrine in limbo in southwestern Kansas, threats of lawsuits discouraaged the establishment of solid functional enterprises.[72] Differences between developments in Kansas and in Colorado can be explained by examining the weak legal rights that were tied with poor water supply and lack of interest in irrigation. In Kansas only one small storage reservoir was built. Instead of trying to develop surface-water resources, farmers used groundwater or blamed their upstream neighbor, Colorado. The main impact in Kansas resulted from actions in Colorado. The Arkansas River ceased surface flows, but subsurface flows allowed the proliferation of cottonwood, a phreatophyte, along the river's bed and banks.

State versus State

Conflicts between cities, irrigators, and industries were resolved under Colorado's appropriation doctrine and the Kansas irrigator's legal/customary practice. However, in 1900 no law existed to settle disputes between states, and jurisdiction over such conflicts was unclear. When Kansas sued Colorado in the U.S. Supreme Court, the Court first had to determine whether they had jurisdiction.[73] The Supreme Court recognizes three ways to resolve interstate water disputes: equitable apportionment by the Court, negotiated compacts between states, and congressional legislation.[74] Within the Arkansas basin, interstate disputes have occurred on the Canadian River (New Mexico, Texas, and Oklahoma) and the Arkansas River (Kansas and Colorado), as mentioned above, as well as the Vermejo River (Colorado and New Mexico).[75]

By 1900 Colorado had 300,000 acres of irrigated land while Kansas had but 30,000 acres.[76] Colorado water use had expanded with 100 ditch systems irrigating 7,000 farms, Pueblo and Colorado Springs providing water for 50,000 people each, and C.F.&I. using ten million gallons daily.[77] Irrigators in western Kansas felt they were being deprived of development opportunities by the increasing Colorado usage. Pressure from farmers, the press, and politicians eventually led to the Kansas "quest" against Colorado. With U.S. intervention in the case, three divergent viewpoints were argued, those of Kansas, Colorado, and the federal Reclamation Service.

Kansas based its case on the riparian-rights doctrine arguing for a continuing flow of the river.[78] As an equity point Kansas claimed this right started before Colorado became a state. Irrigators in western Kansas were not pleased with their state's position, because the continuous flow doctrine, if enforced within Kansas, would preclude irrigation. Some

Kansans even hoped their state would lose.[79] Kansas also argued that the Arkansas was two streams, one on the surface and another underground.[80] By claiming the subsurface water was a distinctive subterranean stream, Kansas hoped to have its flow continue unchanged as well.

Colorado liked the two-river idea, but their version referred to a "broken river," with one river ending in Colorado and another beginning in Kansas.[81] Because the Arkansas was sometimes dry under natural conditions at the Colorado–Kansas border, Kansas could have no riparian rights on a river ending in Colorado. Colorado also claimed absolute sovereignty over the river using the "Harmon Doctrine," as argued by an 1895 attorney-general opinion on a Rio Grande dispute with Mexico.[82] This claim would give Colorado absolute power over the river, including the power to consume the river's entire flow as long as it was within Colorado's borders. A supportive brief by C.F.&I. argued the Rocky Mountains deprived eastern Colorado of moisture that the region would have received if the mountains had not been there. The irrigators and other water users were simply righting a natural injustice caused by the mountains' location.

Because Colorado advanced sovereignty arguments, the newly formed Reclamation Service sought federal intervention. If absolute sovereignty existed, states could restrict development authorized under the Reclamation Act. Also, if Kansas won, recognition of riparian rights would limit land available for irrigation. The federal government argued against the state claims and asserted that the states had surrendered their rights to interstate streams as they had surrendered their "right to make war."[83]

The Supreme Court referred the case to what today is called a Special Master, who gathered evidence. The process took three years, included 8,559 pages of testimony from 387 witnesses, and had 122 exhibits.[84] After gathering evidence the case was referred back to the Supreme Court. The Court's opinion makes it clear the sciences of meteorology and hydrology were not well understood in general and certainly not by the Court. Although not accepted as undisputed scientific fact, the Court seemed to believe rain "followed" the plow. Plowed land absorbed water rather than allowing rain to run off overland. The absorbed water eventually evaporated increasing regional rainfall. Also, vegetation attracted rain. The Court concluded that irrigation in Colorado might make more land arable in Kansas. Although the Court felt this process had occurred in central Kansas, they conceded the process might be more difficult in eastern Colorado, where cultivated land at higher elevations was less likely to retain water.[85]

The Court did not favor any one side completely in reaching its final decision. They limited the expansive federal power claimed by the

Reclamation Service, extending it only to existing federal territories and on federal property.[86] In rejecting Colorado's arguments for absolute sovereignty the court said "[n]either State can legislate for or impose its own policy upon the other."[87] Into the vacuum left by the absence of federal and state control over other states, the Court placed the doctrine of "equitable apportionment" which became the Court's rule for dividing interstate water. This "fairness" standard establishes rights based on the circumstances of a particular controversy. But rather than allocating specific amounts of the Arkansas to each state, the Court found no harm had occurred to Kansas. The Court left open future litigation if Kansas' "subtantial interests" were injured by a "material increase" in Colorado's depletion of the Arkansas.[88]

Without question the amount of water flowing into Kansas had declined prior to the suit, but Kansas had weak arguments. Depriving Colorado water users of water they were already using in order to benefit Kansas farmers would simply shift the location of the benefits. The Court was reluctant to harm one group of farmers to increase the possibility of benefits to another group of farmers. Also, the pseudoscience of the day indicated Kansas rainfall would increase as a result of Colorado irrigation. Priority—first in time, first in right—became a major element in equity considerations as a result. In many ways the Court was simply ignoring the boundary between the states, an approach used later in a dispute between two appropriation-doctrine states.[89] By failing to allocate specific amounts to each state and by allowing reviewed litigation under changed circumstances, the Court set the stage for ongoing legal conflict. The first step was a string of law suits leading eventually to *Colorado v. Kansas II*.

By 1910 Kansas irrigation companies were suing Colorado ditch companies using the appropriation doctrine. The Kansans felt their priority dates were earlier, which would give them better rights. Although some disputes were settled by a negotiated contract, the Finney County Irrigation Association was excluded. Their litigation in 1916 and 1923 led Colorado to the Supreme Court in 1928. Colorado wanted the "nuisance" suits halted, but Kansas claimed a detrimental change in circumstances which reopened the previous litigation. Once again the Supreme Court referred the controversy to a special master who collected 7,000 pages of testimony and 368 exhibits. The master's recommendation allocated the 1,110,000 acre-feet of dependable flow with Colorado getting five-sixths and Kansas one-sixth. The Supreme Court, fifteen years after the litigation began, rejected the recommendation, granted an injunction against the Finney County association, and held Kansas had not proved substantial changes in conditions.[90] In Colorado 300,115 acres were irrigated in 1902, 464,236 acres in 1909, but only 5,000 more were added between 1909 and 1939. Irrigated acreage in Kansas increased from 15,000 in 1895 to 56,000 in 1939. Both states increased acres irrigated in the time between court cases, but Kansas relied on groundwater hydrologically connected to the Arkansas rather than the Arkansas' surface flows. Indeed Kansas's failure to build more than one reservoir to capture Arkansas floodwaters was used against them. The Court strongly recommended Colorado and Kansas negotiate an interstate compact to resolve their dispute and allocate Arkansas River water.[91]

The John Martin Reservoir, begun in 1939 and completed in 1948, was the key to successful negotiation. Even before Colorado sued Kansas in 1928, a technological solution was being sought. Surveys conducted in the 1920s laid the groundwork for major projects increasing water availability in the Arkansas Basin.[92] The John Martin Dam, in eastern Colorado, was beyond the financial capability of irrigation districts or state governments. Early proponents tried to interest the Bureau of Reclamation, but the cost–benefit ratio was unacceptable. With the technical solution stalled, the states proceeded until another federal agency was hooked. In 1933 the Corps of Engineers found the project economically sound for flood-control purposes, but wanted Kansas and Colorado to agree on administration of reservoir water. After considerable political manipulation Congress authorized the dam in 1936, construction began in 1939, and after a war delay completion occurred in 1946.

Compact negotiation began in 1945, was completed in 1948, and was ratified by Congress in 1949.[93] Colorado received 60 percent of the water developed by the reservoir, with Kansas obtaining the reminder. Kansas's water was measured at the state line allowing Coloradans to irrigate between the reservoir and the border. The compact protects Kansas by requiring that "waters of the Arkansas River . . . shall not be materially depleted in usable quantity or availability."[94] Because "usable quantity" and "materially depleted" are values hard to quantify, Kansas is once again suing Colorado.[95] Today, Kansas claims the increased number of wells hydrologically connected to the Arkansas has increased, leading to dramatically decreased Arkansas River water. Also, the Trinidad Reservoir, completed in 1977 on the Purgatoire River near Trindad, and the Pueblo Reservoir, completed in 1974 on the Arkansas River near Pueblo, have reduced inflow to John Martin Reservoir. In spite of this, Kansas's irrigated acreage increased from 68,000 acres when the compact was signed to 200,000 acres in 1989.[96] At this time the case has been assigned to yet another Special Master.

The Supreme Court decisions and the compact determine where the environmental impacts resulting from irrigation will occur. The Court did not discuss whether irrigation was good or bad for the environment but simply assumed all water available would be used. Although the compact between the states allows some water in John Martin Reservoir to be used for fish and recreation purposes, the main purpose is to divide irrigation water. In a broader geographic context, these legal mechanisms determine *where* the impacts will occur not *whether* they will occur. Colorado gains most, but not all, of the economic benefits from irrigation development, and the harms and benefits from the resulting environmental modification. Kansas, although using some Arkansas surface flows for irrigation, is largely impacted by the reduction in flows, including those which would have caused floods.

The Federal Role

The federal government has deferred to the states in allocating private rights to water, but public rights have been recognized from the earliest times. Federal involvement with navigation began after the Revolutionary War,[97] included flood control by the mid-1800s,[98] promoted irrigation by the end of the 1800s,[99] and sponsored power generation by the 1920s.[100] Although federal spending on public projects occurred in the 1800s, the major impact has been since 1930. On the Arkansas, the western basin had less federal influence than the eastern. Flood-control projects, including the John Martin Dam and local urban protection projects, were constructed in Colorado. Also constructed was the Fryingpan–Arkansas Project, which provides irrigation and municipal water, generates power, and provides flood-control storage in the Pueblo Reservoir. In the eastern basin flood control, navigation, and power generation have had a much greater impact. More recently, federal involvement in water quality and environmental protection have had impacts along the entire river. This section concentrates on the major navigation and flood-control projects within the basin's eastern portion and the Fryingpan–Arkansas Project in Colorado.

Free navigation on navigable waterways emerged as federal policy from the economic chaos created by the Articles of Confederation. Trade rivalry and economic discrimination were focal points at the Constitutional Convention. The push for free trade is reflected in the Ordinance of 1787 which states that all navigable waters tributary to the Mississippi and St. Lawrence rivers shall be open for navigation without taxes or tolls.[101] The concept of free navigation persists in federal policy.[102] Although federal power to fund internal waterways improvements was questioned, Congress passed a resolution in 1818 stating they had the power. Federal support for a series of river- and harbor-improvement bills collapsed in the late 1830s when states became active, but many states were not financially secure enough to take on major projects. By the mid-1840s state actions declined with limited federal involvement continuing through the 1800s. In this century, although the constitutionality of internal improvements was challenged,[103] federal subsidies increased, including those on the Arkansas.

The Arkansas was a historic route used by French traders and Indians. Navigation was relatively easy on the river's lower portion, but variations in flow made navigation on the upper portion seasonal at best. Even when the river could not be navigated, the Arkansas provided a source of water for those crossing the dry plains by land. A portion of the Santa Fe trail followed the river for this reason. In the 1820s steamboats regularly traded along the Arkansas as far upstream as Ft. Gibson where the Arkansas, Grand (Neosho), and Verdigris rivers join. During low water the seven-foot-high Webber Falls formed a barrier to upstream traffic making Fort Smith the head of navigation.[104] Keel boats were hauled up the Grand and Verdigris rivers with one steamboat making it to Wichita where it was stranded for several months. Regular traffic was generally limited to the river below Fort Gibson and served eastern Indian tribes being removed to Indian territory. In 1871 the first railroad into the area crossed the Arkansas at Muskogee, ending the Arkansas River's transportation monopoly.

The first federal action to benefit the Arkansas was the River and Harbor Act of 1832, which gave the Corps $115,000 to keep the Arkansas open to its conjunction with the Grand River.[105] Improvements were frequently destroyed by floods, but in good economic times federal money was available. In 1869 a specially designed snag boat with extremely shallow draft was put into service. "By 1902, after seventy years, the Engineers had spent $1 million on improvement of the Arkansas above Pine Bluff, and a total of $2.25 million on the entire stream. The operation of snag boats had cost slightly over $1 million."[106]

The Arkansas was a hazardous river to navigate, but until the railroad boom at the end of the 1800s, the river was the major means of transporting goods, carrying about 25,000 tons annually. After 1872 the river traffic slowed and in essence died by 1900.[107] The Corps made eighteen studies between 1870 and 1921 on improving Arkansas navigation, and promoters in Little Rock and Muskogee bought steamboats to encourage traffic. One of the first acts of the newly created Oklahoma legislature was to request federal improvement of a six-foot-deep channel between Tulsa and Fort Smith.[108] For over seventy years proponents of river navigation worked toward improving the Arkansas, but major changes waited until 1957 when the McClellan–Kerr Navigation System began.

Getting approval for major improvements to Arkansas River navigation was a long process persued vigorously by Oklahoma boosters, especially those from Tulsa. Their unrelenting efforts convinced the Corps, an essential step in the project's implementation. Between 1946 and 1971 the Corps was firmly committed to major civil-works projects along the Arkansas and its tributaries. During the early part of this period, flood-control dams and local levees dominated the Corp's improvements, but by 1957 construction on the navigation system began. The major forces behind final federal approval were two powerful senators, Kerr from Oklahoma and McClellan from Arkansas. In 1955 Robert S. Kerr was chairman of the Flood Control and Rivers and Harbors Subcommittee of the Senate Public Works Committee. In 1960 he was chair of the Senate Select Committee on National Water Resources. This, plus his position on the Appropriation Committee, placed him in a powerful position to influence development on the lower Arkansas. On Kerr's death in 1963, Senator John L. McClellan assured continued development along the Arkansas. This $1.3 billion project cost four times more than the Panama Canal and, when completed in 1971, was the largest public works project ever undertaken by the Corps.[109]

The McClellan–Kerr Arkansas River Navigation System consists of seventeen locks and dams strategically placed along the system's 450-mile length (Fig. 8-2). A total of 420 feet in elevation is gained between the Mississippi River and the Port of Catoosa on the Verdigris River near Tulsa. The channel has a minimum depth of nine feet with the width narrowing from 250 feet to 150 feet on the Verdigris River section. Locks are 100 feet wide and 600 feet long. In 1988 the port at Little Rock handled 250,000 tons of cargo.[110] The navigation route leaves the Mississippi, goes up the White River ten miles then through the Arkansas Post canal where, after another ten miles, the Arkansas River is reached. In the last 50 miles the navigation route leaves the Arkansas to follow the Verdigris. Seven upstream lakes in eastern Oklahoma control the system's water flow. The multipurpose system provides electricity, flood control, water supply, recreation, and wildlife habitat as well as navigation. The dams and reservoirs are Keystone on the Arkansas River, Tenkiller on the Illinois, Oologah on the Verdigris, Eufala on the Canadian, and Hudson, Grand, and Ft. Gibson on the Grand River.

While the need for improved navigation was being promoted by various civic groups and politicians, a coincident demand developed for federal support of flood-control measures and power generation. As early as 1850 the Corps conducted studies on Mississippi River flooding, but no real financial commitment was made until the 1917 Flood Control Act.[111] At that time $45 million was appropriated for levees on the

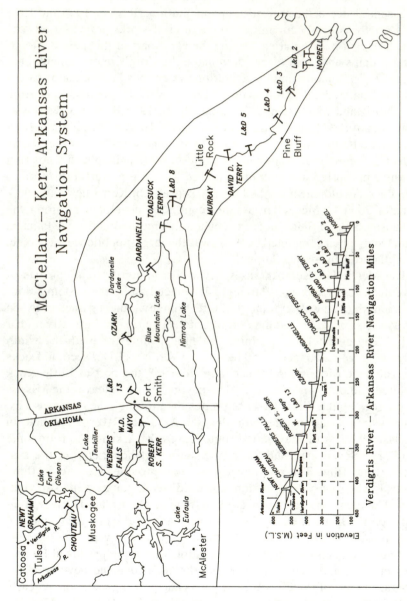

Figure 8-2.

Mississippi River. After a catastrophic flood in 1927 the Corps abandoned levees as the exclusive solution and began to survey tributaries of the Mississippi, including the Arkansas, for possible flood-control reservoir sites.[112] The 1936 Flood Control Act gave the Corps power over flood-control reservoirs which led to the construction of 300 to 400 mostly multipurpose dams. Besides the Corps involvement in flood control and power generation, Congress created the Federal Power Commission, now the Federal Energy Regulatory Commission, in an attempt to establish a comprehensive national policy for hydropower. Private power facilities have needed a federal license to generate power since the Federal Power Act of 1920 was passed.

Authorized in 1928 and completed in 1935, a Corps study recommended three large storage reservoirs in the Arkansas basin.[113] Because these would have no impact on Mississippi River flooding they were not initially funded. Eventually the Flood Control Act of 1936 authorized six projects in the Arkansas Basin with seven more approved in 1938. The Conchas Dam in New Mexico and the John Martin Dam in Colorado were part of this authorization.[114] Although much construction was halted during World War II, the Conchas Dam was completed as were two small dams in Oklahoma—Fort Supply on the North Canadian and the Great Salt Plains Dam on the Salt Fork of the Arkansas River. One major nonfederal dam was also completed before the war, as was one small dam in Arkansas (Fig. 8-3).

The Pensacola Dam, forming Grand Lake, illustrates the evolving federal power over water. Although proposals had been made to dam the Grand (Neosho) River for power purposes since the 1890s, no venture was successfully started until the 1930s. As late as 1930, Corps reports found no economic justification for dams on the Grand River. In spite of this gloomy federal report a private corporation, Grand-Hydro, applied for an Oklahoma license to build Pensacola Dam. Although Oklahoma granted the license, political moves by Tulsa led to the Grand River Dam Authority's formation. As a public utility the Authority was given exclusive power to develop power on the Grand River.[115] Grand-Hydro's property interest was condemned, but a high price was paid for the value of the water "current" granted them by their Oklahoma license.[116] The federal Public Works Administration agreed to help finance the project.[117] In spite of these plans, a 1939 Corps report recommended that the three dams to be constructed on the Grand River be operated as a single unit under Corps control.[118]

The Corps wanted large flood-storage capacity behind the three dams, the Public Works Administration wanted less flood capacity so more power could be generated to recoup their subsidy, and the newly created Fed-

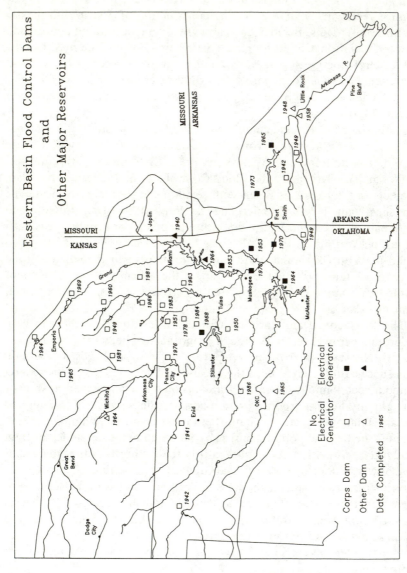

Eastern Basin Flood Control Dams
and
Other Major Reservoirs

No
Electrical   Electrical
Generator   Generator

Corps Dam   □   ■

Other Dam   △   ▲

Date Completed   1965

Figure 8-3.

eral Power Commission insisted on a federal license before construction began. Because the Grand River was not considered navigable, the Grand River Dam Authority contended federal law was inapplicable. But Supreme Court decisions allow Congress to protect a river's navigable capacity,[119] and Congress can authorize dams on non-navigable streams even when states object.[120] The Authority eventually obtained a federal license and completed the Pensacola Dam in 1940, with a small flood-storage capacity. Although the Authority continued with its plans, further dam development was interrupted by World War II. While the Authority's progress was halted, Congress authorized construction of two more Grand River dams, but disputes over whether the Corps or Federal Works Agency should do the construction delayed matters.[121]

A series of floods in the early 1940s, damaging $30 million in property, demonstrated the need for flood control. During one flood event the Arkansas River at Fort Smith discharged 850,000 cubic feet per second and was forty-one feet above flood stage.[122] Even before World War II was over, plans were made for additional multipurpose dams in the Arkansas basin. In 1945 the Corps recommended flood control and navigation improvements on the Arkansas.[123] The following year the Federal Power Commission recommended cost-effective improvements, and Congress approved $55 million for the projects.

The Fort Gibson Dam near Muskogee was begun in 1946. The Corps took this project from the Grand River Dam Authority, which claimed as property the waterpower rights granted them by their license. Although, the property right was similar to the one condemned from Grand-Hydro on Pensacola Dam, the Supreme Court held, "[w]here the United States appropriates the flow of either a navigable or non-navigable stream pursuant to its superior power under the Commerce Clause, it is exercising established prerogatives and is beholden to no one."[124] The Grand River Dam Authority did build another dam on the Grand River, but the Corps determined flood control and navigation needs.

One other major use received significant federal subsidies—irrigation development.[125] Although this was not important in the eastern basin, impacts occurred in the western half. Most of the major players or events are absent from the Arkansas basin. The Reclamation Service, later the Bureau of Reclamation, did assist western Kansas farmers with windmill projects, but the impact was slight until the Fryingpan–Arkansas Project was started. This major project, funded in 1962, diverts water from the Colorado River basin across the continental divide. Although the Bureau of Reclamation had proposed diverting water from the Gunnison River, the approved project takes water from the Fryingpan and Roaring Fork rivers, both tributaries of the Colorado. The project consists of six reservoirs, with two being very small. On the western slope in the Colorado River basin, 26.7 miles of tunnels along with 4 miles of conduit collect and transport water to Turquoise Lake near Leadville. From there 16.7 miles of conduit and canals transport water to Mt. Elbert and Otero power plants. Farther downstream 265 miles of conduit carry water from Pueblo Reservoir to Colorado Springs and other eastern Colorado cities. The Mt. Elbert power plant has a capacity of 200,000 kilowatts, and Otero 11,000 kilowatts.[126]

The project was designed to divert 69,200 acre-feet across the continental divide. Of this, 20,100 acre-feet go to Colorado Springs and 9,650 acre-feet are sent through the Arkansas Valley conduit to Colorado cities as far east as Lamar. The remaining water will be used to provide supplemental irrigation to 280,600 Colorado acres.[127]

Through a series of storage dams, federal actions attempted to control the Arkansas flow to prevent floods, provide water for power and navigation, supply the needs of irrigators, and in later years for recreation. The primary environmental impacts result from the reservoirs themselves and the variety of canals and ditches needed to collect and distribute water. In spite of federal attempts to control nature, floods and droughts still occur. Although inundated land, habitat modification, and species changes are primary effects of federal action, the secondary effects may be more significant in the long run. Reduction in economic loss from floods coupled with economic growth from irrigation development, hydroelectric power, inland navigation, and recreation development have increased the population in the Arkansas basin. The impacts of this population growth significantly affect the environment.

Conclusion

The environmental impacts of state and federal policy in the Arkansas Valley cannot be completely evaluated in the remaining space. Impacts extend from the Colorado River to the Mississippi delta. State and federal policy promoted irrigation which led to the tilling of over 500,000 acres of prairie. In addition to the change in land use, irrigation practices changed the nature of the river. Diversions evened out the flow while diminishing the river's total volume. Erosion from fields increased sedimentation, narrowing the river's banks and raising its bed. Controlling prairie fires and reducing floods allowed the phreatophyte cottonwood to become established along the river which in turn consumed enormous amounts of water. Increased salinity from irrigation practices changed the nature of the river's water, impacted soils, and encouraged the spread of salt cedars, another phreatophyte.[128] Wildlife types and numbers changed as the habitats along the river and in the irrigated fields were modified.

In the lower river the major environmental impacts resulted from the reservoirs constructed and modifications to the river's flow. Farmland was inundated, removing thousands of acres from production. Wildlife habitat was modified, creating large riparian zones diverse in plant life and beneficial to wildlife. Silt normally suspended in the river settles out in reservoirs, reducing the sediment carried to the Mississippi River and filling reservoirs. The large fishery established in the reservoirs encourages recreation uses which in turn have secondary environmental impacts.

Although the environmental impacts are significant, so are the economic and human impacts. Power generation, flood control, navigation, and irrigation were the main thrusts of federal and state policies, but other impacts occurred as well. The many reservoirs provide a place for recreation and have enhanced fish and game habitats. Tourism is a major segment of the economy around many lakes. Increasingly, federal and state policies are addressing environmental quality.

Not all federal and state policies are mutually complementary. Irrigators want to store water for release during times of water shortage. Water stored for this purpose reduces the volume available for flood control and while stored cannot be used to generate electricity. Water released from a reservoir to provide power and flood storage capacity may increase the river's rate of flow, making upstream navigation more costly. Providing a minimum level of water for fish and wildlife in a reservoir may interfere with established irrigation water rights. Conflicts between policy goals are an inherent problem in managing any resource with multiple uses. Conflicts increase when the resource is mobile and the policy is set by seven states and multiple federal agencies. Although integrated river basin management has been suggested, multipurpose management by multiple political units and agencies is the rule. The resulting "law" of the Arkansas is truly a tale of two rivers.

Notes

1. In Kansas the river is pronounced ArKANsas. To avoid regional conflicts over pronunciation, some river managers simply refer to the Ark River.

2. U.S. Army Corp of Engineers, *Water Resource Development in Oklahoma 1989* (Tulsa: U.S. Army Corps of Engineers, 1989), 5. The Columbia River is shorter (1,214 miles), the Colorado is about the same (1,450 miles), and the Missouri is longer (2,315 miles). The Arkansas drainage basin is the smallest of the four major western rivers: Columbia (259,000 square miles), Missouri

(530,000 square miles), and Colorado (250,000 square miles). Ed Marston, "Western Water Made Simple" *High Country News* (September 29, 1986), 11.

3. *Kansas v. Colorado*, 206 U.S. 46 (1907), 116.

4. Oklahoma Water Resources Board, *Oklahoma Water Atlas* (Oklahoma City: Oklahoma Water Resources Board, 1990), 38.

5. Oklahoma Climatological Survey, *Oklahoma Climate Atlas* (Norman: Oklahoma Climatological Survey, in press).

6. George C. Coggins, "Grizzly Bears Don't Stop at Customs: A Preface to Transboundary Problems in Natural Resource Law," *University of Kansas Law Review* 32 (1983): 1.

7. Olen P. Matthews, *Water Resources, Geography and Law* (Washington, D.C.: Association of American Geographers, 1984).

8. Graham A. Tobin et. al. "Water Resources" in *Geography in America*, Gary L. Gaile and Cort J. Willmott, eds. (Columbus, Ohio: Merrill, 1989), 112–40.

9. Olen P. Matthews, "Resources, Boundaries, and Law—A Spatial Classification," Centre Paper Series (Dundee, Scotland: Centre for Petroleum and Mineral Law Studies, 1988), 4. Two additional types, unstable boundaries and access, have been identified.

10. Ibid., 14.

11. Stephen R. Munzer, *A Theory of Property* (Cambridge: Cambridge University Press, 1990), 16.

12. Frank J. Trelease, "Policies for Water Law: Property Rights, Economic Forces, and Public Regulation," *Natural Resource Journal* 5 (1965): 1.

13. Coggins, "Grizzly Bears Don't Stop at Customs," 2.

14. *Omaechevarria v. Idaho*, 246 U.S. 343 (1918).

15. Frank J. Trelease, *Federal-State Relations in Water Law*, National Water Commission, Legal Study No. 5 (1971).

16. *Tyler v. Wilkinson* 24 Fed. Cas. 472 (Case No. 14, 312 C. Ct. R. I. 1827). Peter N. Davis, "The Riparian Right of Streamflow Protection in the Eastern States," *Arkansas Law Review* 36 (1982): 47.

17. National Water Commission, *Water Policies for the Future*, Report of the National Water Commission (Washington, D.C.: National Water Commission, 1973), 280–93.

18. James Michener, *Centennial* (New York: Random House, 1974), 568.

19. Richard Ausness, "Water Rights, the Public Trust and the Protection of Instream Uses," *University of Illinois Law Review* 1986 (1986): 407.

20. U.S. Constitution, Art. I, § 8, cl. 3.

21. U.S. Constitution, Art. I, § 10, cl. 3.

22. U.S. Constitution, Art. IV, § 3, cl. 2.

23. U.S. Constitution, Art. I, § 8, cl. 3. Indian reserved rights are based on the Indian commerce clause or perhaps the property clause.

24. *United States v. Winters*, 207 U.S. 564 (1908).

25. *Arizona v. California*, 373 U.S. 546 (1963).

26. *Cappaert v. United States*, 426 U.S. 128 (1976).

27. *United States v. New Mexico*, 438 U.S. 696 (1978).

28. *Kleppe v. New Mexico*, 426 U.S. 529 (1976).

29. *Sporhase v. Nebraska*, 458 U.S. 941 (1982).

30. Reclamation Act of 1902, 43 U.S.C.A. §§ 371–615; Carey Act of 1894, 43 U.S.C.A. § 641.

31. River and Harbor Acts, 33 U.S.C.A. §§ 401–476, 540–633.

32. Flood Control Act of 1936, 33 U.S.C.A. § 701.

33. Clean Water Act, 33 U.S.C.A. §§ 1251–1376; Safe Drinking Water Act, 42 U.S.C.A. § 300 f-j-10.

34. Federal Water Power Act of 1920, 16 U.S.C.A. § 801.

35. Fish and Wildlife Coordination Act., 16 U.S.C.A. §§ 661–66c; Endangered Species Act 16 U.S.C.A. §§ 4321–4347; Pacific Northwest Electric Power Planning and Conservation Act, 16 U.S.C.A. § 839.

36. Wild and Scenic Rivers Act, 16 U.S.C.A. §§ 1271–1287.

37. *City of Tacoma v. Taxpayers*, 357 U.S. 320 (1958); *First Iowa Hydro-Electric Co-op v. Federal Power Commision*, 328 U.S. 152 (1946).

38. *League to Save Lake Tahoe v. Tahoe Regional Planning Agency*, 507 F. 2d 517 (9th Cir 1974), cert. denied 420 U.S. 974 (1975).

39. *Kansas v. Colorado*, 185 U.S. 125 (1902).

40. Boulder Canyon Project Act of 1928, 43 U.S.C.A. § 617; *Arizona v. California*, 373 U.S. 546 (1963).

41. *Kansas v. Colorado*, No. 105 Original (Pending); *Oklahoma and Texas v. New Mexico*, No. 109 Original (Pending).

42. *Intake Water Co. v. Yellowstone River Compact Commission*, 769 F. 2d 568 (1985), cert. denied 106 Sp. Ct. 2288 (1986).

43. *Kansas v. Colorado*, No. 105 Original (Pending); *Colorado v. Kansas*, 320 U.S. 383 (1943); *Kansas v. Colorado*, 206 U.S. 46 (1907); *Kansas v. Colorado*, 185 U.S. 125 (1902).

44. *Oklahoma and Texas v. New Mexico*, No. 109 Original (Pending).

45. W. Robbins, "Arkansas River Controversy," *Boundaries and Water: Allocation and Use of a Shared Resource* (Boulder, Colo.: National Resource Law Center, 1989), 3.

46. *Clark v. Allaman*, 80 Pac. 571 (Kan. 1905). Kansas Statutes Annotated § 82a–703 (1988).

47. James E. Sherow, *Watering the Valley, Development along the High Plains Arkansas River, 1870–1950* (Lawrence: University of Kansas Press, 1990).

48. Ibid., 37.

49. *The La Junta and Lamar Canal Co. v. Hess*, 25 Colo. 513 (1898); *The La Junta and Lamar Canal Co. v. The Fort Lyon Canal Co.*, 31 Colo. 1 (1903); *Blakely v. The Fort Lyon Canal Co.*, 31 Colo. 224 (1903).

50. Sherow, *Watering the Valley*, 45.

51. Ibid., 51.

52. *Middlekamp v. Bessemer Irrigating Co.*, 46 Colo. 102 (1909); *Barnum v. Bessemer Irrigating Co.*, 46 Colo. 125 (1909); *Brown v. Bessemer Irrigating Co.*, 46 Colo. 126 (1909); *Patry v. Bessemer Irrigating Co.*, 46 Colo. 127 (1909); *Vail et al. v. Bessemer Irrigating Co.* 46 Colo. 128 (1909).

53. Sherow, *Watering the Valley*, 43.

54. Ibid., 54.

55. *Baker et al. v. City of Pueblo*, 87 Colo. 489 (1930).

56. Bureau of Reclamation, "The Fryingpan–Arkansas Project" (Washington D.C.: Bureau of Reclamation, 1979).

57. Sherow, *Watering the Valley*, 59.

58. *Strickler v. City of Colorado Springs*, 16 Colo. 61 (1891).

59. Sherow, *Watering the Valley*, 61.

60. *Empire Water and Power Co. v. Cascade Town Co.* 205 F. 123 (8th Cir. 1913).

61. Bureau of Reclamation, "The Fryingpan–Arkansas Project."

62. Sherow, *Watering the Valley*, 70.

63. Three tunnels from across the continental divide now feed into the Turquoise Lake watershed.

64. Sherow, *Watering the Valley*, 74.

65. William E. Smythe, *The Conquest of Arid America* (London: McMillan Co., 1907 reprint), 110.

66. Sherow, *Watering the Valley*, 79.

67. Smythe, *Conquest of Arid America*, 111.

68. Sherow, *Watering the Valley*, 96.

69. *U.S. Irrigating Co. v. Graham Ditch Co.*, settled out of court, ibid.

70. Early Kansas Statutes referring to irrigation include Kansas Gen. St. 1868, subd. 34, § 5, art. 2 c. 23; Kansas Laws 1872, p. 241 c. 105; Kansas Laws 1885, p. 205 c. 133 and c. 134; Kansas Laws 1886, p. 154 c. 115; Kansas Laws 1889, p. 239 c. 165; Kansas Laws 1899, p. 223 c. 133; Kansas Laws 1899, p. 191 c. 95 and p. 316 c. 151. The statute passed in 1945 is found at Kansas Statutes Annotated § 82a–703.

71. *Clark v. Allaman*, 80 Pac. 571 (Kan. 1905).

72. Sherow, *Watering the Valley*, 92.

73. *Kansas v. Colorado*, 185 U.S. 125 (1902).

74. Felix Frankfurter and James M. Landis, "The Compact Clause of the Constitution—A Study in Interstate Adjustments," *Yale Law Journal* 34 (1925): 685; Frank P. Grad, "Federal-State Compact: A New Experiment in Cooperative Federalism," *Columbia Law Review* 63 (1963): 825; Douglas L. Grant, "The Future of Interstate Allocation of Water," *Rocky Mountain Mineral Law Institute* 29 (1983): 977; Kevin J. Heron, "The Interstate Compact in Transition: From Cooperative State Action to Congressionally Coerced Agreements," *St. John's Law Review* 60 (1985); Jerome C. Muys, "Interstate Compacts and Regional Water Resource Mangement" *Natural Resource Law* 6 (1973): 153; Richard A. Sims, Leland E. Rolfs, and Brent E. Sprock, "Interstate Compacts and Equitable Apportionment," *Rocky Mountain Mineral Law Institute* 34 (1989): 23-1; A. Dan Tarlock, "The Law of Equitable Apportionment Revisited, Updated and Restated," *University of Colorado Law Review* 56 (1985): 381.

75. *Colorado v. New Mexico*, 467 U.S. 310 (1984); *Colorado v. New Mexico*, 459 U.S. 178 (1982).

76. *Kansas v. Colorado*, (1907), 70.

77. Sherow, *Watering the Valley*, 103.

78. *Kansas v. Colorado*, (1907), 53.

79. Sherow, *Watering the Valley*, 115.

80. *Kansas v. Colorado*, (1907), 61.

81. Ibid., 62.
82. 21 Op. Att'y Gen. 274, 283 (1895).
83. *Kansas v. Colorado*, (1907) 65.
84. Ibid., 105–6.
85. Ibid., 101.
86. Ibid., 88.
87. Ibid., 95.
88. Ibid., 118.
89. *Wyoming v. Colorado*, 259 U.S. 419 (1922).
90. *Colorado v. Kansas*, (1943), 391.
91. Ibid., 391.
92. Sherow, *Watering the Valley*, 130.
93. Arkansas River Compact, 63 Stat. 145 (1948).
94. Arkansas River Compact, Art. IV.
95. *Kansas v. Colorado*, No. 105 Original (Pending).
96. Robbins, "Arkansas River Controversy," 4.
97. Robert W. Harrison, *History of the Commerical Waterways and Ports of the United States*, (Washington, D.C.: U.S. Army Corp of Engineers, 1979); William J. Hull and Robert W. Hull, *The Origin and Development of the Waterways Policy of the United States* (Washington, D.C.: National Waterways Conference, 1967); Aubrey Parkman, *History of the Waterways of the Atlantic Coast of The United States* (Washington, D.C.: U.S. Army Corps of Engineers, 1983).
98. U.S. Army Corps of Engineers, *The History of the U.S. Army Corps of Engineers* (Washington, D.C.: U.S. Army Corps of Engineers, 1986).
99. Roy E. Huffman, *Irrigation Development and Public Water Policy* (New York: The Ronald Press, 1953); Walter M. Kollmorgen, "The Woodsman's Assault on the Domain of the Cattlemen," *Annals of the Association of American Geographers* 59 (1969): 215; Timothy J. Rickard, "The Great Plains as Part of an Irrigated Western Empire, 1890–1914," in *The Great Plains, Environment and Culture*, Brian W. Blouet and Fredrick C. Luebke, eds. (Lincoln: University of Nebraska Press, 1977), 81–98.
100. Note, "Federal Power Commission Control Over River Basin Developments," *Virginia Law Review* 51 (1965): 663.
101. An Ordinance for the Government of the Territory of the United States northwest of the river Ohio (July 13, 1787) reprinted at 1 Stat. 51 n.(a) (1789), Art. IV.
102. Hull, *The Origin and Development of Waterways*, 27. Cases on free navigation include *James v. Dravo Contracting Co.*, 302 U.S. 134 (1937); *Economy Light & Power Co. v. U.S.*, 256 U.S. 113 (1929); *Sands v. Manistee River Co.*, 128 U.S. 288 (1887); *Huse v. Glover*, 119 U.S. 543 (1886); *Leverich v. City of Mobile*, 110 F. 170 (Cir. Ct. S. Dist. Ala. 1867); *Jolly v. Terre Haute Drawbridge Co.*, 6 McLean 237 (Cir. Ct. Dist. Ohio 1853).
103. *U.S. v. Gerlach Livestock Co.*, 339 U.S. 725 (1950); *Oklahoma v. Atkinson*, 313 U.S. 508 (1941); *Ashwander v. Tennessee Valley Authority*, 297 U.S. 288 (1936); *Jackson v. U.S.*, 230 U.S. 1 (1913).

104.   Bill Burchardt, "The Arkansas River and the Red," in *Water Trails West*, Western Writers of American, ed. (Garden City: Doubleday, 1978), 30–42.

105.   William A. Settle, Jr., *The Dawning, A New Day for the Southwest* (Tulsa: U.S. Army Corps of Engineers, Tulsa District, 1975), 147.

106.   Settle, *The Dawning*, 14.

107.   Ibid., 17.

108.   Ibid., 17.

109.   Oklahoma Water Resources Board, *Oklahoma Water Atlas*, 39.

110.   U.S. Army Corps of Engineers, *Water Resources Development in Arkansas 1989*, (Little Rock: U.S. Army Corps of Engineers, Little Rock District, 1989).

111.   Flood Control Act of 1917, 39 Stat. 948.

112.   U.S. Army Corps of Engineers, *History of the U.S. Army Corps*, 50.

113.   Settle, *The Dawning*, 29. The reservoirs were Caddoe (later named John Martin), Conchas in New Mexico, and Ft. Reno on the North Canadian River.

114.   H. Doc. No. 308, 74th Cong., 1st. Session.

115.   Oklahoma Session Laws, 1935, c. 70 Art. 4 § 1.

116.   *Grand River Dam Authority v. Grand-Hydro*, 335 U.S. 359 (1948).

117.   Settle, *The Dawning*, 39.

118.   H. Doc. No. 107, 76th Cong. 1st. Session (1939), 2–7.

119.   *U.S. v. Rio Grande Dam and Irrigation Co.* 174 U.S. 690 (1899).

120.   *Oklahoma v. Atkinson* 313 U.S. 508 (1941).

121.   Settle, *The Dawning*, 41.

122.   Ibid., 47.

123.   H. Doc. No. 758, 79th Cong. 2d. Session (1947).

124.   *U.S. v. Grand River Dam Authority*, 363 U.S. 229, 231 (1960).

125.   See note 99.

126.   Bureau of Reclamation, "The Fryingpan–Arkansas Project."

127.   Ibid.

128.   Sherow, *Watering the Valley*, 31.

9

Illinois River Pollution Control, 1900–1970

Craig E. Colten

Eliminating pollution through the passage of legislation is much easier said than done. Public policy, despite well-meaning proponents, seldom arrests poor water-quality problems as recent experiences with the clean-water laws attest.[1] A policy or environmental-management approach to pollution history covers only one dimension of the problem. The pollution history of the Illinois River, in particular, demands a geographic perspective on the disparity between environmental conditions and public policy.[2]

With its drainage basin largely situated within one state and thereby subject to only one set of laws, use of the Illinois River as a sewage outlet exemplifies the geographic inequity of public regulation of waterways. The Illinois General Assembly allowed Chicago's public-health needs to override the concerns of other sections of the state. This caused severe deterioration of water quality and effectively destroyed a thriving commercial fishery and mussel industry. This occurred despite increasing authority held by the state's water-quality agency, whose efforts were negated by special allowances for the Chicago metropolitan region where excessive releases of urban and industrial wastes continued to overwhelm the river. Although state policy provided means to regulate discharges of liquid wastes to waterways, the Illinois River remained severely polluted through the 1960s. Not only were exemptions allowed for Chicago-area sewage, but water-quality conditions often became extreme before action was taken. Belated efforts seldom achieved the intended goals of restoring the river to a healthful condition.[3] Furthermore, early legislative policy focused on general urban sewage and largely overlooked industrial wastes.

This chapter focuses on environmental changes caused by introduction of urban and industrial pollution into the Illinois Waterway. State agencies monitoring water quality repeatedly pointed out problems, but the spatial inequity in legislation and the lack of attention directed toward sources of industrial wastes created a sharp contrast between stated policy goals and the condition of the river.

Illinois River Pollution History

Before 1900

During the last third of the nineteenth century, the rapidly growing city of Chicago realized that its domestic sewage was fouling Lake Michigan, and thus its drinking-water supply. Consequently, local officials sought a means to divert the urban effluent away from municipal water intakes. Chicago proposed to excavate a canal that would carry a mixture of sewage and fresh lake water into the Illinois River where it would be diluted and transported to the Mississippi River (Fig. 9-1). The Sanitary and Ship Canal, or drainage ditch as it was commonly called, would also serve as an improved navigation channel. The few industrial cities along the Illinois River welcomed the prospects of increased commerce and saw no danger in using the river as an open sewer since none obtained its drinking water from the waterway.[4] The state, however, noted that the upper reaches of the river were already polluted by limited quantities of Chicago sewage entering via the older Illinois and Michigan Canal and expressed concern over additional degradation. Although seemingly committed to the Chicago plan, the state carried out a series of investigations under the pretext of protecting the "sanitary interests" of residents throughout the valley.[5]

In its initial investigation, the state's public health agency reported that nearly half of the water reaching Peoria during dry years was a combination of Lake Michigan water and Chicago sewage and concluded that this mixture had no ill effect on the fish above Peoria, except in winter. It suggested that the impending diversion might actually improve water quality by increasing the river's dilution capacity below Peoria.[6] Additional reports pointed out that water quality was particularly poor along the upper reaches, above La Salle, and immediately downstream from Peoria and Pekin. The majority of pollution in the upper river was the result of urban and industrial sewage from Chicago, and along the middle stretches pollution resulted from the dumping of vast quantities of biological wastes into the river. Yet the state concluded that "so far as science may now determine, the cities of the Illinois must, perforce, use the river for sewage disposal."[7]

Other state agencies presented mixed conclusions about industrial

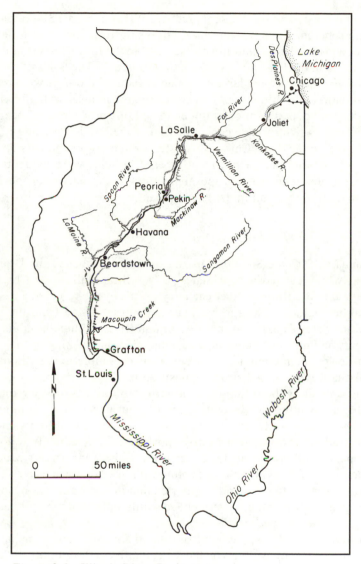

Figure 9-1. Illinois River Basin.

discharges into the Illinois River system. The Illinois Fish Commission cited the increasing load of sewage as a beneficial food supply to fish populations.[8] The annual commercial catch from the Illinois River rose from six million pounds in 1894 to nearly twelve million pounds in 1900.[9] Nevertheless, the commission voiced concern about pollution in general and called for legislation to control industrial wastes in particular.[10]

Illinois had laws in place before 1900 that allowed municipalities to restrict offensive waste-disposal practices.[11] However, the State Board of Health concluded that "no nuisance will result from sewage at Joliet and below, and that the palatability of the water in the Illinois River at Peoria will not be in the least affected from that source."[12] The Sanitary District of Chicago, in which the largest volume of industrial wastes was created, relied entirely on dilution as a means of treatment until well after 1900, and the state department of health endorsed this procedure.[13] Local nuisance laws, which forbade contamination of the Des Plaines and Illinois rivers, did not apply to Chicago's wastes, which originated outside their areas of jurisdiction.[14] Thus, locally based policies were ineffective in restricting upstream waste-disposal practices that relied on self-purification and dilution to minimize their impact.

After the Opening of the Drainage Canal

In January 1900 the Sanitary District of Chicago opened the Drainage Canal, which carried approximately 274 million gallons of Chicago's sewage into the Illinois River each day.[15] This event heralded a new era in public health in Chicago by diverting sewage away from the city's drinking-water supply and into the Illinois River. Although public controversy and political subterfuge accompanied the opening of the canal, most downstream communities welcomed its completion. St. Louis officials, however, voiced strong opposition based on fears that the canal would deliver typhoid and cholera germs to the city's water intakes, located a few miles downstream from the confluence of the Illinois and Mississippi rivers. Reports in the Peoria press that the Illinois had become "turbid" and was temporarily "poisonous" immediately following the opening of the canal did little to allay the concerns of Missouri residents.[16] Two days after the full volume of Lake Michigan water reached Peoria, however, the local press reported that Peoria Lake was becoming pure again, as the amount of suspended solids and the number of bacteria and germs decreased.[17]

Initially, the increased volume of diluted Chicago sewage apparently had minimal negative effects on the water quality in the vicinity of Peoria. Icemen in Peoria noticed no color or odor problems, although they had concerns about long-term effects.[18] The Fish Commission had nothing to say about the Illinois River in 1902, although it reported that one of its tributaries was very polluted and urged legislative action to "prevent the existence of present conditions."[19] Investigations of water quality that sought to determine the public-health impact at St. Louis found that the upper stretches were very polluted, as was the water below Peoria. Testimony presented before the U.S. Supreme Court revealed that some of the most offensive practices originated in the Peoria area. Distillery and feed-lot operators admitted that they heaped stable refuse on the banks of the river, which carried away small islands of manure and straw during high water.[20] After hearing an array of testimony on pollution, the U.S. Supreme Court concluded that there was insufficient evidence to determine that Chicago's sewage would cause typhoid outbreaks in St. Louis— thereby supporting the argument that the Illinois cleansed itself before merging with the Mississippi.

Furthermore, there was no immediate impact on the commercial fishing industry. The Illinois River fishery continued to bring in larger catches each year until 1908, when fishermen reported selling over 23 million pounds of fish.[21] The rapid increase in the commercial harvest reflected several factors, and many observers hailed the drainage canal as a positive influence. They claimed increasing water levels made flooding more frequent and benefited breeding conditions, thereby making the industry more reliable.[22] Another reason for the improved yields was the increased supply of microorganisms, which thrived on the partially decomposed sewage and served as a food supply for fish.[23] A final factor was the carp: an introduced species which flourished in the turbid and polluted water and propagated rapidly to become the most abundant species of commercial fish. Carp made up about a tenth of the total catch in 1894, but constituted over 65 percent in 1908. The number of fishermen also rose dramatically between 1900 and 1910 and undoubtedly contributed to the rising volume of fish landed each year.[24] Nevertheless, the interpretation of sewage as a beneficial influence ran contrary to appeals from the Fish Commission for legislation to halt the use of streams as sewers, especially by industries.[25]

The astounding expansion of the commercial fishery during the first few years of the twentieth century was followed by a precipitous decline after 1908. The chief explanation for the drop in fish yields was the conversion of wetlands along the lower river to leveed farmland, and the consequent loss of nearly half the spawning areas.[26] Also, the important catfish and buffalo populations declined in relative abundance in the lower river and virtually disappeared along the upper reaches as a result of poor water quality. Although pollution played a role in limiting where fish could survive, authorities believed that the extensive conversion of wetlands to drained farm fields caused the greatest harm to the fishery.[27]

By embracing the notion that pollution was only a minor factor, and only in the upper river, public officials delayed any attempts to restrict industrial pollution. Illinois law contained a pair of options whereby the state or private citizens could object to stream pollution. The criminal code provided for a fine of up to $1,000 for anyone willfully or maliciously contaminating a spring or other source of water. The National Committee on Pollution of Water Supplies considered this legislation among the most advanced in the country.[28] However, the fact that no communities drew their drinking water from the Illinois River rendered this statute ineffective. Nuisance law prohibited the corruption of the water of any spring, river, pond, or lake as early as 1845 and provided a fine of $100. Nevertheless, the use of the Illinois River as a sewage sluice for municipal and industrial wastes was sanctioned by laws authorizing the Sanitary District of Chicago.[29] During the decline of the fishery, the Illinois legislature created the Rivers and Lakes Commission with the expressed duty of halting "the unlawful pollution of streams." Its mandate called for the commission to prevent the defilement of waterways to the extent that they are rendered useless for human consumption or *lead to the destruction of aquatic life*. The Rivers and Lakes Commission did not seek out pollution cases, rather they took complaints from individuals or units of local government, investigated the complaint, and held hearings on the matter. The commission had the authority to order polluters to cease their actions or to work out compromises, and in situations where pollution persisted, they could levy fines. If an incident fell within a municipality, they turned the complaint over to local health authorities.[30]

Although expressing a policy of permitting some degree of stream pollution to prevent losing industries, the Rivers and Lakes Commission took a surprisingly firm stand with industrial polluters. In a total of forty industrial cases between 1913 and 1916, the commission issued twenty-four orders to halt discharges; and in another five cases they induced industries to install treatment equipment. The commission referred only one case to a municipality and took no action on seven complaints. In effect, the actions of the pollution-control agency exceeded their stated policy. Nevertheless, agreements with the Sanitary District of Chicago precluded enforcement in cases involving trade wastes on the Illinois River.[31]

Water-quality analyses of the Illinois River proceeded throughout the 1910s and 1920s as production of commercial fish continued to fall. Natural scientists proposed in 1919, for the first time, that urban sewage was a significant cause in the decline of the riverine environment. Biologists with the Illinois Natural History Survey found that the increased flow of Lake Michigan water and sewage reduced the normal summer warming of the river water and that slightly lower temperatures inhibited biological decomposition of the sewage. The increased volume of fluids in the river speeded its passage down the valley, allowing sewage to travel further downstream before decomposing. Consequently, polluted water existed further downstream than in previous years.[32]

Based on the analyses of pollution-tolerant organisms, the Natural History Survey reported that serious changes in the biological environment progressed nearly to Peoria by 1915 and throughout the relatively still water of Lake Peoria by 1925 (Fig. 9-2). They also identified "subpollutional" conditions (emerging populations of pollution-tolerant riverbed dwellers) as far downstream as Beardstown. These bottom fauna that were replacing clean-water species by the mid-1920s were poor food supplies for commercial fish and waterfowl.[33] Thus, the creeping wedge of pollution made inroads into principal fishing areas south of Peoria before 1930. Its impact on the mussel population was even more severe than on the mobile fish (Fig. 9-3). Pollution had decimated the mussel population in Peoria Lake (both commercial and noncommercial species) and eliminated about seventy kinds of benthic organisms near Havana by 1920.[34]

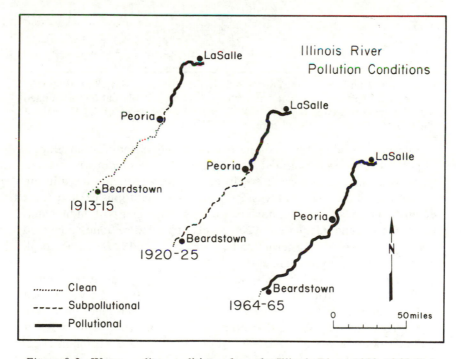

Figure 9-2. Water-quality conditions along the Illinois River, 1913–1965. Pollutional conditions indicate a predominance of pollution-tolerant aquatic life. (After H.B. Mills et al., *Man's Effect on the Fish and Wildlife of the Illinois River*, 1966.)

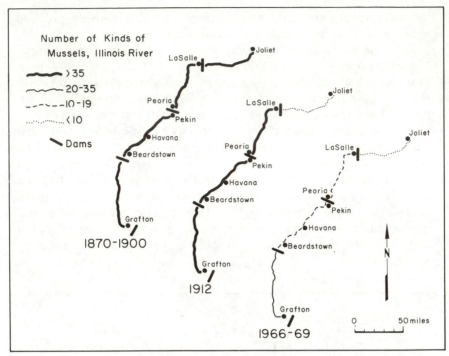

Figure 9-3. Numbers of kinds of mussels in the Illinois River, 1870–1969. The elimination of mussel diversity indicates a loss of suitable habitat associated with declining water quality. (After W.C. Starrett, "A Survey of the Mussels of the Illinois River: A Polluted Stream," 1971.)

Subsequent studies provided a more refined understanding of the impact of pollution. Severely polluted conditions pushed farther downstream in warm years during low-water conditions, thereby reducing the diluting capabilities of the river. At low stage, anaerobic conditions existed as far downstream as Chillicothe; however, during a summer with high water, researchers found adequate oxygen levels at La Salle. State-sponsored research discovered long-term trends, which indicated 1920 was the peak year of pollution by organic wastes.[35]

As part of a series of stream-pollution studies, and also at the request of the Sanitary District of Chicago, the U.S. Public Health Service joined state researchers in their examination of Illinois River water quality in 1921. Together they found that urban population in the Illinois River drainage basin increased from 2.7 million in 1910 to 3.6 million in 1922. The majority of the population lived in the Chicago metropolitan area and contributed to the sewage load carried to the Illinois River through the drainage canal. Federal investigators discovered that "practically none of the sewage reaching the Illinois River or its tributaries is treated before discharge. . . . As a result, the upper Illinois is notoriously polluted."[36] Although the Sanitary District of Chicago opened sewage treatment plants on the Des Plaines and Little Calumet rivers in 1922, culminating a decade of efforts to offset the increasing flow of raw sewage, these facilities handled mostly domestic wastes and effluent from meat-packing plants. This accomplishment represented a pioneering effort at large-scale sewage treatment in Illinois and probably accounted for the state's observation that conditions improved after 1920.

In 1922 the U.S. Public Health Service observed that "very few of any of these [Chicago's] industrial wastes receive any treatment before discharge."[37] In fact, over 140 manufacturers continued to discharge some 500 million gallons of untreated organic and inorganic wastes into the river system daily.[38] As Chicago put its treatment works on line, the proportion of untreated wastes contributed by factories increased. During the 1920s the state Department of Public Works and Buildings held the authority to take action against polluting industries. However, like their predecessor, they had no jurisdiction over the watercourses carrying sewage within the Sanitary District of Chicago. As a result, the state was unable to deal with the increasingly significant volume of toxic and hazardous effluent that entered the Illinois River during the 1920s.[39] In the late 1920s, manufacturing wastes throughout the Illinois valley constituted about 42 percent of the total waste load.

By the end of the decade, the U.S. Public Health Service described the upper Illinois River as being populated by only pollution-tolerant organisms and showing the obvious odor and color of polluted water downstream to La Salle. The continued growth of Chicago and its industries overwhelmed the ability of the Illinois River to decompose the large volume of biological wastes. Polluted conditions continued to advance downstream at a rate of sixteen miles annually. This condition threatened the valuable fishery of the lower river with extinction; a prediction supported by the catch of roughly ten million pounds of fish in 1922 and approximately five million in 1931. Still, the U.S. Public Health Service found no visible evidence of conditions that it believed to be unhealthy to humans below Beardstown.[40]

Response to Industrial Wastes, 1927–1940

A combination of factors brought about a politically vigorous but ineffective response to industrial pollution during the 1930s. The involvement of the federal government in water-quality and sewage-treatment issues directed attention toward factory effluent. Meanwhile, advances in sewage-treatment systems offered encouragement for dealing with many industrial wastes, and a growing corps of sanitary engineers advocated this emerging technology. Furthermore, the state legislature created a new agency with the specific responsibilities of monitoring water quality and enforcing pollution regulations.

The first signs of policy change can be seen in political statements and public referenda on sanitary-district formation. Congressmen from the affected region called for reductions in the volume of untreated urban effluent. One, Henry Rainey, told his constituents that "the Illinois River with all of its romance and its beauty gone, has now become the greatest and most offensive open sewer to be found anywhere on the face of the earth."[41] The gradual adoption of sewage treatment along the Illinois River, and on other waterways in the state, exemplified growing public support for pollution control. Peoria voters, for example, passed a referendum to organize a sanitary district and begin planning a treatment works in 1927.[42] In evaluating the city's needs, engineers noted that manufacturers discharged approximately 28.65 million gallons of wastes a day into the Illinois River, more than half the city's total. Completed in 1931, the Peoria sanitary works had inadequate capacity to treat this large volume of factory wastes. After the repeal of prohibition in 1934, the industrial discharges increased when the numerous distilleries resumed large-scale operations. Consequently, the Peoria Sanitary District reported that a serious condition existed on the Illinois below Peoria and encouraged industries to reduce their discharges.[43] The installation of treatment facilities at Peoria had little impact on the release of industrial effluent.

As local officials grappled with Peoria's wastes, two other political developments unfolded. First, in 1929 the U.S. Supreme Court ruled that Chicago must reduce the volume of water diverted through the Sanitary and Ship Canal. To offset this loss of dilution water, the court ordered Chicago to install additional treatment works by 1935 and instructed other river towns to provide treatment by 1938. Although the court demanded improved sewage treatment, it became essential for municipalities to discharge their effluent to the river to maintain adequate water levels for navigation and to offset the reduced flow from Chicago.[44] Second, the Illinois General Assembly created the Sanitary Water Board (SWB) in 1929. The legislature assigned the board duties of investigating and determining ways of eliminating "all substances and materials which pollute" the streams and waters of Illinois. The board also received powers to order those who polluted "waters of the state" to cease and to issue a fine of $100 for each day the offense continued. This wording expanded the SWB's authority beyond public water supplies and eliminated any upper limit to the penalty.[45]

The legislative mandate appeared stronger than that of the Rivers and

Lakes Commission, but the SWB had to seek voluntary, rather than court-ordered, abatement actions. To enforce the law, they had to prove an industry was harming the quality of the stream. For a large and severely contaminated stream like the Illinois, this was extremely difficult. Furthermore, prior legislation excluded the Sanitary District of Chicago from enforcement actions by the state. Consequently, the SWB made greater progress in curtailing industrial pollution through cooperative arrangements than through legal action. In the late 1930s, the board's efforts became more vigorous as Works Project Administration funds for constructing municipal sewage-treatment works became available and as reductions in the volume of Lake Michigan diversion were impending.[46]

In 1935 the SWB wrote to Joliet officials that area residents had filed numerous complaints about the "sewage nuisance and insanitary conditions" there. They also stated that "the discharge of untreated domestic sewage and industrial wastes have contributed to the pollution of the Illinois River." This came as a follow-up to an earlier letter urging Joliet to undertake voluntary installation of treatment facilities or face action from the SWB. Voters in Joliet apparently did not share the SWB's concerns and rejected a petition to form a sanitary district. As a consequence, the SWB and Joliet remained in conflict over sewage treatment for several years. In 1938, the SWB surveyed industrial waste sources and noted several manufacturers discharging untreated wastes to the Sanitary and Ship Canal. Among the sources were an agricultural-implements manufacturer, a paint factory, and a producer of rubber products. A cooperative approach did not work in Joliet.[47]

SWB efforts proceeded further downstream as well. La Salle, the next industrial community, received notification from the Sanitary Water Board that they must "give serious consideration to the question of sewage treatment." Clarence Klassen, the SWB Technical Secretary, wrote:

> Quite naturally the municipalities along the Illinois River were reluctant to proceed with any such improvements [adequate sewage treatment] in view of the pollution which Chicago was discharging to that particular stream.[48]

Subsequent to its initial letter, the SWB called for a meeting with local officials and industries. The local newspaper reported that "some of the river men believe this reduction [the court-ordered reduction in Lake Michigan flow] of fresh water will, in times of drought, cause the Illinois to become a stagnant cesspool because the sewage from other cities aside from Chicago will still be pumping into it." The technical secretary for the Sanitary Water Board implored the community leaders to begin immediate work on treatment facilities with the stated objective of "restoring the Illinois to its original state." He reported that "75 per cent of the industrial wastes have been cleaned up" and "many communities on streams tributary to the Illinois are already treating their sewage." By 1941 La Salle had submitted plans for a treatment facility to the SWB for its approval. Yet, despite a strong policy, vigorous attempts to enforce it, and promises to comply, La Salle failed to get its treatment facility operational by 1950.[49]

The Sanitary Water Board claimed that its program of encouragement was making significant inroads on the pollution problem and reported that five communities had treatment plants under construction within nine months, and six others passed bond issues clearing the way for construction. Success was tempered by the inability of communities to treat all industrial wastes or even maintain their new plants. Havana responded to the state's 1938 appeal for improved treatment facilities but found its plant was the object of frequent inspections and letters of reprimand during the 1940s, after it failed to operate efficiently for six years.[50]

Even manufacturers that undertook pollution-control projects encountered difficulties. In 1930, the Commercial Solvents Corporation of Peoria began experimenting with methods to reduce the volume of organic solids it was dumping into the Illinois River. By 1938 Commercial Solvents had developed a process to recover corn waste and resell it as feed, but there was no market for the product. Ultimately, fifteen years passed before the company ceased to discharge the daily pollution equivalent of 470,000 people into the Illinois River, even though it was constantly under pressure to reduce this load. In this situation neither policy nor technology provided an effective control of environmental deterioration.[51]

Surveys of stream pollution found that industrial wastes equivalent to the sewage of two million people continued to foul the Illinois River in 1937. The National Resources Committee mentioned that pollution in the Illinois River "threatens public health and has partially destroyed desirable fish and other aquatic life." Several years later, the state planning commission surveyed the status of treatment facilities in the Illinois River valley. On the upper river, the commission reported that thirteen industries discharged effluent into tributaries of the Illinois; only six of these operations had some form of treatment, albeit inadequate. Industrial effluent created polluting situations at ten communities along the lower river. Furthermore, the report discounted several sources of toxic metal and gashouse discharges—operations that were frequent targets of abatement orders during the 1910s. Even after overlooking these sources, the authors concluded that the lack of treatment facilities caused pollution and presented a health hazard.[52]

The SWB recognized the importance of industrial wastes and called for pollution-abatement policies that would accommodate industrial expansion while still protecting water quality, especially in the Peoria and Pekin reach of the waterway.[53] Effective action, however, was delayed during World War II, while most of the professional staff were drawn into the military sanitation service. Consequently, those pushing to improve treatment awaited federal involvement in the late 1940s.

Post-1945 Period

Following World War II and subsequent passage of the Federal Water Pollution Control Act (1948), the Sanitary Water Board intensified its pressure on municipal treatment facilities. A survey of the industrial waste situation in Peoria identified numerous sources of factory effluents entering the Illinois River and reported that industries discharged the annual pollution equivalent of nearly 700,000 people. The SWB recommended that those discharging the greatest quantity either must develop improved recovery systems or install some type of primary treatment. Nevertheless, such advice did not always elicit the desired results. For example, National Cylinder Gas Company in Peoria constructed a lagoon to hold its effluent, thereby preventing suspended solids from directly entering the river. However, the company periodically cleaned the sludge from the bottom of the lagoon, and workers simply dumped it along the banks of the Illinois, where it washed into the waterway at high stage or when transported by storm runoff.[54]

In response to the federal legislation, the SWB inventoried municipal treatment facilities and surveyed pollution in the Illinois River. The inventory identified existing treatment facilities, without directing attention to the well-known industrial-waste problem. The inventory did point out, however, that most larger towns had treatment works, but many were outdated, in disrepair, or had insufficient capacity for postwar demands.[55] Peoria sought to improve its facilities, but found large-volume waste generators unwilling to pay a fair price for sewage treatment. The sanitary district complained that industries refused to consider the cost of waste treatment as part of their production costs; and as a consequence, it was unable to raise funds required to expand and update its facilities. Nevertheless, as complaints of industrial-waste problems flowed into the state Sanitary Water Board, Peoria sanitation officials attempted to persuade its industrial customers to bear a greater share of the costs.[56]

A survey of water quality in 1950, although fairly optimistic, found that over 110 miles of the waterway had pollutional life forms and that clean conditions existed in only very short stretches (Fig. 9-4). One of

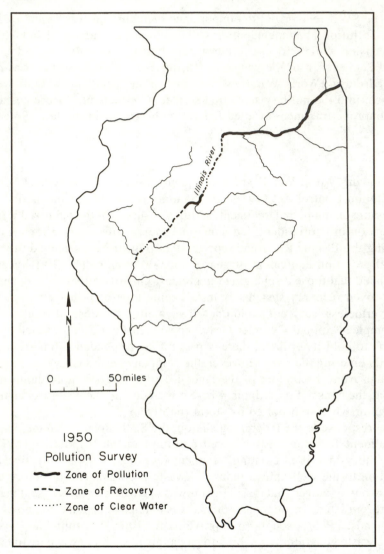

Figure 9-4. Pollution conditions on the Illinois River in 1950. (After Illinois River Pollution Commission, *Report*, 1951.)

the clean areas was Peoria Lake, where organic pollutants from upstream nearly reached complete decomposition before the river received large quantities of industrial wastes at Peoria. Clean water conditions also existed at intervals downstream from Beardstown. Most of the rest of the river was characterized as in "recovery." Industrial wastes entering the river were equivalent to that of 1.9 million people (only slightly reduced

from the 1937 total), or twice the domestic sewage load, and were recognized as a far greater problem than municipal sewage. Although over
90 percent of factory effluent received some form of treatment, phenols,
acids, and oils still caused serious degradation of water quality. A report
of the Illinois River Pollution Commission discussed the serious problem
created by industrial wastes and spelled out the legal authority under
which the SWB could take action against manufacturers.[57]

Illinois law defined pollution as conditions that caused "kills or was
injurious to fish life." Water quality, as reflected by the commercial
fishery, deteriorated through the 1950s. Fishermen reported landing 5.6
million pounds of fish in 1950. Although slightly higher than the total for
1931, the 1950 catch represented a postwar peak. Over the next ten years,
the total catch fell to about two million pounds. The decline reflects poor
conditions for commercial species such as buffalo, catfish, and even the
hardy carp. There was no loss of breeding grounds comparable to what
had occurred during the first third of the century; poor water quality and
the associated loss of food sources were much more of a factor during
the 1950s. Species diversity declined and carp seldom reached commercial size, thereby limiting the viability of the fishing industry. Mussels
and mussel gathering declined as well, but the near disappearance of this
trade from the Illinois reflected the displacement of shell buttons by
plastics. By the 1960s, the cumulative effects of deteriorating water quality
and loss of breeding grounds had effectively eliminated the commercial
fishery on the Illinois River.[58]

Investigations of water quality and waste treatment have accepted the
decline of fishing and offered little mention of salvaging the once-im-
portant commercial activity. Additionally, there has been no prosecution
of polluters who contributed to the destruction of aquatic life. In 1957,
the U.S. Department of Health, Education, and Welfare (USHEW) inventoried waste-treatment facilities and sources of pollution along the Illinois River. By including industrial sources, the inventory clearly indicated the growing concern with factory wastes and the increasing inability
of municipal treatment works to accommodate the complex industrial
effluent. The USHEW reported 156 sources of factory effluent in the
state, and of those, 53 offered no treatment. Along the Illinois River, the
lack of treatment was concentrated in the upper reaches of tributary
streams—in the Chicago metropolitan region—where water quality was
already the poorest. Most of the industries providing treatment simply
removed suspended solids (primary treatment) by allowing them to settle
out in lagoons or by passing the effluent through a mechanical screening
device. This type of treatment reduced the oxygen demand placed on the

receiving stream but did nothing to eliminate toxic or acidic substances. Dilution remained the treatment for such wastes.[59]

In 1963, the USHEW reported that the amount of industrial wastes entering the Illinois River was equivalent to the pollution load of a population of nearly 900,000 people (down from approximately 2 million in 1937) or about 36 percent of the total sewage load. This study recommended that industries either send their wastes through municipal works or install facilities on site; by complying, the sewage's population equivalent could be reduced to less than a quarter of a million people. This report also indicated that treatment facilities installed during the twentieth century had offset human population increases, but biological studies showed the reductions in sewage and industrial wastes were not sufficient to allow the river to recover. Furthermore, primary and biological treatment of industrial wastes failed to eliminate toxic elements in the final discharge. The loss of twenty-five species of mussels between 1900 and 1966 (Fig. 9-3) is the strongest evidence of the long-term impact of continued use of the Illinois River as a sewage sluice.[60]

Conclusions

Following decades of appeals for improved industrial and municipal sewage treatment and on the eve of the passage of the federal Clean Water Act, the Illinois River and its flora and fauna remained severely impacted by pollution. The state and federal governments continuously called for more sewage treatment and were largely successful in reducing the impact of domestic wastes. Yet every biological examination of the Illinois River after 1919 indicated extreme pollution in the upper reaches and an advancing wedge of pollutional conditions downstream. Dilution, the initial form of treatment called for by state law, introduced extremely heavy loads of mixed wastes into the upper river which largely wiped out aquatic life within two decades. When Chicago put its treatment facilities on line during the 1920s, many industrial sources never tied into the service network, and manufacturers located downstream continued to use the river as a sink for untreated effluents. The first state agency to police water quality took a vigorous stand against industrial polluters, but only on small watercourses. Later, agencies tried to work within the confines of unenforceable laws and inadequate sewage-treatment technologies. Even when pressed by federal courts or aided by federal subsidies, local governments failed to provide sufficient treatment facilities. Furthermore, the state relied on local governments and manufacturers to handle industrial wastes which were expensive and difficult to handle, and neither provided adequate treatment. Finally, during the 1950s and early 1960s federal programs provided financial means to improve municipal sewage-treatment facilities but allowed the industrial-waste problem to continue.

An examination of environmental legislation and related public policy is only a partial portrait of the environmental history of the Illinois River. Certainly, one has an impact on the other in the long run, but the environmental degradation of the Illinois River and the destruction of a major commercial fishery and mussel industry are long-term impacts of a slow-moving policy apparatus. For nearly a century, a variety of state and federal laws attempted to redress the biological damage done to the Illinois River by industrial and municipal wastes. Although some success can be measured, particularly since the early 1970s, the 1930s desire of the Sanitary Water Board to return the river to its original condition has never been achieved. Construction of treatment works for existing or even projected populations barely managed to maintain adequate capacity for the increasing numbers of urban residents and industrial customers, and was unable to reduce pollution to acceptable levels. The continuation of severe pollution was largely the result of a conflicting policy that allowed the Chicago area to use the river with near impunity.

The biased statewide legislation sanctioned the use of the Illinois River for sewage dilution, and it remained in effect long after treatment technologies existed that could have minimized the impact of Chicago's sewage. Yet, the fact that the largest city in the state had the legal right to use the waterway to protect its drinking-water supply rendered opposing arguments useless. Politics and policy obviously played an important role, yet the geographic characteristics of the waste-disposal needs of Chicago and legislation that sanctioned its practices overrode subsequent laws and hindered the effectiveness of the regulatory agencies. The very policy that protected Chicago's potable water supply was incompatible with actions taken to protect the water quality of the Illinois River and indirectly authorized destruction of public biological resources. The agreements reached between the state and the Sanitary District of Chicago seriously reduced the effectiveness of the state water-quality authority and caused uneven enforcement of water-pollution statutes. Policy was applied to small streams but not to the larger waterway. Furthermore, industry remained in the background of policy, with the exception of the Chicago stockyards, until the late 1950s. Manufacturers were encouraged to provide treatment, although progress in this area remained inadequate according to contemporary observers.

Policy, therefore, cannot be viewed as uniform in its geographic impact or consistent over time. To equate the passage of laws with pollution control, at least in terms of the Illinois River, is misleading. Environmental histories must consider the environment as well as the policies that impact it.

Acknowledgments

This project was funded in part by grants from the Illinois Hazardous Waste Research and Information Center and the National Endowment for the Humanities. I thank Ted Samsel and Julie Snider for their valued cartographic contributions, Doug Moore for research assistance, and Steve Havera and Clarence Klassen for comments on an earlier draft.

Notes

1. A critique of the post- 1960 water pollution laws is A. Myrick Freeman, "Water Pollution Policy," *Public Policies for Environmental Protection*, P.R. Portney, ed. (Washington, D.C.: Resources for the Future, 1990), 97–150. Donald Worster criticizes the historians' traditional emphasis on policy in "Seeing Beyond Culture," *Journal of American History* 76 (1990): 1142–47. Two excellent examples of environmental history not limited to policy matters are W. Cronon, *Changes in the Land: Indians, Colonists, and the Ecology of New England* (New York: Hill and Wang, 1983) and R. White, *Land Use, Environment and Social Change* (Seattle: University of Washington Press, 1980).

2. An extensive discussion of pollution policy is found in J.A. Tarr, "Industrial Wastes and Public Health: Some Historical Notes, Part I, 1876–1932," *American Journal of Public Health* 75 (1985): 1059–67. Tarr examined industrial wastes specifically in "Searching for a 'Sink' for an Industrial Waste: Coke Production and the Environment," paper presented to the American Society for Environmental History, Houston, Texas, March 2, 1991. See also, J.A. Tarr, "The Evolution of Wastewater Technology and the Development of State Regulation: A Retrospective Analysis," *Retrospective Technology Assessment*, J.A. Tarr, ed. (San Francisco: San Francisco Press, 1977), 165–90; "The Search for the Ultimate Sink: Urban Air, Land, and Water Pollution in Historical Perspective," *Records of the Columbia Historical Society of Washington, D.C.* 51 (1984): 1–29.

3. The lag between the recognition of poor water quality and public policy on the Mississippi River is discussed by P.V. Scarpino, *The Great River: An Environmental History of the Upper Mississippi, 1890–1950* (Columbia: University of Missouri Press, 1985), esp. chs. 1 and 3.

4. Illinois Department of Public Health, *Data on Illinois Public Water Supplies* (Springfield, Ill.: 1938), 16 and *Examination of the Municipal Water Supplies of Illinois* (Springfield, Ill.: 1908).

5. J.H. Rauch, ed., *Water Supplies of Illinois and the Pollution of its Streams*, Illinois Department of Public Health, (Springfield, Ill.: 1889), 1.

6. Rauch, *Water Supplies*, xvii.

7. Quote in Rauch, *Water Supplies*, xvii. J.H. Long, "Chemical Investigations of the Water Supplies of Illinois," in Rauch, *Water Supplies*, 14–29; this point is echoed in J.A. Harmon, *Report of a Preliminary Sanitary Survey of the Illinois River Drainage Basin*, Illinois State Department of Health, (Springfield, Ill.: 1901), 100–1.

8. Illinois Board of State Fish Commissioners, *Commissioners' Report, 1899–1900* (Springfield, Ill.: 1900), 12 (hereafter cited as Fish Commissioners, *Report*).

9. J.W. Alvord and C.B. Burdick, *Report of the Rivers and Lakes Commission on the Illinois River and Its Bottom Lands* (Springfield, Ill.: 1915), 65.

10. Fish Commissioners, *Report, 1896–1898*, 20 and *Report, 1899–1900*, 11.

11. The nuisance law is found in *Hurd's Illinois Revised Statutes* (Springfield, Ill.: Illinois Journal, 1874), para. 221.

12. Illinois State Board of Health, *Report of the Sanitary Investigations of the Illinois River and its Tributaries* (Springfield, Ill.: 1901), xiii.

13. L.P. Cain, *Sanitation Strategy for a Lakefront Metropolis* (DeKalb: Northern Illinois University Press, 1978), 107–109.

14. City of Joliet, *Charter and Revised Ordinances* (Joliet, Ill.: Joliet Republican, 1902), 274 and City of Peoria, *Laws and Ordinances* (Peoria, Ill.: J.W. Franks and Sons, 1892), 597.

15. M.O. Leighton, *Pollution of Illinois and Mississippi Rivers by Chicago Sewage*, 59th Cong., 2d sess., 1907, H. Doc. 788, 149.

16. *Peoria Journal*, January 23, 1900, 6.

17. *Peoria Journal*, January 25, 1900, n.p.

18. *Peoria Journal*, January 18, 1900, 6.

19. Fish Commissioners, *Report, 1900–1902*, 13.

20. Leighton, *Pollution*, 144–45.

21. Alvord and Burdick, *Report*, 65.

22. L.E. Cooley, *The Diversion of the Waters of the Great Lakes* (Chicago: Sanitary District of Chicago, 1913), 44.

23. Alvord and Burdick, *Report*, 70.

24. Alvord and Burdick, *Report*, 74; in 1899 2,341 fishermen worked the Illinois, and by 1908 the number had risen to 4,359.

25. Fish Commissioners, *Report 1902–1904*, 32.

26. An extensive account of the process of levee building and wetland drainage by John Thompson is tentatively titled *From Carp to Corn* and is being prepared for publication by a major university press. Also see John Thompson, *Case Studies in Drainage and Levee District Formation and Development on the Floodplain of the Lower Illinois River, 1890s to 1930s*, University of Illinois Water Resources Center, Special Report 016 (Urbana: 1989).

27. Alvord and Burdick, *Report*, 72 and LeRoy Sherman, *Stream Pollution and Sewage Disposal with Reference to Public Policy and Legislation, Illinois Rivers and Lakes Commission Bulletin* 16 (Chicago: 1915), 6.

28.   *Illinois Revised Statutes* (Chicago: Hurd's, 1889), para. 202, 487. See J.L. Leal, "Legal Aspects of Water Pollution," *Public Health: Reports and Papers of the American Public Health Association* 27 (1901): 103–12.

29.   *Illinois Revised Statutes* (Chicago: Hurd's, 1899), 687–88. *Illinois Revised Statutes* (Chicago: Hurd's, 1889), 305–13 gave the Sanitary District of Chicago legal authority to release wastes into the Illinois River system as long as they maintained a certain volume of discharge. By 1927 state law prohibited the discharge of any "chemicals, industrial wastes or refuse, poisonous effluent or dye-stuff, . . . or any other substance deleterious to fish life" into waterways of the state, with the exception of the Des Plaines (which fed Chicago's wastes into the Illinois River). See A.M. Bushwell, "Pollution of Streams in Illinois," Illinois State Water Survey *Bulletin* 24 (1927): 10.

30.   See Sherman, *Stream Pollution*, 15. Also 16, for a discussion of local nuisance law which effectively applied only to discharges within municipal limits.

31.   Illinois Rivers and Lakes Commission, *Annual Report* (Chicago: 1913–1916). Each annual report contained a listing of cases heard and resolved by the commission.

32.   S.A. Forbes and R.E. Richardson, "Some Recent Changes in Illinois River Biology," Illinois Natural History Survey *Bulletin* 13:6 (1919): 139–56.

33.   H.B. Mills, W.C. Starrett, and F.C. Bellrose, *Man's Effect on the Fish and Wildlife of the Illinois River*, Illinois Natural History Survey Biological Notes 57 (Urbana, Ill.: 1966).

34.   W.C. Starrett, "A Survey of the Mussels of the Illinois River: A Polluted Stream," Illinois Natural History Survey *Bulletin* 30:5 (1971): 267–403, see 351.

35.   R.E. Greenfield, "Comparison of Chemical and Bacteriological Examinations made on the Illinois River during a Season of Low and a Season of High Water—1923–1924," Illinois State Water Survey *Bulletin* 20 (1925): 16–17 and C.S. Boruff and A.M. Buswell, "Illinois River Studies, 1925–1928," Illinois State Water Survey *Bulletin* 28 (1929).

36.   The U.S. Public Health Service saw the Illinois River as an excellent laboratory for continuing its investigation of natural purification of streams. The summary of 1921–1922 fieldwork is J.S. Hoskins, C.C. Ruchhaft, and L.G. Williams, "A Study of the Pollution of the Illinois River," U.S. Public Health Service, *Public Health Bulletin* 171 (1927): 10–18. Also see Cain, *Sanitation Strategy*.

37.   Hoskins et al., "Study," 26.

38.   H.R. Crouhurst, *Report on an Investigation of the Pollution of Lake Michigan in the Vicinity of South Chicago and the Calumet and Indiana Harbors, 1924–1925* (Chicago: Sanitary District of Chicago, 1926); and Cain, *Sanitation Strategy*, 107–25. Also, Borduff and Bushwell, "Illinois River"; and Bushwell, "Pollution of Streams in Illinois."

39.   C.E. Colten, "Industrial Wastes in Southeast Chicago: Production and Disposal, 1870–1970," *Environmental Review* 10 (1986): 93–106; and Bushwell, "Pollution of Streams," 10.

40. W.C. Purdy, "A Study of the Pollution and Natural Purification of the Illinois River," U.S. Public Health Service *Bulletin* 198 (1930): 2; and Mills et al., "Man's Effect."

41. A 1925 speech by Illinois Congressman Henry T. Rainey quoted in R.A. Waller, "The Illinois Waterway from Conception to Completion, 1908–1933," *Journal of the Illinois Historical Society* 65 (1972): 254.

42. *Peoria Journal* April 1, 1927, 6 and June 7, 1927, 1.

43. Pearse, Greeley, and Hansen, Engineers, *Peoria, Illinois: Report on Sewerage and Sewage Disposal* (Chicago: 1926), 72; Greater Peoria Sanitary District, *Past, Present, Prospective* (Peoria, Ill.: 1966), 21; Peoria Sanitary District, *The Illinois River Below Peoria* (Peoria, Ill.: 1935), 1.

44. Wisconsin et al. vs. Illinois 281 U.S. 179 (1929); C. Lynde, "The Controversy Concerning the Diversion of Water from Lake Michigan by the Sanitary District of Chicago," *Illinois Law Review* 25 (November 1930): 243–60.

45. *Hurd's Illinois Revised Statutes* (Chicago: Hurd's, 1929), 239–40.

46. Clarence Klassen, former Director of the Illinois Sanitary Water Board (hereafter referred to as SWB), interview with author, January 17, 1986. "The Sanitary Water Board," *The Digester* 2 (August 1935), 2.

47. SWB to City of Joliet, May 7, 1935, microform records, Illinois Environmental Protection Agency, Water Pollution Control Division, Springfield, Illinois (hereafter referred to as IEPA records); SWB to City of Joliet, March 25, 1935, IEPA records; SWB, Joliet Pollution Survey, November 10, 1938, 1, IEPA records.

48. C. Klassen to Mayor H.M. Orr of La Salle, Illinois, June 28, 1937, IEPA records.

49. *La Salle Daily Post-Tribune* April 25, 1938, 1–2 and April 26, 1938, 1. City of La Salle to SWB, June 26, 1941 and SWB to City of La Salle, April 11, 1950, IEPA records. See also, "A New Stage in Illinois River Pollution Abatement," *Public Works* 69 (1938): 34–35.

50. "Give it Back to the Indians," *The Digester* 1 (February 1939), 1 and SWB to City of Havana, September 24, 1948, IEPA records.

51. M. Wheeler, "Commercial Solvents Corporation Waste Disposal Plan—Peoria, Illinois, Plant," *Proceedings of the Fifth Industrial Waste Conference Purdue University, November 1949*, 175–80. SWB, Summary of Industrial Waste Situation at Peoria, unpublished manuscript, April 16, 1945, IEPA records.

52. National Resources Committee, *Drainage Basin Committees' Reports for the Upper Mississippi Basins* (Washington, D.C.: 1937), 38. Illinois State Planning Commission, *Report on the Upper Illinois River Basin* (Chicago: 1939), 32 and *Report on the Lower Illinois River Basin* (Chicago: 1939), 40–41. Population equivalent was a term frequently used to allow comparison between different pollution sources. It referred to the BOD (biochemical oxygen demand) of biological wastes and chiefly serves as a measure of the volume of putrescible wastes in a waterway.

53. J.A. Tobey, "Legal Aspects of the Industrial Wastes Problem," *Industrial and Engineering Chemistry* 31 (November 1939), 1322. Also, C. Klassen, interview with author, January 17, 1986.

54.   SWB, Summary of Industrial Waste Situation at Peoria, April 1945, IEPA records. SWB to National Cylinder Gas Company, Peoria, July 27, 1950, IEPA records.

55.   SWB, *Data on Municipal Sewerage Works* (Springfield, Ill.: 1949) and Illinois River Pollution Commission, *Report*, Submitted to the 67th General Assembly of the State of Illinois (Springfield, Ill.: 1951).

56.   W.C. Starrett, Illinois Natural History Survey, to Sam Parr, Illinois Department of Conservation, January 19, 1951, complained of harmful wastes causing fish kills near Peoria, IEPA records. The Peoria Sanitary District lamented its inability to convince industry to pay a fair share of the costs of improved treatment. N.C. Seidenberg, "Special Charges for Treatment of Industrial Wastes at Peoria," paper presented to the annual meeting of the Illinois Sanitary Districts, Urbana, Illinois, September 14, 1951.

57.   SWB, *Report of Pollution Study, 1950* (Springfield, Ill.: 1950), Fig. 21, 40. Illinois River Pollution Commission, *Report*. Also, Illinois Legislative Council, "State Supervision over Local Water Pollution," Research Memorandum File 1–235, December 1950, M-7. This report states that the SWB's power to regulate industrial wastes rested in their authority to issue or deny permits for sewage-discharge outlets and their exclusive jurisdiction to determine when harmful pollution conditions existed.

58.   Mills et al., *Man's Effect* and Starrett, "Survey of the Mussels."

59.   U.S. Department of Health, Education, and Welfare, Public Health Service, *Municipal and Industrial Waste Facilities: 1957 Inventory*, V. 5 (Washington, D.C.: 1958).

60.   U.S. Department of Health, Education, and Welfare, Public Health Service, *Municipal Waste Facilities: 1962 Inventory, Region V* (Washington, D.C.: 1963) and Starrett, "Survey of the Mussels."

Part Four
Playing with Nature

10

Historical Coastal Environmental Changes: Human Response to Shoreline Erosion

Klaus J. Meyer-Arendt

The origins of coastal erosion as a perceived "problem" can be traced directly to the historical sequence of human settlement on wave-washed shores, a process stimulated by recreational predilections for this dynamic geomorphic environment and its idealized ambience. Concurrent with beachfront urbanization was a change in attitude toward the prevailing physical processes. Initial respect for marine forces prior to the late nineteenth century evolved into complacent acceptance and finally to combat and dominance—an attitude shift facilitated by a displacement of liability from the individual to government. Although the folly of this transition is today being realized, past legislative commitments to protect coastal communities from erosion are hard to undo. In this chapter, the evolution of policy responses to shoreline erosion in the United States will be outlined.

The Seaside Tradition in the United States

Although human attraction to the seashore may have its antecedents in the thallasotherapeutic (seawater therapy) pursuits of the ancient Greeks, the modern history of beach recreation is an outgrowth of the elitist spa phenomenon which swept northwestern Europe during the Middle Ages.[1] The "taking of the waters" at such resorts as Bath, Vichy, Espa, and Baden-Baden gradually became augmented by a "salt" component. The first modern sea bathing is traced to Scarborough, England (circa 1700), where a natural springs emptied out onto the beach.[2] Although sea bathing was initially confined to members of the elite, the Industrial Revolution—characterized by increasing urbanization, increasing wealth, a secularization of "holy days," and a corollary rise in leisure time—increasingly popularized spa and seaside resort visitation and development through-out England and continental Europe.[3] Diffusion of spas and seaside re-sorts to the overseas English colonies followed rapidly, and by the late eighteenth century, distinct spa-resort and seaside-resort landscapes had evolved in the new United States.[4]

As the seaside resort became popular in the United States, it was in-creasingly developed along exceptionally fragile and dynamic coastlines. Unlike in England where much of the coast is cliffed, the coast of the eastern United States—from Cape Cod to the Rio Grande—largely con-sists of low-elevation sandy beaches, barrier islands, and sand spits, environments that are geologically young and highly dynamic. While shoreline transgression associated with late Holocene and present-day sea-level rise affects all types of coasts, narrow strips of sands are par-ticularly vulnerable to erosion. Furthermore, conditions of equilibrium in barrier environments are easily upset by events such as storms or interference with longshore transport processes.[5]

In terms of human settlement, the dynamic character of sandy shore-lines dictated that permanent occupation would be subject to various levels of adversity. In England settlements could be located on bluff tops and removed from the adverse impacts of transgression and storms. In the United States, direct shorefront settlement was very vulnerable to ero-sion and destruction by wave action. This was recognized by the aborig-inal Indians, who did not select wave-exposed shorelines for permanent settlement sites. The first European settlers generally also avoided ex-posed shorelines, and where they did not (e.g., the Spanish at Pensacola, Florida), severe storms or hurricanes quickly stimulated shifts in settle-ment location.[6] With few exceptions, America's coastal cities became established in sheltered locations such as baysides, riversides, or leesi-des of barrier islands.

The Nineteenth Century: Changes in Attitude

Colonization of seashores for recreational and touristic pursuits in the nineteenth century led to changing attitudes toward coastal environments. Until about the 1870s, America's "recreational coastal frontier" expand-ed as recreationists experimented with, learned about, and attempted to adjust to a dynamic Nature that more or less remained in control. By the late nineteenth century, however, as ever more Americans flocked to the coast, the first signs of more brazen attitudes toward shore erosion ap-peared. Terms such as "stabilize" and even "combat" became more prev-alent.[7] With few exceptions, however, human reactions to beachfront losses were unorganized, and no policies resulted during the nineteenth century.

In the early 1800s, America's seaside resorts—still rather elitist and almost exclusively concentrated in the northeastern states—were mostly linked with the major urban hinterlands. Bostonians frequented Nahant, New Yorkers visited Coney Island and Long Beach, New Jersey, and Philadelphians sojourned at Cape May, New Jersey.[8] Wealthy Southerners—mostly from Virginia and the Carolinas but also planters from the lower Mississippi valley—traveled to northern resorts such as Cape May as well as Newport, Rhode Island, which was more an elitist summer-home colony than a beach resort.[9] Little is known about the impacts of storms and coastal erosion upon these resorts during this period, although the diminishing appeal of Cape May throughout the century has been attributed partly to the gradual disappearance of the sand beach.[10]

The diffusion of seaside resorts to the rest of the United States took place throughout most of the nineteenth century. This "frontier period" of coastal urbanization may be attributed to a complex interplay of cultural, economic, and technologic factors: (1) sea bathing remained extremely popular, and increasing numbers of Americans had sufficient disposable time and money to partake in the "pleasures of the seashore"; (2) technological advancement in transportation, notably the invention of the steam engine, facilitated—and lowered the cost of—travel, initially by steamship and later by railroad, to the popular resorts; (3) the late antebellum social rifting between the North and the South both reduced southern travel to the northern resorts but also propelled Southerners to establish their own resorts; (4) the post–Civil War opening of the West by railroad facilitated resort diffusion to Pacific shores (hence Newport, Oregon—perhaps the oldest seaside resort in the West);[11] and (5) a renewed interest in "thermalism" popularized winter recreation, which was, by the latter 1800s, both reinforced as well as stimulated by the southward extension of rail lines. The settlement histories of both southern California and Florida are integrally linked with resort development.[12]

Throughout the nineteenth century, the interaction of recreationists and dynamic shorefront environments was one of learning, experimenting, and coping. On the Gulf Coast, there was very little construction directly upon exposed shorelines until the late 1800s. Although wave-washed beaches were recreationally desirable, not only for bathing but also for sensory stimulation, the hazards of periodic hurricanes—well known by long-term residents—were acknowledged by early coastal recreationists. On the other hand, lower wave energy shorelines, such as Mississippi's mainland shores of Mississippi Sound and the Eastern Shore of Mobile Bay, were perceived as being safer. Many recreational settlements developed in such "sheltered" locations, from which excursions to the undeveloped exposed shores were easily made—e.g., Port Isabel to Padre Island in Texas. Also, hotels and cottages were built on higher ground, often a considerable distance from the beach, and only structures such as bathhouses or dance pavilions were built directly along the beach. In locales where suitably high elevations were absent, such as on Grand Isle, Louisiana, structures were raised several feet off the ground to keep ground floors dry during periodic storm-overwash events (Fig. 10-1).[13] Also, driftwood and sand dunes were usually left in place, as their role in retarding beach erosion was recognized. Until the onset of the winter recreation phenomenon, the summer-only tourism season normally ended by September 1, a date popularly regarded as the onset of hurricane season.[14]

Along with the expansion of rail lines, the diffusion of grand resort hotels to southern shores, and the institutionalization of annual southward migrations, the earlier precautions regarding shorefront settlement began to be ignored during the affluent Gilded Age. Sand dunes were mined for fill material, beach debris was removed to aesthetically improve the recreational resource, and hotels were built in previously undeveloped beachfront locations, many of which were known to be unstable by aboriginal and long-term residents.[15] The removal of natural protection from storms, coupled with often-rampant urbanization in the late nineteenth century, set the stage for direct confrontation between coastal residents and nature.

Variations of human response to storm-induced erosion and destruction during this period may be illustrated by case studies of Grand Isle, Louisiana, and Galveston, Texas. Both sites first experienced beachfront urbanization in the 1880s, and both were soon hit by major hurricanes: Grand Isle by the infamous Cheniere Caminada storm of 1893 and Galveston by the even more infamous Hurricane of 1900.[16] In Louisiana, where the entire settlement of Cheniere Caminada (population of circa 2,000) was destroyed, as were the three major hotels on Grand Isle, the response was one of abandonment. Cheniere Caminada was not rebuilt, and the surviving residents moved inland, some to the New Orleans area. Tourism development on Grand Isle was set back four decades. Not until highway access was provided in the 1930s did recreational urbanization recur.[17] The response in Galveston was different, perhaps in part because that city, the largest in Texas at the time, was a major commercial shipping center as well as a seaside resort. Even prior to the 1900 hurricane, beach erosion had been recognized as a problem, and the city had erected bulkheads and groins, and had outlawed the excavation of beach sand.[18] Following the storm, in which an estimated 6,000 inhabitants lost their

Figure 10-1. Surf bathing at Grand Isle, Louisiana, circa 1880. (Painting by John Genin, 1830–1895. Courtesy of the New Orleans Museum of Art, gift of Sam Friedberg.)

lives, a commitment to rebuild meant strengthening the coastal defense system to withstand future hurricanes. The result was one of the greatest coastal engineering projects ever undertaken in the United States. With local bond money, a five-mile-long (now expanded to ten miles), seventeen-foot high seawall was built, and 11,000,000 cubic yards of dredged sand were used to raise the grade of the entire city.[19] By 1911, a "new and improved" Galveston was ready to usher in a new era of shorefront tourism development.[20]

Elsewhere along America's developing shoreline in the late nineteenth century, responses to storms and accelerated erosion fell somewhere in between those of Grand Isle and Galveston. In this pre–Automobile Age period, a general reluctance to build on exposed coasts prevailed. Storm-damaged structures, although occasionally abandoned, were usually rebuilt by individual owners, and isolated efforts at installing shore-protection measures were made. For example, the same 1893 hurricane that temporarily halted tourism on Grand Isle struck the Mississippi coast, causing additional damage and loss of life. Although complaints were voiced, reconstruction was largely left up to individuals. Little evidence of organized resistance or policy response to erosion was noted.[21]

The Twentieth Century: Organization, Scientific Assistance, and Federal Involvement

The trend of organized involvement in "combatting encroachment of the seas" pioneered by the City of Galveston became more prevalent along America's shores as beachfront urbanization continued into the twentieth century. The beach became increasingly valued as a natural resource, and as the dollar value of coastal development increased so did the calls for protection from erosion.[22] Because early-twentieth-century demand for protection from erosion was increasingly directed at political bodies ranging from local governments to the U.S. Army Corps of Engineers, a better understanding of coastal processes was necessary. The growing field of coastal engineering needed scientific input from coastal geomorphologists, of which there were few at the time.[23]

At about the same time that coastal populations demanded more knowledge about the coastal environment, coastal process theories began to change. Previous explanations for coastal erosion—and perhaps for the nineteenth-century patterns of caution regarding beachfront structural development as well—relied upon a prevailing theory of land submergence. As the seaward edge of the eastern United States subsided at rates of one to two feet per century, wave action slowly moved landward in response. Thus, coastal erosion was seen as an integral aspect of the forces of nature, and organized political entities were reluctant to assist coastal property owners who had dared to defy nature and lost. However, after having studied several decades worth of sea-level data, Dr. Douglas W. Johnson, geology professor and later author of *Shore Processes and Shoreline Development* (1919), set out to debunk the land-submergence theory.[24] This change in thinking had the effect of giving the public an impression that (1) shorelines should theoretically be stable, (2) beachfront construction should not be as vulnerable to erosional forces as previously thought, and (3) any beach erosion that did occur should be able to be offset by structural or nonstructural countermeasures. In view of Johnson's premature dismissal of the land-submergence theory, the need for more research in coastal morphology and coastal engineering became evident.

The new attitudes toward coastal erosion, coupled with a rapidly expanding beachfront infrastructure, made apparent the need for more organized responses to erosion. First, individual property owners' attempts at structurally modifying the shore zone often were not only ineffective but also counterproductive. Second, highways, rail lines, and utilities were increasingly occupying beach-proximate corridors, and protection of such public and semipublic service infrastructure was considered implicit. Also, there was strong public support to keep beaches in the public domain. As early as the 1890s seaside communities in New Jersey were buying up private beach properties seaward of new coastal roads or boardwalks.[25] (The fact that this incipient beach-preservation movement began in response to an intensification of coastal development is somewhat analagous to the beginning of the national park movement at a time of increasing wilderness tourism only a few decades earlier.) When a series of severe storms in New Jersey during the winter of 1913–1914 caused much damage to coastal development, public demand for state involvement quickly increased. The State Board of Commerce and Navigation stressed to the state legislature "the importance of the protection of the the New Jersey beaches, realizing their tremendous value to the state and to the nation at large."[26] In Mississippi, petitions for state involvement in coastal protection followed a 1909 hurricane which caused serious damage to the shell road and a new interurban trolley along the rapidly urbanizing mainland coast (Fig. 10-2). After a much more severe hurricane in 1915 destroyed over half of the beach roadway, the state legislature in 1916 passed a law committing itself to protection of the beach highway. Although the law was soon declared unconstitutional, legislative lobbying continued.[27]

World War I temporarily interrupted trends of both coastal urbaniza-

Figure 10-2. Harrison County, Mississippi, circa 1911, the view looking east from the lighthouse toward Biloxi. (Photo courtesy Murella Hebert Powell, Biloxi Public Library.)

tion and organized efforts to stem shoreline erosion. However, the boom years of the Roaring Twenties witnessed a resumption of both, and for the first time, the federal government became involved. In 1922 the New Jersey legislature appropriated money for a comprehensive study of beach erosion, and an Engineering Advisory Board on Coast Erosion was formed.[28] Numerous federal agencies, including the U.S. Army Corps of Engineers (USACE), were represented on the board in advisory capacities. Although U.S. Army involvement in beach erosion began as a by-product of the military mission to construct coastal fortifications in the 1820s, not until this time was the erosion of privately developed lands seriously investigated.[29] The inclusion of the USACE in the new movement to halt erosion was party rationalized on the basis that navigational improvements—especially jetties—commissioned under the numerous Rivers and Harbors acts of the nineteenth century had resulted in increased erosion of adjacent beaches.[30] In one spectacular case that was not acknowledged until many years later, the resort of Bayocean, Oregon, gradually tumbled into the sea, as the shoreline readjusted to a new equilibrium after the USACE in 1917 constructed only a north jetty to maintain a navigation channel into Tillamook Bay.[31] Studies commissioned by the New Jersey Engineering Advisory Board on Coast Erosion resulted in the release of two technical reports (in 1922 and 1924) which did place the blame for some coastal erosion on nearby jetties constructed to maintain navigation channels.[32] The upshot of the studies was the increased role of the federal government, specifically the USACE, which was viewed as the logical agency to coordinate erosion-control efforts.[33] The USACE formed a Board on Sand Movement and Beach Erosion in the late 1920s, which was replaced by the Beach Erosion Board (BEB) in 1930. The BEB, in turn, was replaced in 1963 by the Coastal Engineering Research Center (CERC), today headquartered in Vicksburg, Mississippi.[34]

Also in the early 1920s, coastal geologist Douglas Johnson was able to form a Committee on Shoreline Studies under the Division of Geology and Geography of the National Research Council. This committee, which included geographers Isaiah Bowman, director of the American Geographical Society, and Nevin Fenneman, professor at the University of Cincinnati, felt that shoreline erosion was a matter of concern because (1) beaches were socially and economically important, (2) the constant attrition of such valuable lands resulted in large economic losses and threatened the existence of many communities, and (3) the scientific basis of shore protection–oriented coastal engineering was inadequate.[35] Among the activities of this committee was a public outreach to representatives of coastal communities and states throughout the country. This, in turn, resulted in the formation of a private organization—composed of coastal scientists, engineers, and public citizens—known the American Shore and Beach Preservation Association (ASBPA) in Asbury Park, New Jersey, in 1926. Established for the "welfare of shore and beach lands," the organization's mission was "to foster sound, far-sighted, and economical development and preservation of these lands."[36] One of the aims of the ASBPA was to get communities and states to recognize the need for federal involvement in shore protection, and the resultant grass-roots support played a part in the USACE decision to form the Beach Erosion Board. The ASBPA, which publishes the journal *Shore and Beach*, is still quite active today in shore protection and preservation issues.

Although the events of the mid-1920s were slowly leading to increased federal involvement in shore protection, local governmental responses to erosion still dominated until the early 1930s. Buoyed in part by successful local structural reactions to erosive forces of nature in Galveston as well as in Europe (notably Holland), local governments embarked on both isolated and comprehensive structural engineering projects. In Mississippi, the state legislature formed a Road Protection Commission (a.k.a. the Seawall Commission) in 1924, and with funds derived from a gasoline tax, it authorized a seawall fronting the entire 26.5-mile-long shorefront of Harrison County. Completed in 1927, the concrete seawall was billed as the world's longest, and similar seawalls subsequently were built fronting the developed portions of the two flanking Mississippi coastal counties.[37] The seawalls, thought to be successful (later to be proved false), afforded a false sense of security which in turn stimulated a tremendous tourism-development boom.[38]

The success stories of the Galveston and Mississippi seawalls notwithstanding, other local efforts at combating beach erosion were often poorly planned and unsuccessful. As in Mississippi, for a brief period individual states took on the financial responsibilities and the USACE provided the technical assistance. Because of lower construction costs, groins and bulkheads became the popularly prescribed structural solutions of the period, and even Miami Beach armored itself with them following the devastating hurricane of 1926.[39] Centrally organized erosion control was deemed essential for successful beach preservation, and the relatively successful groin fields of south Florida were contrasted by the often haphazard responses along the New Jersey coast.

Changes in Federal Policies: From the Flood Control Act to the Coastal Barrier Resources Act

In the aftermath of the Stock Market Crash of 1929 it became apparent that states or local governments could not finance comprehensive erosion control.[40] And although the BEB had been created in 1930 to provide technical expertise and coordinate local erosion control projects, there was strong opposition in Washington to using federal funds to protect private property. By 1934, however, Congress agreed to recognize that shoreline erosion was a public problem.[41] In the aftermath of severe storms during the winter of 1935–1936 which caused extensive flood damage in various interior states, Congress passed the Flood Control Act of 1936, which established that flood control was a proper activity of the federal government and that both public and private property could be protected by federal projects.[42] This policy was extended to shorelines, although "federal interests" had to be proved. The term was not clearly defined, but it has come to be interpreted in terms of public recreational resources, including public beaches even if backed by private property.[43] The Flood Control Act quickly stimulated federal involvement in beach-preservation/shore-protection projects on both coasts, including the creation of many miles of beaches in Southern California.[44] It also led to the first federal acquisition of a beach, in 1937—the Cape Hatteras National Seashore.[45]

The term "federal interests" in the Flood Control Act of 1936 was interpreted differently by the myriad federal agencies created in the economically depressed 1930s. Several "jobless-relief" agencies justified putting people to work on erosion-control projects throughout the United States, including a massive Works Progress Administration (WPA) dune-construction project on North Carolina's Outer Banks.[46] As with the Mississippi seawall, this project imparted a false sense of security which subsequently allowed much private development to take place on these fragile "ribbons of sand." In contrast, the Beach Erosion Board interpreted the 1936 act much more critically and refused to support federal financing of hard structural methods of erosion control throughout the 1940s and 1950s.[47] The emplacement of groins, bulkheads, and jetties remained quite popular at the local level during this period because of their relatively low cost, but the effectiveness of such structures would be increasingly questioned. The USACE did, however, endorse artificial nourishment as a compatible solution to beach erosion, and it completed numerous projects on both coasts. By the early 1950s, the USACE had received authorization to include potential impacts of hurricanes in its benefit-to-cost analyses when evaluating the feasibility of beach-nourishment projects.[48] As a result, beach construction projects flourished, and Mississippi was soon able to boast of "the longest manmade beach in the world" fronting what had become an erosion-threatened seawall in Harrison County.[49] Between 1936 and 1978, the USACE assisted coastal communities in the construction of seventy-five shore-protection/beach-nourishment projects at total costs of $109 million.[50]

During the rise of environmental consciousness in the 1960s and 1970s, legislative policies were increasingly perceived as contradictory. While the federal government on one hand tried to ensure a continuance of "public interest" which implied the preservation of nature and public accessibility, on the other hand it encouraged private development through subsidized flood-insurance and disaster-relief funds. Federally subsidized disaster insurance became available in the early 1950s, and federally subsidized flood insurance was made widely available to residents of flood-prone riverine and coastal environments following the National Flood Insurance Act of 1968.[51] The effect of this was to remove the individual risk in building in erosion-prone coasts, actually stimulating coastal construction and thereby increasing benefit–cost ratios used to justify shore-protection/beach-nourishment projects (Fig. 10-3). For example, the most costly federal shore protection project to date has been the beach nourishment of Miami Beach. In the discussion stage since the late 1950s, a federal commitment was made in the 1960s, and—after various delays, especially over issues of public access—the project was finally completed in 1980 at a total cost of about $80 million, half of which were federal dollars.[52]

However, the Miami Beach project was destined to be the last of the great federally funded beach-nourishment projects, as legislative policy

Figure 10-3. Atlantic City boardwalk, 1987. (Photo by Klaus J. Meyer-Arendt.)

shifted from subsidization of development to preservation. The National Environmental Policy Act (NEPA) of 1969 gave a new Environmental Protection Agency jurisdiction over coastal development to ensure "a balance between population and resource use which will permit high standards of living and a wide sharing of life's amenities."[53] In 1972, the federal Coastal Zone Management Act (CZMA) was passed, and coastal states were given incentives to prepare coastal-management programs which would outline development guidelines and monitor development practices.[54] Also, the National Park Service was given the mission to expand its national seashore program, and by 1972 the remaining nine of the present national seashores had been authorized for preservation.[55] Scientific evidence that sea level was indeed rising—and at accelerated rates—further supported the shift toward a policy of preservation.[56]

Although the various guidelines and legislation were intended to minimize development of coastal areas and to preserve and conserve the natural resources, coastal development has increased substantially since the laws were first enacted. First, the state governmental policies were not very effective due to both loose interpretation and lack of enforcement, and second, the federal flood-insurance program continued to stimulate new and more elaborate beachfront construction. (In spite of constantly changing minimum required ground-floor elevations, claims paid out in the wake of hurricanes continued to increase rapidly.) Various other federal programs were providing direct supports in the form of highway funds, sewer improvement funds, and other infrastructural assistance. By the late 1970s, a loosely organized coalition of coastal scientists, environmentalists, and fiscal conservationists called for more stringent legislation.[57]

In 1982, Congress passed the Coastal Barrier Resources Act (CBRA), which effectively withholds federal monies from any development on designated undeveloped barrier islands and mainland barrier shorelines of the Gulf and Atlantic coasts.[58] A 1985 proposed amendment to the act, adding existing protected land and near-shore water bottoms to the previously designated barriers, was adopted as the Coastal Barrier Improvement Act of 1990.[59] Although the acts preclude the federal government from legally preventing structural development on privately owned land, they could theoretically lower rates of development by withholding federal subsidies and passing on risks and higher costs to the private sector. Preliminary results showed that the CBRA legislation has indeed slowed rates of development at some of the designated CBRA barrier units, but land use is becoming more intensified (e.g., condominiums) as only major developers can afford to take the added financial risks.[60]

Although legislative policies are today reverting back to the "be cautious at the coast" attitudes that prevailed until almost a century ago, a commitment to protect existing coastal communities remains. Construction guidelines have become more stringent, federal flood insurance is still available, and in cases of severe storm damage and other (natural) causes of erosion, shore-protection projects are still completed. Structural methods of shore protection—including groins, breakwaters, and seawalls—have largely been replaced with more "nature-compatible" beach nourishment, including creative uses of dredged spoil.[61] However, there are increasing demands that federal involvement in beach nourishment be lessened. Orrin Pilkey of Duke University's Program for the Study of Developed Shorelines has argued that money spent on beach nourishment is essentially being flushed into the sea.[62] Although the USACE has not retreated from its mission of coastal "flood control," the federal government has been slowly decreasing its share of financial commitment and thereby increasingly placing responsibility for costs and risks in the hands of the local communities—as it used to be.

Conclusions: The U.S. Coastal Landscape in the Twenty-first Century

The present coastal landscape of the United States has evolved as a result of both "spontaneous occupation" and also regulatory policies. Until the onset of the twentieth century, coastal development proceeded slowly because of infrastructural hindrances coupled with a certain degree of respect for marine forces. More brazen attitudes toward shoreline erosion, reinforced by successful efforts at "combatting the sea" (such as erecting the Galveston seawall) and subsequent shifts in the science and engineering fields' attitude on erosion control led to increasing coastal urbanization and shorefront armoring. Although this rampant urbanization stimulated a shift to preservation, and the national seashore program, flood insurance, and infrastructural subsidization by various federal agencies actually permitted coastal construction to proceed at unprecedented rates during the 1970s. By the 1980s, the detrimental effects of tampering with beachfront ecosystems by structural means was realized and even "soft" shore-protection measures such as beach nourishment were being questioned. More importantly, environmentalists joined forces with fiscal conservatives to preclude further rampant urbanization of the country's shorelines by the withdrawal of federal subsidies.

As we enter the twenty-first century, the impacts of policies will continue to be manifested in the landscape. The historical record has given indications that the public attraction for the seashore is not diminishing, although rates of visitation and urbanization may fluctuate with the state of the economy. Since this finite resource will have been effectively parceled into preserved coastal segments and developed coastal segments and the latter perhaps subdivided into "grandfathered-in" federally subsidized development and CBRA (nonsubsidized) private development, the real-estate values will rise in response to demand for property. High-value real estate will effectively restrict development to low-density residential construction by the wealthy (again, a reversion to patterns of the past) or to high-density development in the form of high-rise hotels and condominiums. For many, enjoyment of the seashore will take only the form of visitation, as high costs will preclude beachfront vacation residence ownership. These patterns, already found along many segments of the United States coastline, will surely be further intensified in the next century.

Notes

1. Patrick Lavery and Carlton Van Doren, *Travel and Tourism: A North American European Perspective* (Huntingdon, Cambs., UK: ELM Publications, 1990).

2. E.W. Gilbert, "The Growth of Inland and Seaside Health Resorts in England," *Scottish Geographical Magazine* 55 (January 1939): 16–35.

3. J. Allan Patmore, *Recreation and Resources: Leisure Patterns and Leisure Places* (Oxford, UK: Basil Blackwell, 1983).

4. Henry W. Lawrence, "Southern Spas: Source of the American Resort Tradition," *Landscape* 27: 2 (February 1984): 1–12.

5. William Kaufman and Orrin H. Pilkey, Jr., *The Beaches Are Moving: The Drowning of America's Shoreline* (Durham, N.C.: Duke University Press, 1983).

6. Klaus J. Meyer-Arendt, "Modeling Environmental Impacts of Tourism Development along the Gulf Coast," *The Compass* 67 (Summer 1990): 272–83.

7. David G. McComb, *Galveston: A History* (Austin: University of Texas Press, 1986).

8. Charles A. Stansfield, Jr., "The Development of Modern Seaside Resorts," *Parks and Recreation* 5 (October 1970): 14–17, 43–46; Robert E. Snow and David E. Wright, "Coney Island: A Case Study in Popular Culture and Technical Change," *Journal of Popular Culture* 9 (1976): 960–75.

9. J.H. Franklin, *A Southern Odyssey: Travelers in the Antebellum North* (Baton Rouge: Louisiana State University Press, 1976).

10. Charles A. Stansfield, Jr., "Cape May: One of America's Oldest Resorts Makes a Comeback," *Vue Touristique* 1 (1977): 7–8 [Brussels].

11. Earl Pomeroy, *In Search of the Golden West: The Tourist in Western America* (New York: Knopf, 1957).

12. Ibid. and David Nolan, *Fifty Feet in Paradise: The Booming of Florida* (New York, Harcourt Brace Jovanovich, 1984).

13. Klaus J. Meyer-Arendt, "The Grand Isle, Louisiana Resort Cycle," *Annals of Tourism Research* 12 (1985): 449–65.

14. Ibid.

15. McComb, *Galveston.*

16. Ibid. and Frederic J. Stielow, "Isolation and Development on a Louisiana Gulfcoast Island, 1781–1962" (Ph.D. dissertation, Indiana University, 1977).

17. Meyer-Arendt, "The Grand Isle Resort Cycle."

18. McComb, *Galveston.*

19. Ibid.

20. Meyer-Arendt, "Modeling Environmental Impacts."

21. Charles L. Sullivan, *Hurricanes of the Mississippi Gulf Coast 1717 to Present* (Biloxi, Miss.: Gulf Publishing Company, 1985).

22. Mary-Louise Quinn, *The History of the Beach Erosion Board, U.S. Army, Corps of Engineers, 1930–63* (Fort Belvoir, Va.: Coastal Engineering Research Center, U.S. Army, Corps of Engineers, 1977).

23. Ibid.

24. Ibid.

25. *Proceedings, American Shore and Beach Preservation Association* (ASBPA) (Trenton, N.J.: MacCrellish and Quigley, 1930).

26. Quinn, *History of the Beach Erosion Board.*

27. *Proceedings, ASBPA.*

28. Quinn, *History of the Beach Erosion Board.*

29. Jamie W. Moore and Dorothy P. Moore, "The Corps of Engineers and Beach Erosion Control 1930–1982," *Shore and Beach* 51 (January 1983): 13–17.

30. Quinn, *History of the Beach Erosion Board.*

31. T.A. Terich and P.D. Komar, "Bayocean Spit, Oregon: History of Development and Erosional Destruction," *Shore and Beach* 42 (October 1974): 3–10.

32. Quinn, *History of the Beach Erosion Board.*

33. Moore and Moore, "The Corps of Engineers."

34. Ibid. and Quinn, *History of the Beach Erosion Board.*

35. Quinn, *History of the Beach Erosion Board.*

36. *Proceedings, ASBPA.*

37. Ibid.

38. Klaus J. Meyer-Arendt, "Human Impacts on Coastal and Estuarine Environments in Mississippi," *Coastal Depositional Systems in the Gulf of Mexico: Quaternary Framework and Environmental Issues,* Proceedings of the GCSSEPM Foundation 12th Annual Research Conference, Houston, Texas, December 8–11 (Austin, Tex.: Earth Enterprises, 1991), 141–48.

39. The Federal Writers' Project, *The WPA Guide to Florida* (New York: Pantheon Books, 1984 [1939]).

40. Moore and Moore, "The Corps of Engineers."

41. William J. Herron, "The Influence of Man Upon the Shoreline of South-

ern California," *Shore and Beach* 51 (July 1983): 17–27 and Moore and Moore, "The Corps of Engineers."

42. Rutherford H. Platt, *Land Use Control: Geography, Law, and Public Policy* (Englewood Cliffs, N.J.: Prentice-Hall, 1991).

43. Moore and Moore, "The Corps of Engineers."

44. Herron, "The Influence of Man."

45. Rutherford H. Platt, "Congress and the Coast," *Environment* 27 (July/ August 1985): 12–17, 34–40.

46. Moore and Moore, "The Corps of Engineers."

47. Ibid.

48. Ibid.

49. Charles L. Sullivan, Murella Hebert Powell, and Nedra A. Harvey, *The Mississippi Gulf Coast: Portrait of a People* (Northridge, Calif.: Windsor Publications, 1985).

50. Platt, "Congress and the Coast."

51. Rodney C. Emmer, "Flood Insurance: A Case Study of a Federal Land-Use Program in the Louisiana Coastal Zone," *Research Techniques in Coastal Environments*, H. Jesse Walker, ed., Geoscience and Man, Vol. XVIII (Baton Rouge: Louisiana State University School of Geoscience, 1977), 299–304. Lynn M. Alperin, *Custodians of the Coast* (Galveston, Tex.: U.S. Army Corps of Engineers, 1977).

52. Moore and Moore, "The Corps of Engineers."

53. Peter H.F. Graber, "The Law of the Coast in a Clamshell: The Federal Government's Role," *Shore and Beach* 49 (January 1981): 16–20.

54. Graber, "Law of the Coast."

55. Rutherford H. Platt, "Cities on the Beach: An Overview," *Cities on the Beach: Management Issues of Developed Coastal Barriers*, Rutherford H. Platt, Sheila G. Pelczarski, and Barbara K.R. Burbank, eds. (Chicago: University of Chicago Department of Geography, 1987), 3–14.

56. V. Gornitz, S. Lebedeff, and J. Hansen, "Global Sea Level Trend in the Past Century," *Science* 215 (1982): 1611–14.

57. William H. MacLeish, "Our Barrier Islands are the Key Issue in 1980, the 'Year of the Coast,'" *Smithsonian* 11 (September 1980): 46–59 and H. Crane Miller, "The Barrier Islands: A Gamble with Time and Nature," *Environment* 23 (November 1981): 6–11, 36–42.

58. David R. Godschalk, "The 1982 Coastal Barrier Resources Act: A New Federal Policy Tack," *Cities on the Beach: Management Issues of Developed Coastal Barriers*, Rutherford H. Platt, Sheila G. Pelczarski, and Barbara K.R. Burbank, eds. (Chicago: University of Chicago Department of Geography, 1987), 17–27 and Platt, *Land Use Control.*

59. Meyer-Arendt, "Modeling Environmental Impacts."

60. David R. Godschalk, *Impacts of the Coastal Barrier Resources Act: A Pilot Study* (Chapel Hill: University of North Carolina Department of City and Regional Planning, 1984) and Godschalk, "The 1982 Coastal Barrier Resources Act."

61. Klaus J. Meyer-Arendt and Karen A. Kramer, "Deterioration and Restoration of the Grande Batture Islands, Mississippi," *Mississippi Geology* 11 (June 1991): 1–5.

62. Orrin H. Pilkey, Jr., "The Engineering of Sand," *Journal of Geological Education* 37 (1989): 308–11 and Katharine L. Dixon and Orrin H. Pilkey, Jr., "Summary of Beach Replenishment on the U.S. Gulf of Mexico Shoreline," *Journal of Coastal Research* 7 (Winter 1991): 249–56.

11

Stemming the Flow: The Evolution of Controls on Visitor Numbers and Impact in National Parks

Lary M. Dilsaver

In May 1918, Secretary of the Interior Franklin Lane sent a letter to National Park Service (NPS) Director Stephen Mather establishing the policies and priorities of the two-year-old agency. They were to be based on three broad principles: (1) that the parks be maintained "absolutely unimpaired" for future generations; (2) that they be used for the observation, health, and pleasure of the people; and (3) that the national interest dictate all decisions affecting public or private enterprise in the parks. So that the priorities would be clearly understood, Lane reiterated, "Every activity of the Service is subordinate to the duties imposed upon it to faithfully preserve the parks for posterity in essentially their natural state."[1]

These instructions embodied both the letter and the spirit of earlier national park legislation. From the 1872 act establishing Yellowstone to the 1916 Organic Act founding the National Park Service, the same complex combination of purposes and the same theoretical priorities were repeated. And from that time forward the inconsistency of the dual goals of use and preservation have been interpreted, argued, and implemented in the more than 360 units of the national park system. Today, as in 1872, a small agency, itself philosophically divided, attempts to manage delicate natural resources in the contexts of both playground and preserve.

Both recreational use and preservation have evolved in practice and purpose. Recreation, vigorously encouraged for the first half-century, began with typical outdoor games and amusements more appropriate today to urban parks and recreation areas. Subsequently it changed to educational and inspirational purposes. However, the vast majority of infrastructural developments occurred during the early period for the larger and older parks. Meanwhile, preservation philosophy evolved at a much slower rate. From early techniques of simply protecting objects such as trees, animals, and wonderful curiosities, park managers generated an immature systemic policy of "atmosphere preservation" to protect entire scenes for solitude and inspiration. There is growing scholarly debate on whether the Park Service from the 1930s to the early 1950s had available sufficient scientific data to challenge this simplistic, image-oriented management and simply ignored it, or whether the science of ecology still could not furnish hard, trustworthy data to be seriously followed. It is probable that the truth lies somewhere between these two options. Nevertheless, by the 1960s, ecological data were both available and accepted. An increasingly science-driven National Park Service adopted ecosystem preservation with priorities ostensibly devoted to protection of ecological process and the biosphere.[2]

The fact that recreation development proceeded rapidly while preservation policy changed slowly allowed many unforeseen recreation impacts on park ecosystems. In descending order of magnitude, buildings, roads, campgrounds, picnic areas, and trails attracted increasing numbers of funseekers transforming delicate areas from wilderness to playground. Additional nonrecreation impacts, such as manipulation of animal populations, habitat clearing, water control and diversion, and ancillary economic functions, further belied the instructions to place preservation above all other policies.

Slowly at first but with increasingly anxious awareness as visitor numbers grew and preservation philosophy changed, the Park Service sought ways to minimize public impact while preserving the democratic spirit of free access for all who desired the park experience. They considered many options which recreation planners have grouped into two categories—indirect controls and direct controls. Indirect controls are those that try to influence or modify behavior, allowing the individual to retain freedom of choice. They include encouraging visitor dispersal and consciously avoiding provision of recreation infrastructure. Direct controls emphasize regulation of individual choice and include restrictions on access, zonation of use, and limits on size of groups, duration of visits, and absolute numbers allowed entry. In addition, deprivation of existing access or removal of extant facilities may also be considered direct controls because the public is aware that its opportunities are being curbed.[3]

As the National Park Service experimented with these controls, a pattern of coping strategies developed with the details dependent on local conditions of both resources and the visiting public. The purpose of this chapter is to examine the methods developed in four national park units

(Fig. 11-1)—limits on development area in Yosemite National Park, a ceiling on lodging capacity in Sequoia National Park, manipulation of visit duration in Muir Woods National Monument, and restrictions on access and absolute numbers in Channel Islands National Park. These strategies illuminate the reasons why visitor impacts occurred, allow construction of a general model of Park Service response to recreation effects, and encourage speculation on why the government will not adopt absolute limits in the most popular and heavily stressed units.

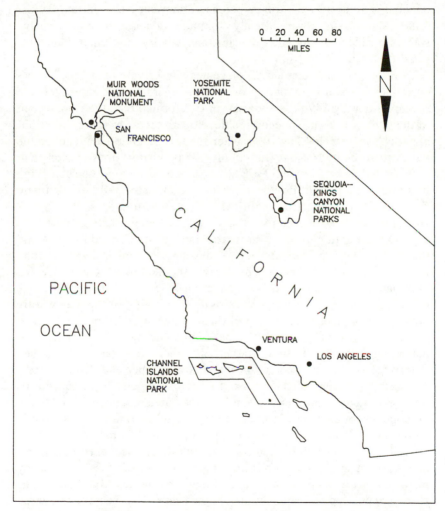

Figure 11-1. Four national park units in California are deluged with visitors from the state's 31 million residents as well as countless tourists from around the world.

Yosemite National Park

The national park movement in America truly began with the withdrawal of Yosemite Valley and the Mariposa Grove of giant sequoias in 1864. The valley with its 3,000-foot cliffs, spectacular waterfalls, and idyllic meadows quickly became a focus of wonder and worldwide attention. The State of California administered the three-quarter-by-ten-mile valley and, despite recommendations against development by a group empaneled to study it, encouraged extensive tourism construction. By the 1880s, some visitors were already complaining about the hotels, roads, stables, residences, orchards, dairies, and tawdry amusements that littered the valley floor.[4]

Development was conducted piecemeal by private enterprise. It occurred so fast and with such profound disregard for the more delicate resources that by 1890 the governor of California urged the Department of the Interior to refuse concession developers access to any new national parks.[5] Nevertheless, by 1906, when the federal government added the valley to Yosemite National Park, only 10,000 visitors arrived each year.

In 1916 the new National Park Service launched a vigorous campaign to attract visitors and provide superior and modern facilities for them. Their motives sprang from political self-preservation as well as philosophical ideals. The creation of the agency came about as part of a cantankerous split between conservationists, led by Gifford Pinchot and the men of the U.S. Forest Service, and preservationists, led by John Muir and Stephen Mather. A considerable segment of the public favored elimination of the apparently redundant Park Service and either transfer of the parks to Forest Service control or elimination of them as wholly unnecessary expenses. As leader of the new agency, Mather saw tourism as the justification for both the parks and the agency committed to managing them. In addition, Mather and other early Park Service men firmly believed in the recreation mandate as proper and democratic.[6]

Yosemite was one of the first and foremost targets for Mather in his tourism campaign. He designed and implemented a policy of concession monopolies for each park, forcing all the major operators in Yosemite to merge in 1925 into the Yosemite Park and Curry Company. With improved roads, considerable capital, vigorous government encouragement, and the promise of protection from competition, the concession company responded with rapid construction of new and improved lodgings. The structural buildup was concentrated at the east end of the valley between Yosemite Falls and Half Dome, in the most scenic and historically popular area. By 1927, park visitors had the luxurious Ahwahnee Hotel to add to their overnight options of tents, cabins, and campsites. All facilities were enormously popular. Over the fifteen years from the formation of the Park Service to 1931, visitors to Yosemite jumped from 33,000 per year to nearly half a million.[7] No longer was Yosemite threatened with elimination. No longer was the Park Service in danger of absorption by the Forest Service. No longer did anyone seriously question the worth of such a rich and enjoyable resort.

Yet with the waning political danger came realization that Yosemite Valley was still a threatened place, not politically, but at its heart. Preservation of the cliffs and waterfalls was easy. Preservation of the meadows, riverbanks, flora, and fauna was not so easy. Evidence of accelerating bank erosion along the Merced River, rutting and forest encroachment on the valley meadows, disappearance of some larger animal species, and cessation of sequoia regeneration troubled park rangers.

At the same time, park personnel were equally bothered by the loss of serenity and solitude. By the late 1920s, the Park Service provision for recreation as outdoor amusement had been replaced with a zealous mission to educate and inspire visitors in the sublimity of nature. The integrity or, if necessary, illusion of a natural "park experience" became the principal goal. It was carried out by a new type of ranger, the naturalist–interpreter, in a program first tried at Yosemite. As the interpretation program grew toward the familiar and popular institution it has now become, the mission grew more difficult among the clutter and crowds of the valley.[8]

In some desperation the Park Service sought advice from experts of natural science and landscape architecture. Beginning in July 1927, the Yosemite National Park Board of Expert Advisors, as part of a congressionally mandated study, examined the crowding problem and searched for ways to mitigate it in Yosemite Valley. The principal members were eminent landscape architect Frederick Law Olmsted, Jr., geologist John Buwalda, and Sierra Club members Duncan McDuffie and William Colby. Although they provided advice rather than mandates, their recommendations were carefully studied and usually followed.[9]

The reports of the advisory board during the decades of the thirties and forties provide a window onto the difficulties and differences of opinion over how to control visitor impact. Initially the board recommended indirect persuasion as a plan for management of visitors. Among the techniques tried were encouragement of off-season visits, travel to areas outside Yosemite Valley or to other parks altogether, and education of visitors to appreciate wilderness rather than resort. The results were winter crowds with no diminishment of summer numbers, new roads and development elsewhere in the parks, and a touring pattern that still focused on the valley, the linkage of other parks to Yosemite in more elaborate vacation trips, and ever-greater numbers seeking wilderness and finding a townscape in Yosemite.[10]

After these measures failed in the first half of the 1930s, opinion split within the board between two options. Buwalda favored some type of direct control on visitor numbers in the valley. Colby emotionally rejected such limits and proposed some kind of control on development which would theoretically allow visitor numbers to come to a natural equilibrium with available services. Other board members fell between these two options but when pressed leaned toward Colby's solution.[11]

As for the Park Service itself, the agency and its top men, all disciples of Mather, still shunned direct curbs on visitors which they feared might bring a perceived loss of recreation autonomy and thus corrupt the message and purpose of the parks as inspirational wilderness. But it soon became apparent that the Yosemite concession intended to continue building and seeking resort-minded visitors for its burgeoning operation. As indirect controls on visitors proved ineffective, the attention of park planners turned more and more to direct limits on the concessioner. This came hesitantly owing to the agency's fresh legacy of tourism promotion and the lingering sense that the concessioner had gone out on an economic limb in the far-flung park as a favor to Mather. Nevertheless, the harsh realities of overcrowding, a daily problem by the mid-1930s, coupled with concessioner calls for continued growth, made the choice of some unpopular solution inevitable.

After considerable philosophical and practical debate, the advisory board settled on a plan of placing spatial limits on structural development both by the concessioner and the government. This solution came about, in part, when by joint decision the company and the Park Service removed several buildings well to the southwest of present facilities. The spatial contraction obviously suggested a spatial solution to Yosemite's principal problem. In 1939, acting upon advisory-board recommendations, Superintendent Lawrence Merriam proposed specific boundaries to contain intensive use (structures) just west and east of the existing facilities (Fig. 11-2). Campgrounds, hotels, cabins, and both commercial and administrative buildings were to remain clustered in an area of approximately one and one-half square miles, or some 20 percent of the valley floor.[12]

After Merriam's proposal, the policy of spatial containment became implicit policy. The western boundary line subsequently became confused with another planning line and was thereafter called the "Olmsted Line," after the chair of the advisory board. In the mid-1970s, park planners revived the tacitly accepted line to block development of a parking

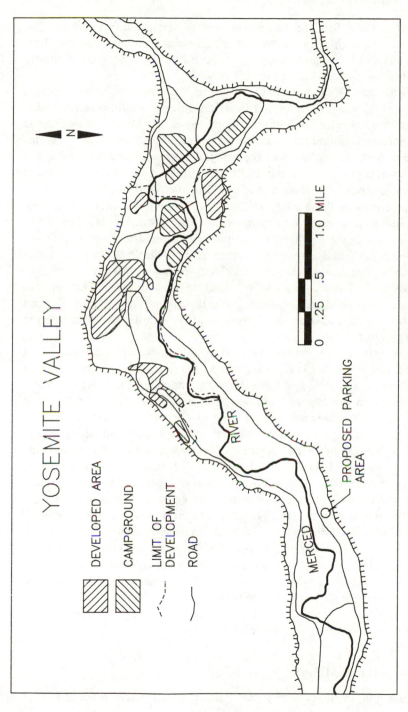

Figure 11-2. The eastern end of Yosemite Valley, tightly constrained by 3,000-foot vertical cliffs, contains five large campgrounds and one of the larger resort complexes in the American West.

lot at the foot of Taft Toe, well to the west of existing infrastructure. The demand for parking was acute, but the traditional integrity of the Olmsted Line and its eastern counterpart caused the Park Service to quietly drop the planned parking project.[13]

By the late 1960s, annual visitation to Yosemite Valley topped two million. Park rangers wondered if visitation ever would reach an equilibrium with service as Colby had suggested. Visitor accommodations had increased, although the combination of spatial limits and maintenance of park atmosphere had kept the increase small, but visitation had shot up 350 percent between 1939 and 1960.[14] Yosemite development became an emotional issue as the mood of the public and the preservation priorities of the agency shifted toward environmental protection. Park visitors now asked how many structures, how many cars, how many people the valley could handle unimpaired. Responding to pressure from the Sierra Club and other preservation groups, the Park Service implemented further spatial controls in 1970 by banning auto use in the easternmost end of the valley and substituting shuttle buses. This shift to direct control of visitors caused grave misgivings in the Park Service over the effectiveness of such a move and, especially, its impact on the general public.[15]

Preservationists remained largely unimpressed and responded that closure of a few roads hardly constituted a solution. They submitted that development had already gone way too far and that they wanted the most extreme extension of spatial containment, nothing less than the complete removal of structures and the banning of automobiles from the valley. They used National Environmental Policy Act (NEPA) planning procedures to barrage the Park Service with their opinions and helped shape a 1980 General Management Plan (GMP) calling for removal of most valley structures to areas outside the park. Meanwhile, entertainment giant MCA purchased the concession and embarked on a plan to maximize recreational activities. They brought pressure to abandon the GMP before MCA itself was purchased by a Japanese company. The negative implications of foreign ownership of a national park monopoly caused the Japanese to divest themselves of the concession and have left its future and that of the GMP in limbo. Amid the confusion and contention, the Park Service still struggles to please everyone by continuing to limit the area of development while allowing a diversity of lodgings and amusements to please any recreationist.[16]

Sequoia National Park

To the south, in Sequoia National Park, the Park Service faced similar pressures but responded differently due in large part to the efforts of one man—Superintendent John White. The focus of visitor and concession attention in Sequoia has always been a spectacular grove of giant sequoias known appropriately as Giant Forest. The 1,400-acre plateau contains more than 2,200 trees with diameters greater than eleven feet, the second largest and unquestionably the finest stand of the seventy-five that remain. In addition, Giant Forest is relatively accessible and sufficiently level to encourage substantial development of infrastructure (Fig. 11-3).

Although the park was established in 1890, Sequoia did not receive large-scale development until 1926, when the Park Service completed a major automobile access road. Then Mather applied his Yosemite-tested tourism policies, helping to establish a long-term concession monopoly, encouraging a rapid structural buildup, and aggressively promoting Sequoia, especially in the vast visitor pool of Los Angeles. In the next six years the concession increased its Giant Forest buildings by 500 percent. Annual visitation shot up from 11,000 in 1916 to more than 140,000 in 1931.[17]

However, unlike Yosemite's rock walls and waterfalls, the principal attraction of Sequoia lay in living trees. Although huge in size, sequoias have a fragile root system bunched within four feet of the surface and seeds requiring untrampled and burned mineral soils to regenerate. Imposition of roads, buildings, water lines, and sewage pipes impacted the trees, although the extent of damage remains difficult to calculate.[18]

Of greater immediate import to White, the forest of giants tolerated the chaos and noise of holiday amusements less comfortably than Yosemite. White was one of the chief proponents and spokesmen for the concepts of atmosphere preservation and parks as inspirational tableaux for the public.[19] In 1931, after witnessing the debacle of a Fourth of July weekend, he proclaimed Giant Forest impaired and demanded removal of all structures from the grove.[20]

Once again, to an agency with recent success in tourism promotion such an idea was clearly an anathema. Hence the Park Service typically resorted to indirect controls. They developed other portions of Sequoia and its neighbor park General Grant (now Kings Canyon National Park). They built trails and vigorously promoted back-country use. They also promoted off-season use and, finally, tried a weak direct control by placing a thirty-day limit on campsite occupancy. None of these measures had any more success in Sequoia than they did in Yosemite.

Concessioner Howard Hays meanwhile categorically rejected White's plan to remove facilities from Giant Forest and balked at infrastructural investment elsewhere. To one of White's encouraging letters Hays acidly responded:

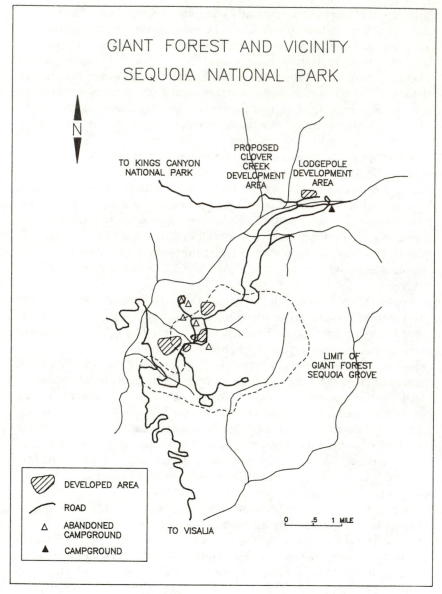

GIANT FOREST AND VICINITY
SEQUOIA NATIONAL PARK

N

TO KINGS CANYON
NATIONAL PARK

PROPOSED
CLOVER
CREEK
DEVELOPMENT
AREA

LODGEPOLE
DEVELOPMENT
AREA

LIMIT OF
GIANT FOREST
SEQUOIA GROVE

DEVELOPED AREA

ROAD

△   ABANDONED
CAMPGROUND

▲   CAMPGROUND

TO VISALIA

0   .5   1 MILE

Figure 11-3. Giant Forest in Sequoia National Park, at once the most super-
lative and most developed of the remaining seventy-five sequoia groves. Plans
to remove some 1,400 structures to the Clover Creek and Lodgepole areas have
met seventy years of concessionaire resistance.

No money payment as damages or expenses could compensate us for the moving of our Hotel from our previous site to (say) Lodgepole [a nearby pine-forested valley]. There is no national park feeling at Lodgepole.[21]

Director Horace Albright, perhaps the quintessential Mather man, who supported tourism in the national parks throughout his long life, also rejected White's removal plan and further chastened him for showing an "attitude problem" toward the concessioner. However, Albright was not insensitive to the potential damage and especially the corruption of appropriate atmosphere brought about by unchecked development. Hence, in 1931, amid some misgivings, Albright imposed a so-called pillow limit of 1,000 on Giant Forest. Although it was boosted to 1,250 in 1965, this absolute limit on lodging capacity has served to prevent runaway development and to mitigate some of the excesses that so troubled White in 1931.[22]

Muir Woods National Monument

Muir Woods, near San Francisco, also protects an ancient and delicate species of gigantic trees, in this case coast redwoods. Its proclamation as a national monument in 1908, under the Antiquities Act, protected the only stand of redwoods on national park land for more than fifty years. Yet in a deliberate departure from the more stringently preservationist spirit of the Antiquities Act, Muir Woods was established because of its proximity to a major urban center and consequent availability to the recreation public. Almost immediately the impractical results of this arrangement became obvious. National monuments were supposed to preserve objects of "historic and scientific interest" found on federal government land and were to be administered by whatever agency held those lands. It was assumed that designation of monument status and periodic administrative inspections would suffice, and no separate funds were provided to care for these "objects."[23] This worked well enough to protect various archaeological sites in the southwest from rampant exploitation and vandalism. However, having established Muir Woods as a visitor destination, the Department of the Interior found itself coping with a crush of visitors and no management funds or personnel. Congressman William Kent, who had donated the land for the monument, hired and paid a custodian for several years until the Department of the Interior could redress the embarrassing situation.[24]

Muir Woods, now some 550 acres in size, has remained a tiny pocket valley monument attracting increasingly huge annual crowds. In 1936 it hosted some 51,422 visitors, with hikers outnumbering auto passengers 2.25 to 1. But in 1939, after the opening of the Golden Gate Bridge and government purchase of the toll road leading to the monument, nearly 180,000 visitors poured into the tiny canyon. Auto passengers outnumbered hikers nearly eleven to one. Travel to Muir Woods in 1990 approached one and one-half million. The Park Service has used Muir Woods as a showplace, hosting hundreds of large parties including that of the founding delegates to the United Nations in 1945. In addition, Muir Woods figures prominently in commercial bus tours from San Francisco. Thus, for most years, foreign tourists account for 20 percent of the total visitors.[25]

As a result of the massive flow of visitors into this small monument, many traditional activities were halted. In 1923 rangers closed the only auto road and the following year banned camping. In 1933 fires were prohibited and fireplaces removed. Two decades later rangers moved all picnic facilities to the parking lot and by 1964 banned picnicking completely. Each of these steps directly curbed the behavior of visitors and shortened their visits by eliminating first overnight stays, then cooking, and finally eating within the forest. Still as the Park Service mission evolved from preserving individual trees to protecting the scenery and serenity of the groves and finally to squarely blocking even minimal environmental disruption, even these draconian measures proved insufficient.[26]

In 1963 Stewart Udall, secretary of the interior, commissioned another board to study wildlife management specifically in Yellowstone but by extension system-wide. The board, chaired by A. Starker Leopold, seized a rare opportunity for academic input and bluntly criticized the Park Service's preservation record.[27] Udall ordered that the recommendations of the Leopold Report for research and ecological management be implemented and officially ushered in a growing commitment to preserve the biosphere and discourage unchecked autonomous tourism, or the illusion of it, through indirect controls.

At Muir Woods, with its history of direct steps against overcrowding, implementation took a drastic turn. In the 1970s, park engineers paved and fenced the trails through the monument and reduced the number of bridges over Redwood Creek from seventeen to four (Fig. 11-4). The ostensible purpose was to protect the roots and understory growth from trampling. However, the net effect of this streamlining was to manipulate the average Muir Woods visit to a brief forty-five minutes. Without the possibility of wandering off-trail, climbing trees, picnicking, or running and playing tag through the grove, most visitors have had all they want within a half-hour. The last fifteen minutes are spent buying souvenirs.[28]

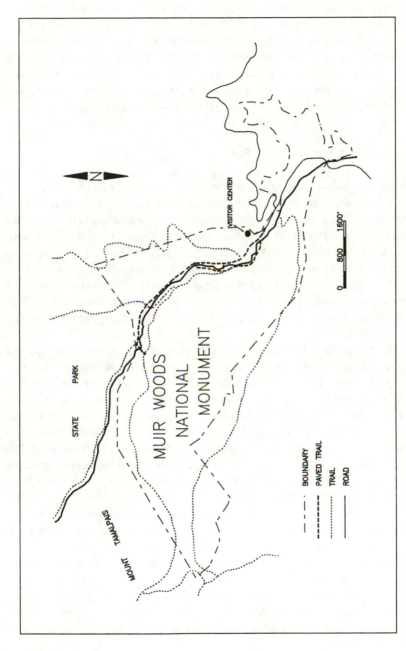

Figure 11-4. A tiny unit of some 550 acres, Muir Woods absorbs 1.4 million visitors per year.

This remarkable strategy has helped the forest and especially its understory to recover. However, it continues to challenge a Park Service confused in its mission. A forest without such artificial constraints as paving and fences ironically looks more appropriate to the untrained eyes of most visitors, more like an unaffected wild area fit for the national park system. A forest with such intrusions provides far better ecosystem protection but looks like what one old-time ranger has disparagingly called, "a botanical garden showing the redwood community."[29]

Channel Islands National Park

Channel Islands as a unit differs in several important ways from the other parks considered in this chapter. First, it consists of islands inaccessible by automobile, a fact of towering significance. Second, it is the youngest unit, established as a two-island national monument in 1938 and expanded to a five-island national park in 1980. Third, of these four California units, it is the most explicitly legislated for preservation, particularly in its 1980 enabling act. It has still faced the same confusion of agency mission and public priority as the other three parks, but has benefited from these three conditions to escape many of the negative impacts they have brought.

Channel Islands National Monument, consisting of tiny Anacapa and Santa Barbara Islands, was proclaimed by Franklin Roosevelt during a flurry of preservation activity in the late 1930s. They remained singularly unappealing to the nearby metropolitan areas of Los Angeles and Santa Barbara, due to their inaccessibility and the domination of both islands by the U.S. Coast Guard and U.S. Navy respectively. Both islands presented steep cliffs and no adequate harbor to whatever pleasure boaters approached them. Park Service management remained aloof, ignoring the two islands from distant administrative offices, first in San Francisco and later at Cabrillo National Monument near San Diego.[30]

Nearly four decades passed before the monument received its own administration along with an elaborate new mainland visitor center at the harbor of Ventura. Six years later a locally generated campaign for an enlarged park succeeded. The new national park took over administration of distant San Miguel Island from the navy and began compliance with congressional mandates to acquire the two largest, privately owned islands, Santa Rosa and Santa Cruz. Congress also charged the Park Service to carefully monitor and preserve both terrestrial and marine resources.[31]

All these recent actions and mandates came about because of the shift

of both Park Service policy and public commitment to ecosystem preservation. NEPA planning procedures, implemented even before national
park status, illuminated a strong public will to ensure preservation of the
islands' unique flora, fauna, and fossils despite damage by prior private
and military use. In response, the Park Service has implemented its traditional dual mission with a decided tilt toward the preservation side.
Most rangers still believe people should be entitled to visit the national
parks. But in the case of Channel Islands, they should constitute a very
small number at a time, carefully monitored and coached by NPS personnel. The three smaller islands have limits of one-hundred visitors each.
If more approach by either private or concession boats, they must wait
until those on the island leave. In addition, many areas are zoned for no
access. Off-trail travel is strongly discouraged, and uniformed personnel
are on hand to enforce the rules. The Park Service has recently acquired
Santa Rosa Island, and its draft-management plan proposed a visitor
capacity of 500 for a 52,794-acre island.[32] Adoption of this staunchest of
direct controls—absolute visitor limits—is a rarity in government resource management. So far it remains untested because the number of
visitors seeking access to the islands exceeds the capacity only two or
three times per year. So far the Park Service has not had to face the
rebuke of a public denied access to its treasures. It remains to be seen
what will happen should Channel Islands suddenly become a popular
destination.

Other Recent Steps

The policies of the National Park Service for Channel Islands reflect the
effects of the ecological revolution in management. Yet the agency continues to recoil from similar limits in the mainland units. Ever tighter
direct and indirect controls are implemented to avoid the obvious but
unpalatable solution. At Muir Woods they refuse to build more parking,
effectively sealing the unit from unending visitor increase. Also recent
discouragement of buses from the twisting access road has lightened the
pressure.[33] Still, defense of Muir Woods continues to rely chiefly on
channeling the swarms of visitors through a series of asphalt picture stops
more reminiscent of a museum than a natural ecosystem.

At Sequoia, reconsideration of Superintendent White's old plan to move
structures from Giant Forest to other sites accompanied the Leopold Report
and ecological preservation. Between 1962 and 1971 the Park Service
relocated four campgrounds and a picnic area from the grove. They
overcame opposition from traditional users by appealing to their height-

ened awareness of environmental issues and subtly suggesting that the areas were unsafe due to unstable, leaning sequoias. Subsequently, the government removed all of its operations to other sites and has recently built the infrastructure for a new concession housing site. With $30 million already spent on the latter, the effort now is concentrated on getting a still recalcitrant concessioner to agree to move.[34]

Meanwhile in both Yosemite and Sequoia–Kings Canyon, the Park Service has tried sterner controls on back-country use. The lessons of Yosemite Valley, Giant Forest, and other auto-access areas are clear—the best development is no development. Even before the Leopold Report, park planners zoned Sequoia back country as a no-development area, successfully defeating three ambitious road-construction projects, similarly zoned most of Yosemite's back country, succeeded in having Kings Canyon National Park legally designated as roadless, and placed limits on stock use of damaged meadows in all the High Sierra parks. These steps mixed direct control of the concessioners with tentative direct limits on tractable, environmentally aware hikers and horsemen. In 1974, the National Park Service took a major step in the two high-country units by establishing a wilderness permit system with absolute capacities by trail head. Again, the back-country users have remained largely supportive.[35]

Finally, in the mid-1980s, reacting to gridlock on roads and in parking lots, Yosemite rangers turned away cars at the entrance to the valley. Experiments with limits at Channel Islands and in the back country, combined with an annual visitation soaring over three million, finally drew the Park Service to a suggestion nearly as old as the automobile. From the 1920s, the advisory board explored John Buwalda's option of forcing cars and their passengers to other parts of the park. Each time, the Park Service rejected or ignored it as an improper curb on the free and democratic enjoyment of public property. And sure enough, each time it happened in the eighties, this temporary exclusion brought a swift and highly publicized angry reaction.[36] There are many controls and checks the public will accept to preserve their beloved national parks. From limits on development area to limits on lodging capacity, from limits on off-trail use to limits on backpacker numbers, from maximization of inaccessibility to clever manipulation of visit time, the experiment to stave off crowd corruption of park resources continues. Yet the American public, autobound and democratically autonomous, will not be denied its due recreation.

Conclusions and Discussion

In the 128 years since the Yosemite withdrawal, national parks have gone from being anomalous scenic curiosities to valued inspirational resorts to treasured islands of a rapidly disappearing natural world. During all those years park managers, particularly the National Park Service, have struggled to interpret their dual mission of recreational encouragement and indefinite preservation. The experience of the Park Service in these four units demonstrates important characteristics of both the agency with its confused mission and the American public, the ultimate source of the parks as legal entities. First, the National Park Service is generally a reactive agency rather than a proactive one. Even the implementation of back-country limits came after decades of despoliation by overgrazing, littering, trail erosion, and vegetation change. Only at Channel Islands is the Park Service trying to begin a national park with definite and absolute controls. This approach has come about because of the lessons of the past and the recency of the unit's creation. Yet that recency has its own negative implications. Alteration of Channel Islands flora and fauna by rabbits, goats, sheep, and other introduced species, as well as naval bombardment and military construction during the last 150 years, has been catastrophic. Earlier park designation and management might have prevented some of these excesses.

Second, the National Park Service is itself to blame for much of the development. Incessant promotion of parks as valued destinations and places almost holy in America's splendid landscape has convinced the public. Implementation of campfire talks, ranger-led walks, museums, and displays has brought them back for more. Encouragement of concession facilities and services has reaped a substantial reward of structures, roads, tours, and amusements. A major proportion of the infrastructural capacity in these four units was developed during the first two decades of the Park Service. Many buildings have been replaced, but surprisingly few have been added in the last fifty years.

Third, the Park Service has followed a distinct pattern of implementing controls on visitor impact. A four-stage model can be proposed from the data provided by these California units. In the first stage, which we might entitle the "Hands-off Stage," the Park Service opts for indirect manipulation of visitors while vigorously encouraging their attendance. Direct controls consist only of laws against specific, exploitative activities, such as setting fires and cutting trees. Much of the infrastructure is built, and recreation is allowed in most forms although the sense of parks as inspirational places is present. Eventually, the agency begins to chafe under increasing visitation, which it senses has developed a cycle of build, fill, and build. It shifts to the "Making a Better Park" stage, recognizing that some limits are inevitable to protect the scenery and serenity that have become the ascendant values. There is elaborate experimentation with indirect controls and public education, a few tentative direct controls on visitors such as limiting camping duration and designating limited campsites, and finally resort to direct controls on the concession. The latter avoids direct public backlash while mitigating the most serious impact on the resources. The third stage develops along with recognition of ecological process and the rise of environmental consciousness among both park planners and the public. In "Controlling the Controllable," direct limits are placed on areas and resources where the clientele is distinctly prosocial and environmentally aware. Some areas are zoned for specific and limited uses. Access and, in some cases, infrastructure are reduced. Permit systems are introduced, and regulations against ignoring the zoning and capacity rules are enforced systematically for the first time. Discussion of large-scale relocation or outright elimination of infrastructure intensifies. Finally, there is a fourth stage; call it "No Room in the Ark." Herein, the Park Service applies direct limits on visitor access and numbers according to scientifically determined carrying capacities. So far stage four remains a much-discussed but still elusive dream of resource-management officers and preservationists in most national park units.

The reasons for the above characteristics can be traced to the slow advance of science, its slower acceptance by an agency top-heavy with men philosophically devoted to recreational democracy and to the culture of America itself. Although men like Joseph Grinnell, Aldo Leopold, and George M. Wright sounded clarions of distress over ecological mismanagement as early as the 1920s, their data were not believed to be sufficiently reliable to challenge the appeal of landscape architects promoting scenic inspiration. It was landscape architects, not scientists, who were repeatedly consulted and hired by the Park Service during the critical years of development. When scientists did present increasingly incontrovertible evidence of harm, they found a Park Service led by Mather men committed to recreation and the public's right of democratic access.

And the American people themselves spawned the culture and attitudes that delayed science, forestalled direct controls by the government, and generated public rejection of absolute limits on visitation. It is the volatile mix of anthropocentrism, autonomy, and the automobile that has so intensified the clash of purposes in the national parks. The belief that parks are islands of the biosphere, that they have rights to exist unaffected by humans, is both very recent and still a rare minority view. Even the Leopold Report called for "vignettes of primitive America," reproductions of the landscape early European explorers saw, rather than ruthlessly guarded bastions of pure ecological process. It is, after all, the national park system, and park is defined as "a tract of land set aside for public use." That public, in democratic America, insists on freedom of access to government and its holdings. All who love their parks should enjoy them in person and without hindrance. Nothing has gone further to promote the execution of spatial freedom and democracy than the family automobile. At the same time it brings in its wake the most devastating alteration to the natural world of the parks. Anthropocentrism, autonomy, and the automobile make a difficult cultural obstacle for a small, infiltrated, and confused agency to confront, scientific evidence or no scientific evidence.

Notes

1. Franklin Lane to Stephen Mather, May 13, 1918, reprinted in "Administrative Policies for Natural Areas of the National Park System," (Washington, D.C.: U.S. Department of Interior, National Park Service, 1970), 68–71.

2. Ronald Foresta, *America's National Parks and Their Keepers* (Washington, D.C.: Resources for the Future, 1984); Alfred Runte, *National Parks: The American Experience*, 2nd. ed. (Lincoln: University of Nebraska Press, 1987); Alfred Runte, *Yosemite: The Embattled Wilderness* (Lincoln: University of Nebraska Press, 1990); Richard Sellers, author of forthcoming National Park Service history of resource management, telephone interview with author, March 26, 1991.

3. Robert E. Manning, *Studies in Outdoor Recreation: Search and Research for Satisfaction* (Corvallis: Oregon State University Press, 1986), 109–17; Tommy Swearingen and Darryll Johnson, "Influencing Visitor Behavior: Rethinking the Direct/Indirect Management Model," unpublished manuscript supplied by its authors.

4. Stanford E. Demars, *The Tourist in Yosemite, 1855–1985* (Salt Lake City: University of Utah Press, 1991), 12–53; Runte, *Yosemite*, especially 13–55.

5. Governor R. Waterman to John W. Noble, September 24, 1890, Microfilm Roll No. 1, "Early National Park Correspondence, 1890–1907," Sequoia National Park Library.

6. Hal Rothman, "'A Regular Ding-Dong Fight': Agency Culture and Evolution in the NPS–USFS Dispute, 1916–1937," *The Western Historical Quarterly* 20 (May 1989), 141–61; Runte, National Parks, 65–105.

7. Runte, *Yosemite*, 135–59.

8. Yosemite National Park (YNP), "Annual Superintendent's Report," 1934, YNP Research Library; Yosemite Board of Expert Advisors, "Meeting of the Expert Advisors Reports 1934–36" File 201–11, YNP Research Library; for a discussion of atmosphere preservation and the origins of NPS interpretation, see Lary Dilsaver and William Tweed, *Challenge of the Big Trees: A Resource History of Sequoia and Kings Canyon National Park*s (Three Rivers, Calif.: Sequoia Natural History Association, 1990), 118–24 and 157–96.

9. Runte, *Yosemite*, 154–59.

10.   See Yosemite Board of Expert Advisors, "Reports 1934–1944," File 201–11, YNP Research Library; and "Superintendent's Reports 1936–1941," YNP Research Library.

11.   Yosemite Board of Expert Advisors, "Reports 1936–1949," File 201–11, YNP Research Library.

12.   Lawrence Merriam, "Memorandum for the Files," September 13, 1939, filed with "Yosemite Board of Expert Advisors Reports," Box 10, File 201–11, YNP Research Library.

13.   Linda Eade, YNP Archivist, telephone interview with author, April 22, 1991.

14.   Demars, *The Tourist in Yosemite*, 122–50.

15.   Frank Dean, YNP Management Assistant, interview with author, YNP headquarters, May 3, 1990; Runte, *Yosemite*, 181–218.

16.   The story of the Japanese buyout of MCA and its succeeding impact is best reconstructed from dozens of columns by reporter Gene Rose and others of the *Fresno Bee* from July 1990 to February 1991.

17.   Dilsaver and Tweed, *Challenge of the Big Trees*, 109–56.

18.   Emilio Meinecke, "Memorandum on the Effects of Tourist Traffic on Plant Life, Particularly Big Trees, Sequoia National Park, California," unpublished report in the Sequoia National Park (SNP) Research Library, 1926.

19.   John White, "Atmosphere in the National Parks," an address to the Special Superintendent's Meeting, Washington, D.C., February 10, 1936, transcript in SNP Research Library.

20.   John White to Newton Drury, November 23, 1944, includes a seven-page summary of the history of the Giant Forest "situation," File D-18, Planning, SNP Archives.

21.   Howard Hays to John White, March 14, 1931, File D-18, Planning, SNP archives.

22.   John White to Newton Drury, November 23, 1944, File D-18, Planning, SNP Archives.

23.   Hal K. Rothman, *Preserving Different Pasts: The American National Monuments* (Urbana: University of Illinois Press, 1989), 61–64.

24.   Muir Woods National Monument (MWNM), "Annual Superintendent's Reports 1935–1940," filed under Muir Woods Resource Management Files, MWNM Archives; MWNM, "Monthly Narrative Report 1930–1937," filed under HDC, folders 33–38, Maritime Museum, Golden Gate National Recreation Area Headquarters.

25.   Margaret Littlejohn and Gary Machlis, "Visitor Services Project, Muir Woods National Monument," (Moscow, Idaho: Cooperative Park Studies Unit, Department of Forestry, University of Idaho, March 1990).

26.   Wes Hildreth, "A Chronology of Muir Woods National Monument," unpublished manuscript filed under History and Chronology, MWNM Archives.

27.   Stanley Cain et al., "A Vignette of Primitive America," *Sierra Club Bulletin* 48 (March 1963): 2–11. A letter from Secretary of the Interior Steward Udall ordering implementation is printed with the report.

28.   Mia Monroe, Muir Woods Ranger–Historian, interview with author at Muir Woods, August 13, 1990.

29.   Lawson Brainerd, Muir Woods Ranger and Volunteer, 1942–1991, interview with author at Muir Woods, July 26, 1990.

30.   Channel Islands National Park (CINP), "Resource Management Plan: Anacapa Island," (January 1968); Dana Head, "Interagency Coooperation Within Channel Islands National Park" (senior thesis, University of California at Santa Barbara, 1981), 10–11.

31.   CINP, "Statement for Management, Revised," (July 1984); Kate Faulkner, Chief of Resources Management, interview with author at Channel Islands National Park Headquarters, July 27, 1990.

32.   CINP, "Draft Environmental Assessment and Development Concept Plan: Santa Rosa Island" (1991).

33.   Mia Monroe, interview with author at Muir Woods, August 31, 1990.

34.   Dilsaver and Tweed, *Challenge of the Big Trees*, 252–55, 289–95; William Tweed, SNP Management Assistant, interview with author at Sequoia National Park Headquarters, December 12, 1990.

35.   Dilsaver and Tweed, *Challenge of the Big Trees*, 265–78, 307–17; Linda Eade, telephone interview April 22, 1991.

36.   Frank Dean, interview with author at Yosemite National Park Headquarters, May 3, 1990.

Index

About the Contributors

Originally from the piney hills of north Louisiana, *Craig E. Colten* has resided on the prairies of "Illinoleum" since relocating to the Midwest in 1984. He holds the position of associate curator of geography with the Illinois State Museum. Schooled in what was then referred to as the "man–land" tradition at Louisiana State University and historical geography at Syracuse University, he currently tracks the evidence of industrial wastes across the western reaches of the manufacturing belt.

Lary M. Dilsaver was born and reared in California, also home to the first land withdrawal for a major park, Yosemite, to the first four directors of the National Park Service, and to the most widely recognized advocacy group for park preservation—the Sierra Club. Through his teens and early college years, he frequented western national parks and forests, becoming keenly aware of the political and philosophical questions of their use and management. He moved to the Deep South as a doctoral student at Louisiana State University and is now professor of geography at the University of South Alabama as well as a researcher for the History Division of the National Park Service. He continues to trek westward annually to pursue both research and renewal in the Sierra Nevada and other rugged landscapes of the mountainous West.

Carville Earle is professor and chair of geography and anthropology at Louisiana State University. He is the author of various books and essays on the historical geography of the United States from initial colonization to the twentieth century. A native of the southernmost northern city and the northernmost southern city (Baltimore), he is unusually appreciative of the differences between the North and the South and the geohistorical myths that enshroud them.

Richard V. Francaviglia's appreciation of art and fascination with science (especially geology) are at the root of his long-standing interest in the design and evolution of the American landscape. In a world of increasing specialization, he values the interdisciplinary role of historical geographer and generalist. He holds a Ph.D. in geography and architectural history from the University of Oregon (1970) and has served in a wide range of teaching and administrative roles. His publications on the American landscape deal with the Mormon region of Utah, cemeteries, and most recently, mining districts. He currently serves as director of the Center for Greater Southwestern Studies and the History of Cartography at the University of Texas at Arlington.

David S. Hardin was raised in the rolling hills of Virginia's northern Piedmont, where he developed his love for the Old Dominion. Appreciation of the past is nearly inescapable among Virginians, but he has combined historical interests with environmental concerns since the first Earth Day in 1970. Once he discovered historical geography as a student at Mary Washington College in Fredericksburg, Virginia, during the early 1980s, he pursued his interest in Virginia's geographical and environmental past at the University of Tennessee, Knoxville, and the University of Maryland, College Park, and through work and research at the Virginia State Library and Archives. Home is now Longwood College in Farmville, where he is an instructor of geography and where he is finishing his dissertation on the interrelationship between environment and agriculture in eighteenth-century Tidewater Virginia.

Western landscapes have provided both a sense of place and area for geographical inquiry for *Martha L. Henderson*. After working for the U.S. Forest Service in central and eastern Oregon, she continued to study landscape processes in Oregon and New Mexico while pursuing graduate studies at Louisiana State University. Currently an assistant professor at the University of Minnesota, Duluth, she commutes regularly to New Mexico, Nevada, and Oregon.

Political boundaries and the problems associated with them have always held a fascination for *Olen Paul Matthews*. That fascination combined with degrees in both law and geography led to a research specialization based on transboundary resource issues. On moving to Oklahoma three years ago, his interest focused on the nearby Arkansas River. Trips up and down the Arkansas are easy from his central Oklahoma home, where he is professor and head of geography at Oklahoma State University.

Perhaps because of his background, *Klaus J. Meyer-Arendt* has a predilection for coastal environments. Born in the Hanseatic port of Hamburg, he first crossed the equator by freighter en route to Brazil—at the age of three. From Oregon's Coast Range, where the family finally settled, he moved to Louisiana, where interests in cultural/historical geography became blended with coastal/deltaic studies. Presently associate professor of geography at Mississippi State University in somewhat landlocked northern Mississippi, he continues to focus his human–environment research on coastal settings—along the U.S. Gulf Coast and shorelines of the Caribbean and Latin America.

Arthur J. Ray is professor of history at the University of British Columbia. He earned his Ph.D. in geography at the University of Wisconsin studying with Andrew H. Clark.

Stanley W. Trimble was trained as a historical-settlement geographer under the mentorship of Louis De Vorsey, Jr., and Kirk H. Stone. Trimble's interest in environmental matters came about when his incipient study of historic riverine settlement in Georgia revealed that most of the relict features had been buried by modern settlement. His primary interests are surface-water hydrology, fluvial geomorphology, and the historical geography of Europe and North America. He has held appointment as hydrologist with the U.S. Geological Survey and is an environmental consultant to several agencies. He has taught at the University of Wisconsin at Milwaukee, the Univeristy of Chicago, and University College, London, and is presently professor of geography at U.C.L.A.